The Daily Telegraph

Book of Canadian Obituaries

CANADA FROM AFAR

The Daily Telegraph

Book of Canadian Obituaries

CANADA FROM AFAR

Edited by
DAVID TWISTON DAVIES

Dundurn Press
Toronto • Oxford

Editor: **Judith Turnbull**
Designer: **Sebastian Vasile**
Printer: **Best Book Mfrs.**

Canadian Cataloguing in Publication Data

Main entry under title:

Canada from afar: the Daily telegraph book of Canadian obituaries

Includes index.
ISBN 1-55002-252-0

1. Obituaries – Canada. 2. Obituaries – England – London. 3. Canada – Biography. 4. Canada – History – 1963–   – Biography.* I. Davies, David Twiston, 1948–.

FC25.C35 1996   920.071   C96–931216–4   F1005.C35 1996

Publication was assisted by the **Canada Council**, the **Book Publishing Industry Development Program** of the **Department of Canadian Heritage**, and the **Ontario Arts Council**.

Care has been taken to trace the ownership of copyright material used in this book. The author and the publisher welcome any information enabling them to rectify any references or credit in subsequent editions.

Printed and bound in Canada

Dundurn Press
2181 Queen Street East
Suite 301
Toronto, Ontario, Canada
M4E 1E5

Dundurn Press
73 Lime Walk
Headington, Oxford
England
OX3 7AD

Dundurn Press
1823 Maryland Avenue
P.O. Box 1000
Niagara Falls, NY
U.S.A. 14302-1000

CONTENTS

v

Contents

Contents

PREFACE

THE LAST FLOWERING of Fleet Street – before the denizens of the medieval printers' district were scattered throughout London with the advent of computer technology – was the newspaper obituary. For most newspapermen, in Britain no less than in Canada and elsewhere, obituary writing is a necessary chore, one to be shuffled onto younger, weaker or older members of staff. "Duffy," the city editor admonishes a hapless reporter in Ben Hecht's *The Front Page*, "if you don't smarten up I'll send you to Obituaries." A death is recognized as news, but the recording of the bare facts together with a few sketchy remarks on a deceased's life, hastily culled from the last three news stories in his or her library file, is all too often deemed more than sufficient.

A change began with the arrival of two people at *The Daily Telegraph*: Conrad Black, who became majority shareholder in March 1985, and Hugh Massingberd, the former editor of *Burke's Peerage* publications, who joined the paper's obituaries section in July 1986. The *Telegraph* had an obituaries editor of 12 years' standing in the estimable Augustus Tilley, but he had been charged with keeping as much material out of the paper as he decently could. Readers were only interested in live people, the previous owners believed, but since the *Telegraph* was a serious broadsheet, it could not ignore the important deaths. A good spread could be allotted on a news page if the dead person was deemed worthy by the powerful and sceptical members of the "backbench" of the senior sub-editors. Nevertheless, Tilley was normally expected to produce half a dozen paragraphs a day; an essential part of the job, he declared, was to bring a book to read in the office.

Massingberd, however, came with the ambition of challenging the *Times,* which was acknowledged as the one serious practitioner in the obituaries field. Ever since the *Telegraph* absorbed the *Morning Post,* which had attached importance to obituaries, in 1937, the *Times* had been the place where people looked to see how the great and the good were summed up on departure. *Times* obituaries had a specific location at the back of the paper. Each notice began with a subject's name, rank and title, followed by a cluster of initials signifying his or her medals and orders. It would then proceed in stately, even pompous, prose to assess the subject's achievement in a way that often left the reader searching for the human being, who seemed to be but the tiniest cog in his or her field of endeavour.

Massingberd was inspired less by such authority than by a one-man show at London's Criterion Theatre. In this, the actor Roy Dotrice played the 17th-century antiquary John Aubrey, whose *Brief Lives* offers vivid, shrewd, entertaining reflections of his contemporaries. When Aubrey remarked of a lawyer, "He gained more by his prick than his practice," Massingberd recognized the model for what an obituaries column should be. Anecdotal, sharp, witty and wise, an obituary should portray the individual as a mixture of strengths and weaknesses which were developed by character and circumstances in the course of a unique life. He or she should be not only assessed, but shown as the person the reader would have encountered. None of this has much to do with death, it should be noted, and this book contains no litany of a deceased's last six months in which the progress from one minor illness to others more serious is gloatingly traced to an inevitable conclusion. Only occasionally is an individual's ending mentioned here, though it can be significant, as in the case of Roger Marshall, who died alone on Mount Everest.

Massingberd's first problem was having to persuade some publication to let him try to produce such a novelty. *The Daily Telegraph* was the obvious choice. The largest-selling broadsheet, it was enjoying an unusually high circulation when he made his approach in 1979 because the *Times* was not printing. The *Times*'s proprietor Ken Thomson, canny Toronto merchant reluctantly transformed into the 2nd Lord Thomson of Fleet, had agreed to halt production for a year in an attempt (which turned out to be unsuccessful) to break the stranglehold of the print unions. Massingberd was told that it would be "unsporting" to steal from a rival who was down. He had to wait six years before he was hired by the war correspondent and historian Max Hastings, who had been given the editor's chair when Black became proprietor. Hastings, keen to bring in some fresh blood, quickly recognized that he had made an exceptionally good decision. The apprentice Massingberd infused new vigour, authority and energy into a section previously governed by the concern to be first. Nobody cared what the *Telegraph* wrote once a *Times* obit had appeared, I remember being told. Ironically, *Times* obituaries went into a sharp if temporary decline at this time; an attempt to make them more frank had given way to a sullen disapproval of the *Telegraph*'s new efforts, which one *Times* obituaries editor sniffily dismissed as "a graveyard gossip column." Despite this, the *Independent*, launched by three former *Telegraph* journalists in October 1986, hesitantly began to run obituaries under the guidance of a former antiquarian bookseller.

After serving alongside his predecessor for five months, Massingberd took over as sole obituaries editor when Tilley retired in December 1986, and I was drafted in to help him. I arrived with considerable ill grace from the comfort of the *Telegraph*'s books department with the instruction to continue his induction into the mysteries of newspaper production. Two decisions had already been confirmed. Obituaries had been allotted a daily space of at least two columns on the Court and Social page since September, and bylines were banned, except in occasional personal tributes tacked onto a main obituary. The latter rule was important because it enabled writers to be more frank about their subjects than they would otherwise have been. It avoided that curse of the signed obituary, noticeable in both the *Independent* and *Guardian*, which is the paean of praise directed at the deceased's widow or widower. Of course, we could never catch up the *Times*, said Hastings, but we could try. Progress was slow and uncertain; nevertheless, we eventually noticed that both *Telegraph* readers and others were telling us that we had outstripped the Olympian leader. Other obituary columns sprang up not only in other British national papers but as far afield as the *Australian*.

Over drinks in a Fleet Street wine bar, Massingberd and I, by now burning with enthusiasm, agreed that there were two great facts of our experience this century – the world wars and the Empire. Canada was, inevitably, first in our thoughts. Through his researches into families at *Burke's,* Massingberd had long been aware of the close personal connections between Britain and the senior dominion; he had just completed a cross-Canada promotional tour for his book *Her Majesty the Queen.* I was a transplanted Canadian who had lived in Britain most of his life but had been keenly aware of his nationality ever since being called "a Yank" at prep school, a word never previously encountered but instantly disliked.

To start with, we found ourselves scraping around for material. The yellowing cuttings in the *Telegraph's* library sometimes contained facts new to a deceased's family, but they often also failed to give much indication of the course of many people's careers, particularly in the case of servicemen. Our original brief was to employ specialist reporters with beats in the News Room, but we soon found that busy hacks would only give the task their most cursory attention. We therefore slowly built up a team of contributors, specialist authors in their own field, who like so many people in Britain seemed to have some personal knowledge of Canada.

The obituaries of Canadians in this book are selected from more than 150 which have appeared in *The Daily Telegraph* during the past 10 years. They are not always written from the same perspective as those appearing in Canadian newspapers. This is partly because, with the exception of the *Globe and Mail,* obituaries come under the direction of news desks. It is also because distance lends different perspectives. Members of the Armed Forces are generally afforded much fuller treatment than in Canadian papers. The broadcaster Stewart MacPherson was a giant of the BBC but never enjoyed the same celebrity in his native Winnipeg. In Britain Eugene Forsey is recognized firstly as a leading Commonwealth constitutional scholar and only secondly as a pundit and socialist. The extraordinary painter Sveva Caetani was little known in Canada and Britain; news of her death came via our Rome obituarist Desmond O'Grady.

Some of the stories here are little known in Canada: Professor George Story's oration dedicated to his dog; General John Rockingham's determination that nobody should forget he was born in Australia; and the diplomat Hugh Keenleyside's experience as secret wartime go-between for Mackenzie King and Franklin Roosevelt.

It can be argued that minority groups are under-represented. The prevalence of subjects of British origin reflects partly the interests of the readers of *The Daily Telegraph* but also the make-up of the Canadian population before the great immigration waves of recent years. Above all, this book is concerned primarily with the Anglo-Canadian relationship. This remains so pervasive in its multitudinous forms – cultural, historical, political, military, commercial and, most important, personal – that, being sub-conscious, it is largely unacknowledged.

Obituary writing is rightly an anonymous art, and only partly to protect authors from the wrath of a deceased's relatives. An obit is often the work of diverse hands, whose individual responsibilities in an obituary are not always clear even to themselves. The creators of any obit are divided into two distinct groups. In the office there are the editors, who commission, amend, polish, check and select for publication the contents for each day's column. After Massingberd himself, who served as obituaries editor with such gusto for eight years, mention should made of his former deputy David Jones, Claudia Fitzherbert, Aurea Carpenter, Robert Gray, Kate Summerscale and Will Cohu. They were ably supported by Diana Heffer and Teresa Moore and aided by my own incomparable secretary Dorothy Brown. Then there are the authors Lieutenant-Colonel Jeffery Williams, Edward Bishop, John Winton, Geoffrey Hattersley-Smith, Eric Shorter, George Galt, the late David Holloway, John Lanchester, Professor R.M. Farquhar, Lord Harris of High Cross and Fred Langan, the *Telegraph's* Toronto correspondent. Perhaps the most significant is Bob Francis, the former Canadian Press and *Newsweek* foreign correspondent, whose earliest memories in Nelson, B.C., are of his father receiving the old *Morning Post* from England and turning first to the obituaries section.

Many others deserve my personal thanks for help with this book, though not all would wish to be acknowledged for the specific aid they supplied. One, whose obituary appears here, is Charles

Ritchie, who died as this book was being prepared. Paul Koring and Richard and Sandra Gwyn have always been ready to advise. The works of Peter Newman have been not only helpful but also inspirational. John Harbron and Professor Peter Neary did much to encourage me to press ahead with the project. Lastly my cousin, the genial C.J. Fox, has provided help in every way possible from both England and Canada. I must also thank Conrad Black for agreeing to write a foreword, Max Hastings for pushing me into the Obituaries Department, albeit temporarily, and the *Telegraph*'s publications manager, Marilyn Warnick, for steering the book through the mysteries of contract law.

David Twiston Davies

FOREWORD

As DAVID TWISTON DAVIES has recounted in his presentation of this volume, obituaries in *The Daily Telegraph* were, until nearly 10 years ago, news stories for the prominent deceased, or rather truncated summaries for the less well known. This was judged appropriate in the long era from shortly after the First World War to the mid-1980s, when *The Daily Telegraph* was a broadsheet newspaper with a mid-market content and price. Features were minimal, comment and letters were rather basic, like obituaries, and news, sports and business were covered fully if concisely, but fairly and with flair where unusually comical or salacious stories arose, as they do on most days in Britain. Informative biographical material on Canadians, living or dead, was rare.

With the change to new (Canadian) ownership and the move to modern and greatly increased capacity presses in 1986 and 1987, *The Daily Telegraph* was effectively relaunched as a full-range quality newspaper offering at least as complete coverage as the *Times* and the *Guardian*. The traditional middle-class readership of *The Daily Telegraph* had prospered in Thatcherite Britain, and it was calculated that the readership could endure cover-price increases provided the product was strengthened and value was given for money. It was also believed that the readership could be broadened to attract many aspirant mid-market readers and previous devotees of competing broadsheet newspapers.

This strategy proved successful, as circulation remained from 400,000 to 650,000 above the nearest broadsheet competitors, despite cover-price increases. The readership was enhanced and rejuvenated (even through the recent cover-price and circulation war), and the newspaper was steadily expanded to offer the fullest and most varied coverage, even of many matters formerly scarcely touched by the traditional, hair-shirted, if not bare-boned version of *The Daily Telegraph*.

Hugh Massingberd, best known as the learned author of coffee-table books about Britain's stately homes, had, as David Twiston Davies recounts, pioneering ideas about how to make obituaries more interesting, and he also had the panache and thoroughness to implement them. Our new press capacity afforded the space for more ambitious obituaries and the new team of obituarists assembled by Mr Massingberd exploited the opportunity.

Emphasis was placed on lively anecdotal material, and while the general tenor of the obituaries, as of the *Telegraph* newspapers generally, was reasonably generous, they ceased to be the unvaried whitewash of the previous era. Under the new regime, *The Daily Telegraph* swiftly established itself as one of the world's most lively and informative newspapers in this field.

On one occasion, when the editor of *The Daily Telegraph,* Max Hastings, the principal architect of the editorial renascence of the newspaper, had added a comment to the obituary of one of his former school teachers, the widow of the deceased educator wrote to me in anguish. Max Hastings responded for me and a lively correspondence ensued in which the editor gave the grieving woman an extensive recitation of her husband's shortcomings and excesses.

When Mr Massingberd moved from obituaries to edit the Peterborough column on topical matters, not to say high-level gossip, Max Hastings admonished him that he would have to treat the living more cautiously than he had sometimes treated the dead.

From the beginning of Mr Massingberd's responsibility for obituaries, an unprecedented stress was placed on Canadian subjects. Because of the intimacy of the two countries during the Second World War, when for over a year they were the only organized combatants against fascism and Nazism in the Northern Hemisphere, there was widespread British interest in accomplished Canadian war veterans. It is this group which now, unfortunately, has reached an age likely to attract the obituarist's attention.

Because *The Daily Telegraph* readers include a very large number of retired officers and senior government officials, there is great interest in many of the Canadians who were known to Britons in analogous positions during and after the Second World War. And because Canadian newspapers do not generally make of obituaries such an ambitious sketch of their subjects as the British broadsheet press does, some of the obituaries included in this collection could be somewhat enlightening to Canadian readers.

Apart from serving *The Daily Telegraph*'s readers with a wide number of well-remembered Canadian acquaintances, this attention paid to prominent Canadians who have died subtly emphasizes the historic and present relationship between the two countries and in particular the fact that the United Kingdom's principal broadsheet newspaper is owned by Canadians. This too is a tradition, one in which I am privileged to continue the important legacy of Lord Beaverbrook when he was the proprietor of the Express Newspapers and of Lord Thomson when he controlled Times Newspapers.

It is the hope of all of us at the *Telegraph* that this volume will make a modest contribution to the valued and historic cause of close and good Anglo-Canadian relations.

Conrad Black
Toronto, September 7, 1995

TROOPER GEORGE IVES

TROOPER GEORGE IVES (who died at Aldergrove, British Columbia, on April 12, 1993, aged 111) was the last surviving soldier of the Boer War.

Determined to surrender to old age only by inches, he retained vivid memories of his service in South Africa as a mounted infantryman – notably of chasing enemy commandos. The Boers never tarried for a pitched battle and were generally content to shoot from the hills, killing more oxen than men, he recalled. Nevertheless, Ives had a scar from a Boer bullet that had ricocheted off a rock. "My job was to get over there and kill Boers," he would recall in his soft Gloucestershire accent. "You went to war to kill someone, and he tried to kill you back."

Like most soldiers, he had mixed feelings about his service. He expressed little enthusiasm for the British cause, felt a deep sympathy for the enemy, and remembered uneasily his time guarding their womenfolk in ill-run concentration camps. Ives was happier to remember the humanity displayed by both sides. On one occasion Christiaan de Wet, the great Boer general, was allowed to enter a British camp during a lull in the fighting to obtain medical supplies for his wounded men. And there was always the soldier's perennial search for beer.

The son of a coachman and a lady's maid, George Frederick Ives was born in France and taken to England to have his birth registered as November 17, 1881, to ensure that he would not be called up for French military service. He was brought up largely in France, where his parents worked for the Tidmarsh family, and until he grew too heavy, he had hoped to become a jockey.

Young George was working in his father's grocery shop in Bristol when news of the British defeats at Colenso, Magersfontein and Stormberg arrived in Black Week, December 1899. In a burst of patriotism, he and thousands of others volunteered to join the Imperial Yeomanry. MPs, barristers, blacksmiths and butchers, few of them with any military experience, poured into half a dozen recruiting centres determined to do their duty.

Ives was one of the 123 who joined the 1st Imperial Yeomanry at Cheltenham. As mounted infantry, they had no sabres and were intended to match the fitness of the Boers' cavalry, but were usually employed in aid of other units. Even so, by their return home only 17 of the original volunteers remained. Like most of his comrades, Ives was not inclined to become a settler on the veld after the war, despite government encouragement, but on his return to Britain he found widespread unemployment.

Ives sent off for literature about emigration to the dominions and decided on his destination by the toss of a florin, with heads for Canada and tails for New Zealand. It came up heads, and Ives joined a group of 2,000 colonists, including a large number of Boer War veterans, to open up a new wheat belt in the unpopulated Northwest Territories. Under the leadership of two Anglican clergymen, the Reverend Isaac Barr and the Reverend G.E. Lloyd, the party muddled west to found an "all British colony" at what would become Lloydminster on the Saskatchewan-Alberta border.

Ives and his father arrived in 1903 and bought a quarter section of 160 acres for $10. Under the preferential laws of purchase they had to break at least 15 acres and build a shack, which would be made of logs with a sod roof; their major problem was to find a well. Ives, who was rejected for service in the First World War because of a heart murmur, proved himself a hard-working and methodical farmer. In 1910 he felt prosperous enough to marry the woman who would be his wife for the next 76 years, Kay Nelson ("I used to call her Cayenne"); they had three sons and three daughters. But his wife disliked the hard life of the prairies, where the washing always froze on the line during the winter. So in 1919 they moved to White Rock, British Columbia, where Ives had a dairy farm until retiring at 60. This retirement proved merely an excuse to change jobs, and for the next 15 years he worked in a shipyard, building wooden scows, before retiring for the last time.

He and his wife continued to live in their house until 1984, when they moved to an old people's home. Ives proved a genial, if critical, resident. He performed chin-ups on a parallel bar until he was well past 100, and like other fathers was critical of his children's generation, complaining that youngsters in their eighties and nineties were apt to let themselves go.

After a story about him appeared in *The Daily Telegraph*'s Peterborough column, he said that he would like to attend the Albert Hall service on Remembrance Day 1992. Within a week he found himself brought over by a television producer and greatly enjoyed meeting Queen Elizabeth the Queen Mother, Lady Thatcher and John Major, the prime minister.

Right to the end Ives liked to talk about going down to the Legion for "a couple of pints." He maintained the ethical standards of his youth, and when a writer half his age who was interviewing him suggested that they retire to the quiet of his room, he was concerned for her reputation lest it became known she had been to a man's bedroom.

PROFESSOR BARKER FAIRLEY

PROFESSOR BARKER FAIRLEY (who died on October 11, 1986, aged 99) became an internationally respected authority on Goethe, then established a second reputation in middle age as a painter.

He played a vigorous part in Canadian intellectual life, becoming the friend, champion and early collector of the Group of Seven painters, who turned to the landscape in reaction to what they saw as Victorian stuffiness. When the political and cultural magazine *Canadian Forum* started in 1920, he was its first literary editor.

The son of an elementary school headmaster, Barker Fairley was born on May 21, 1887, at Barnsley, Yorkshire. He won a county scholarship to Leeds University, from which he emerged with first-class honours in modern languages to take a job as *lektor* at Jena in 1907. A chance meeting in a German boarding house with a Canadian professor who was seeking staff for the new University of Alberta at Edmonton led him to Canada in 1910. Five years later he moved to the University of Toronto, with which he remained associated for the rest of his career, except for four years in the 1930s when he went to Manchester University. The face of England's blighted north in the Depression sent him thankfully back to Toronto as head of English.

Fairley wrote *Goethe as Revealed by His Poetry* (1932), *A Study of Goethe* (1947), which drew an admiring letter from the novelist Thomas Mann, and a respected translation of *Faust* (1970). He also produced works on the novelists Heine and Raabe.

Fairley wrote a biography of the Arabist C.M. Doughty (1927) and claimed to have been "a poet for a year" when, in 1922, 58 complete poems sprang suddenly into his head. They were eventually published in 1972, dedicated to the painter A.Y. Jackson.

Once he had taken up painting, it became the major preoccupation of his life. He preferred portraits, the best of them gaunt and penetrating, but also found his landscapes, which were spare compositions using minimum colour, in demand. Prices ranging from $2,000 to $5,000 for each picture made welcome additions to his retirement pension, particularly as he worked fast.

Fairley had been a regular lecturer at Columbia University when he found himself barred from entering the United States to lecture at Bryn Mawr College in 1949 – an event which saw him honoured and dishonoured at the same time, he claimed. The ruling, probably due to his being vice-president of the Canadian Council of American-Soviet Friendship, was never explained or altered. He finally crossed the border the year before he died when he went to have lunch at Lewiston, New York, "just for kicks."

CHARLIE RUTHERFORD, VC

CHARLIE RUTHERFORD was the last survivor of the 633 winners of the Victoria Cross in the First World War when he died on June 11, 1989, at the age of 97.

On August 26, 1918, the recently commissioned Rutherford was commanding a platoon of the 5th Canadian Mounted Rifles advancing towards the strongly held village of Monchy-le-Preux, whose capture would give observation over the powerful defences of the Hindenburg Line. Beginning their move in driving rain shortly after midnight, Rutherford and his men overran a battery of four German guns, their crews completely surprised by the speed of the advance. With daylight, as the artillery began to shell the rubble which had been Monchy, Rutherford left his men to co-ordinate the assault with the company on his left.

When he returned 10 minutes later, his men had disappeared. Unaware that they had taken cover in a wood, he assumed that they had moved into the town and ran forward to join them. Rutherford was within 100 yards of the ruins before he saw a group of fully armed Germans outside a pillbox. In the words of his VC citation: "He beckoned them with his revolver to come to him but they in turn waved to him to come to them. This he boldly did and informed them that they were his prisoners. This fact an enemy officer disputed and invited Lieutenant Rutherford to enter the pillbox, an invitation he discreetly declined. By masterly bluff, however, he persuaded the enemy that they were surrounded, and the whole party of 45, including two officers and three machine-guns, surrendered to him."

At that moment a nearby enemy machine-gun began firing on another company of the Mounted Rifles. Rutherford ordered a German officer to stop it, and then went back to prevent his own men opening fire. As soon as he was out of sight of the Germans, Rutherford took off his helmet and waved his platoon forward. They soon joined him, and he sent the prisoners under escort to the rear. By now he could see that the assault on the right was being held up by heavy machine-gun fire from another pillbox. Indicating a further objective to the remainder of his platoon, he attacked the strongpoint with a Lewis gun section, captured a further 35 prisoners and opened the way for the advance to continue.

According to the official account: "The bold and gallant action of this officer contributed very materially to the capture of the main objective and was a wonderful inspiration to all ranks in pressing home the attack on a very strong position." A brother officer put it more memorably: "The newspapers reported that Monchy had fallen to the 3rd Canadian Division – that morning, Charlie Rutherford *was* the 3rd Division."

Charles Smith Rutherford was born in Haldimand Township, Ontario, on January 9, 1892. He spent his early years on the family farm and was educated at Dudley Public School. In June 1916 he joined the 5th Canadian Mounted Rifles as a private and later that year took part in the Somme battles, being wounded in Regina Trench. He returned in time for the victorious assault on Vimy Ridge the next April and was wounded again at Avion in June. As a sergeant at Passchendaele he was one of the 13 survivors of a company of Mounted Riflemen who captured Vapour and Source Farms on the left of the Canadian advance, then held them against repeated enemy counter-attacks. For their gallantry that day his company commander, Major George Pearkes, won the VC and Rutherford the Military Medal. Commissioned in April 1918, Rutherford returned to his battalion in time for the opening on August 8 of the great offensive in front of Amiens. That day he won a Military Cross by capturing and holding the village of Arvillers until relieved by the French troops whose objective it was.

After the Armistice, Rutherford returned to the family farm in Ontario. On the outbreak of the 1939–45 war, he joined the Veterans Guard of Canada, with whom he protected the Duke of Windsor in the Bahamas and guarded prisoner-of-war camps in Canada, finally leaving the army as a captain in July 1945. Like most VCs, Charlie

Rutherford saw himself as anything but a hero. He enjoyed the company of his old comrades, men who could understand that his most terrible experience at the front was carrying back the body of a close friend from an outpost through a water-filled tunnel.

After the Second World War he became the postmaster at Colborne, Ontario, and in later years enjoyed the quiet of his daughter's farm to the north of the town. He married Margaret Helen Haig in 1921, and they had a son and three daughters.

AIR VICE-MARSHAL SIR VICTOR TAIT

AIR VICE-MARSHAL SIR VICTOR TAIT (who died November 29, 1988, aged 96) played a key role in the preparations for the Normandy landings in 1944 when he led the team responsible for spoofing or destroying the Germans' radar stations.

In May 1944 Tait was director of radar and director-general of signals at the Air Ministry when, a few weeks before D-Day, he was ordered to Fighter Command's former Battle of Britain headquarters at Bentley Priory at Stanmore, Middlesex. This was the result of a meeting between Professor R.V. Jones, the radar backroom boy, and Air Chief Marshal Sir Arthur Tedder, Eisenhower's Deputy Supreme Allied Commander, at which Jones had pressed for an Allied Expeditionary Air Force team to counter the radar protecting Normandy.

Jones told Tedder that Tait was the man for the job, and no sooner had Tait been appointed than he recruited Jones to look after the intelligence side. Their collaboration contributed significantly to the success of the invasion. Apart from seeking to knock out radar installations by pinpoint air strikes, the team at Bentley Priory came up with a number of ruses to confuse the enemy. Particularly successful in implementing Tait's plans was No. 617 – the "Dam Buster" squadron – which spoofed the Pas-de-Calais radar sites with spurious radar reflectors to give the impression that a large naval force was on the point of invading that area.

Victor Hubert Tait was born in Winnipeg on June 8, 1892, and read electrical engineering at the University of Manitoba. At the outbreak of the First World War he enlisted as a sapper in the 2nd Field Company, Canadian Division Engineers. In 1916 he was commissioned in the 8th Battalion, London Regiment, and was then seconded to the Royal Flying Corps, with which he specialized in navigation and wireless. When the Royal Air Force was formed in 1918 he was commissioned in the new service. After wireless duties with

9

No. 4 Squadron at Constantinople in the early 1920s Tait continued to specialize in that area until 1932, when he was seconded to the Egyptian Air Force and flew out with eight aircraft to Cairo.

In recognition of his services King Fuad ordered Squadron Leader Tait to be known as Miralai Tait Bay, with the rank of *kaimakan* (lieutenant-colonel) and in 1937 he appointed him Commander of the Order of the Nile. By 1940 Tait had returned to the directorate of signals at the Air Ministry, where he was successively deputy-director and director of radio until his appointment in 1942 to head Radar and Signals for the remainder of the war. He also carried out special liaison duties with the RAF delegation to the U.S. Army Air Corps.

On his retirement from the RAF in 1945 Tait joined British Overseas Airways Corporation as operations director. He remained in the post until 1956, also becoming technical director. In 1946 he was founding chairman of International Aeradio, and he was director, too, of several other concerns. Tait, who was married three times, was an accomplished Olympic hockey player in the 1920s; he retained his relish for the game and was president of the British Ice Hockey Association from 1958 to 1971. He was appointed OBE in 1938, CB in 1943 and KBE in 1944.

HOWARD GREEN

HOWARD GREEN, Canada's last imperially minded senior minister (who died on June 26, 1989, aged 93), brought down John Diefenbaker's Progressive Conservative government in 1963 by his passionate opposition to nuclear arms.

Increasingly mistrustful of the tightening economic embrace of the United States, Green took a cool view, as external affairs secretary, of the aggressive American response to Khrushchev's support for the building of the Berlin Wall in 1961. When the Kennedy administration sought Canadian support during the Cuban missile crisis of the next year, Green made an impassioned plea in cabinet, saying: "If we go along with the Americans now, we will be their vassals forever." He dissuaded Diefenbaker from supporting demands by Douglas Harkness, the national defence minister, for Canada's Honest John rockets and Bomarc missiles to be loaded with nuclear warheads under the terms of a treaty their government had signed. But while Diefenbaker correctly sensed, like Green, the growing opposition to nuclear weapons in Canada, his inability to come down on one side or the other led to Harkness's resignation and, two days later, the defeat of the minority government on the floor of the House. With the active encouragement of the American administration, the Liberal party won the subsequent election, and Green's career ended with the loss of his seat – though the Liberals later reverted to a supposedly anti-nuclear policy.

A shopkeeper's son of United Empire Loyalist stock, Howard Green was born at Kaslo, British Columbia, on November 5, 1895, and educated at the local high school and the University of Toronto. During the First World War he was mentioned in dispatches while serving in France and Germany with the 54th Kootenay Battalion, and he subsequently served on the staff of the 2nd Canadian Division. He was called to the British Columbia Bar in 1922 and elected a Vancouver MP in 1935. A teetotal non-smoker who refused to work on Sundays and never learned to drive a car, Green was so successful in checking the "continentalist drift" that the American-born Minister C.D. Howe once remarked that Howard stalked the corridors of Parliament "with a Bible in one hand and a stiletto in the other." Green was the most outspoken Tory supporter of the 1944 speech by the Earl of Halifax, British ambassador to the United States, which urged a closely unified Commonwealth after the war and earned a fierce rejoinder from Mackenzie King, the prime minister. He helped to prevent the introduction of a new Canadian flag in 1946, but could only protest at the way the Liberals dropped the title "Dominion"- which, he pointed out, was a long-standing Canadian-devised term recalling the 72nd Psalm: "He shall have dominion also from sea to sea."

In 1957, when the Tories returned to power after 22 years in opposition, Green first received the Ministry of Public Works, where he proved an inflexible opponent of "pork-barrel" contracts for government supporters. He moved next to the Ministry of Defence Production for a year. His promotion to External Affairs came as a surprise, not least because he had not crossed the Atlantic for 40 years. Suspicions that he would be merely Diefenbaker's tool seemed to be confirmed when he unofficially urged the Opposition to be gentle with him one week because he had been too busy meeting people to come up with sensible answers. But Green showed keen interest in Laos and South America, and threw much of his energy into trying to prevent the spread of nuclear arms – a campaign he refused to relax despite American concern over the volatile Khrushchev. As one of those who had been loudest in condemning the Liberal government for stabbing Britain and France in the back during the Suez crisis, Green strongly opposed Britain joining the Common Market. It was an American plot, he declared, not entirely without foundation, to make British ministers betray British interests.

Green's concern for Canada's survival as an independent nation found an echo in the 1988 general election debate on free trade with the United States. But his plain Anglo-centric beliefs were out of place in the self-consciously sophisticated 1960s. When asked by reporters to explain the significance of his defeat, he replied: "I have given the matter the fullest consideration and, having examined the problem from all its angles, reached the conclusion that it was because I did not get enough votes."

CAPTAIN ERIC BRAND

CAPTAIN ERIC BRAND (who died on November 22, 1991, aged 95)
served as the Royal Canadian Navy's director of intelligence and trade
throughout the Second World War.

From their headquarters in Ottawa, Brand and his staff collated
intelligence on all shipping movements in North and South America,
which they then fed into the Admiralty's world-wide intelligence
organization in London. They also had the immense task of organizing
the naval control of shipping in North America, which involved the
formation and routing of scores of Atlantic convoys, and the defensive
arming of hundreds of merchantmen.

The RCN expanded from a few destroyers in 1939 to more
than 400 ships, mostly corvettes, by 1945. This unprecedented and
unforeseen growth meant that almost all RCN ships in the Battle of the
Atlantic were manned largely by reserve officers and men with little sea
experience or fighting qualities. They had to learn their business at sea,
and they did it well. But there were many casualties in some of the
early convoys, which led to questions about the RCN's competence.

As the war progressed, Brand, who arrived on loan from the
Royal Navy in June 1939, did much to change the RCN's touchiness
over criticism from the RN. Older Canadian naval officers remembered
the "upstage" officers who had come over to tell them how to do their
job in the First World War, but they quickly found Brand a friendly
and cultivated man as well as an outstanding leader. They were
surprised to learn that he had been passed over for promotion to
commander in the RN, and promoted him captain at first shot in
January 1940.

Eric Sydney Brand was born at Ipswich, Suffolk, on May 14,
1896, and had a boyhood ambition to join the navy – "even if I had to
do it as a doctor or dentist." Although he failed the Admiralty
interview for the junior Royal Naval College at Osborne, Isle of Wight,

he joined the training ship *Conway* in 1909 and passed into Dartmouth as a cadet the next year. His first visit to Canada was in the cruiser *Cumberland*, in 1913 when Prince Albert (the future King George VI) was a fellow cadet.

Later that year he joined as a midshipman the battleship *Dominion* (named in honour of the Dominion of Canada). Brand served throughout the First World War in the Grand Fleet, and afterwards specialized as a navigating officer. It was while instructing on a pilotage course at HMS *Dryad*, the navigation school at Portsmouth, that he taught his charges how to take the sun's meridian altitude with his patent "Astronomical Spotting Table." This involved the schoolmaster leaning out of an upstairs window and slowly hauling the large shining brass gong, which normally stood in the wardroom entrance, up and down the wall on a length of string. Since the wall was whitewashed for its first four feet, it made an excellent artificial horizon, and Brand's class would stand in the courtyard with their sextants, measuring the maximum altitude of the brass "sun" from the "horizon."

Brand was then navigating officer of the battlecruiser *Renown* and of the battleship *Barham*. He became executive officer of the cruiser *Vindictive* and the aircraft carrier *Courageous* and commanded *Saltburn*, the minesweeper attached to *Dryad* as a training ship, and carried out some of the earliest pre-war trials of seaborne radar.

In Canada he was the naval member of the Canadian Shipping Board from 1942 to 1946, and a member of the Merchant Shipping Policy Committee from 1943 to 1947. He retired from the navy in 1946 and became government controller of Great Lakes and St Lawrence shipping. After becoming a Canadian citizen in 1947, Brand was employed by the Department of Reconstruction as adviser on merchant shipping; he was later posted to the Department of Immigration to advise on the transportation of immigrants to Canada. In 1959, after almost a decade as executive director of the newly formed Canadian Maritime Commission, he was appointed to the new post of director of marine operations in the Department of Transport, responsible for the organization of the Canadian Marine Service, which later became the Canadian Coast Guard.

He retired in 1963 with the honorary rank of commodore in the Coast Guard. The next year he was recalled to assist in setting up the Canadian Coast Guard College at Sydney, Nova Scotia. When he found another old *Conway* hand on the staff, Brand sought the Queen's permission to revive the custom of awarding the annual *Conway* Gold Medal, which had lapsed in Britain with the wrecking of the last *Conway* in 1974. It had been first awarded by Queen Victoria in 1865, and Brand used the same 100-year-old *Conway* procedure in which each cadet votes for a candidate from a select list.

Brand, who was appointed OBE in 1943 and Commander of the U.S. Legion of Merit in 1946, was married with a son and a daughter.

MAJOR-GENERAL HARRY LETSON

MAJOR-GENERAL HARRY LETSON (who died on April 11, 1992, aged 95) enjoyed a life of remarkable success and versatility: he was a university professor, ran his own engineering company, revived shipbuilding in British Columbia, was adjutant-general of the Canadian Army and served as secretary to the Governor General.

Having joined the militia in 1910, he was with the Western Universities Battalion on the outbreak of war in 1914 and was soon promoted NCO. In 1916 he moved with them to England where he was commissioned. The next year, as a lieutenant in the 54th Battalion in France, he won an MC and was severely wounded by machine-gun fire, which left him with a lifetime limp. After the war Letson returned to Vancouver, where he graduated in engineering from the Pacific coast branch of McGill University. He returned to England to gain his doctorate from London University, and from 1923 to 1935 he was associate professor of engineering at the University of British Columbia.

Harry Farnham Germain Letson was born in Vancouver on September 26, 1896, when it was still a shantytown. On the day of his birth his father founded the pioneer engineering firm of Letson & Burpee, which Harry later inherited and developed into one of the largest in western Canada. As chairman of the metal trades section of the Canadian Manufacturers' Association and a member of its national defence committee, Letson played an important part in the revival of shipbuilding on the Pacific coast. He was largely responsible for organizing the supply of machinery and equipment to be fitted in the bare hulls built in the yards of British Columbia – an industry which proved to be of vital importance during the Second World War.

Military affairs were of absorbing interest to Harry Letson. In 1927 he became the commanding officer of the British Columbia Regiment (Duke of Connaught's Own Rifles), a militia unit in

Vancouver. At his own expense he spent some months in England attached to units of the British army for training. In Canada he took every military course available to him. He was a crack shot and went to Bisley five times, last appearing there, in 1934, as commander of the Canadian team. For six years from 1930 he commanded the Canadian Officers Training Corps at the University of British Columbia. He was then promoted colonel to command the militia's 14th Infantry Brigade and the Vancouver defences.

In 1939 Letson once more volunteered for active service, and in August of the next year he was posted to Washington as military attaché at the Canadian Legation. His subsequent promotion to the rank of brigadier was an indication of the growing military co-operation between Canada and the United States. In February 1942 Letson was again promoted, to be adjutant-general in Ottawa. In 1944 he returned to Washington as chairman of the Canadian Joint Staff Mission, responsible for planning Canada's participation in the invasion of Japan. When the vastly popular Field Marshal Earl Alexander of Tunis was appointed Governor General in 1946, Letson – as a soldier with wide connections in business and society – proved an admirable choice as his secretary. He held the post until 1952 but, on retiring from it, continued to take an active part in military affairs. From 1954 to 1958 he was adviser on militia to the army and in 1963 was appointed honorary colonel of the British Columbia Regiment. Letson was appointed CBE in 1944 and CB in 1946. He also held the Efficiency Decoration and the Canadian Forces Decoration. He married, in 1926, Sally McKee Lang. They remained in Ottawa after his military service, where he was on the advisory board of a trust company and was close to the excellent fishing of the Gatineau Hills.

BILLY BROWNE

BILLY BROWNE (who died on January 10, 1989, aged 91) had a political career – after Newfoundland joined Confederation in 1949 – that was dominated by an epic war against Joey Smallwood, the premier.

Browne and Smallwood were born to be enemies. Smallwood, an agnostic of Methodist descent, led the island into Confederation as a Liberal. Browne was a devout Catholic of Irish stock and a determined anti-confederate who joined the mainland's Progressive Conservative party. Where Smallwood's financial style was open to question, Browne was an upright lawyer – though an amused electorate noted that his sanctimonious mien did not prevent him marrying four times. (His first three wives died.)

The first open clash came when the new premier prevented Browne, a district court judge of 15 years' standing, from receiving a Canadian salary raise. Browne resigned and promptly brought bribery charges against Smallwood for telling Ferryland district voters in the federal election, with typical Newfoundland forthrightness, that they would only receive aid by voting Liberal. Browne dropped the case after he was elected an MP for St John's West, but he caused a sensation in the House of Commons by producing a pamphlet accusing Smallwood's economic guru Alfred Valdmanis of collaborating with the Nazis.

On his federal defeat four years later, Browne won a seat in Newfoundland's House of Assembly, where he savaged the province's harebrained schemes for new industries so successfully that Smallwood tried to smear him with accusations that he was a slum landlord. Browne met with only token opposition when he ran for a federal seat in 1956. But his standing first as minister without portfolio and then as solicitor-general in Ottawa was destroyed when John Diefenbaker, the prime minister, vented his own hatred of Smallwood by threatening to end Newfoundland's federal subsidy. At the next election Smallwood declared that Browne and the Tory party had cut Newfoundland's throat and stabbed her in the back. Browne duly paid the price with his seat. He was re-elected to the Assembly, failed again to win a federal seat and finally retired, leaving Smallwood triumphant for seven more years.

The son of a schooner-master, William Joseph Browne was born in St John's on May 3, 1897, and educated at St Bonaventure's College. He studied engineering at the University of Toronto and then won a Rhodes scholarship to read law at Merton College, Oxford. A keen supporter of Irish independence who regularly visited Ireland while an undergraduate, he once earned two pounds from the *Irish Independent* and *Cork Examiner* for taking a photograph from a train of the Royal Mail's first delivery to the island by plane.

After being called to the Bar by Gray's Inn and then in Newfoundland, Browne set up practice in St John's. He was briefly assistant clerk of the House of Assembly before being elected member for St John's West in 1924. He lost the seat four years later but won it back in 1932 for what promised to be a successful ministerial career. But Browne reached cabinet rank as minister without portfolio, one of six appointed to avoid costs, as the Depression began to bite and the dominion approached bankruptcy. Britain suspended all political activity and substituted rule by a commission of civil servants the following year.

Browne spent the succeeding years on the bench, where he helped to set up workers' co-operatives and opposed British plans for the island to join Canada after the 1939–45 war. Although he never returned to active politics after 1965 he remained a figure behind the scenes of Tory politics, earning considerable criticism by chairing meetings for the South African ambassador to Canada and staying in legal practice until he was 90. Increasingly devout in his old age, Browne liked to offer lifts to hitch-hikers, then invite them to say the Rosary with him.

PAULINE VANIER

PAULINE VANIER (who died on March 23, 1991, aged 92) was in her element as wife of the Governor General Georges Vanier, but then dedicated most of her long widowhood to the L'Arche community for the mentally handicapped founded by her son Jean outside Paris.

A tall, elegant woman with a musical laugh, Mme Vanier possessed a formidable air that could chill the nervous at official receptions; yet the sick and infirm never hesitated to embrace her. She put her husband, daughter and four sons unequivocally first in her own life, and was a determined champion of the family ideal against the threat posed by the growth of postwar prosperity and sexual permissiveness. After Major-General Vanier died in office in 1967, she organized a conference in Ottawa which led to the formation of the Vanier Institute of the Family. Her greatest satisfaction, however, derived from the L'Arche at Trosly-Breuil, near Compiègne, where she settled in a house containing several patients and few luxuries.

Pauline Archer was born in Montreal on March 28, 1898, daughter of a judge with Devonian roots and a mother from the seigneurial family de Salaberry, which had emigrated to Canada in 1730 and counted the French General Philippe Leclerc as a kinsman. In 1921 she married Georges Vanier, an officer in the Royal 22e Régiment (the Vandoos), who had lost a leg on the Western Front and was just about to become the first French Canadian ADC to the Governor General, Lord Byng of Vimy. The young couple soon became firm favourites with Byng, who used to throw stones at their cottage window after his early-morning ride, calling out, "Get up, you little Vaniers." In return, they asked Byng to become godfather to their first son Georges – now a Trappist monk at Oka, Quebec – whom they called Byngsie at home.

After two years Vanier was posted to the Staff College at Camberley, where he and his wife never lacked invitations after their reception at Windsor Castle. King George V asked Vanier how he managed his duties with his tin leg, and teased Pauline about women looking older than they seem. Queen Mary surprised them, though, with her fulsome praise for the Canadian climate. Vanier returned home to command his regiment and to serve as ADC to Byng's successor, Lord Willingdon, after which he became a military representative to the League of Nations in Geneva. On Jean's birth, Byng wrote to ask if Pauline was "thinking of starting a little League of Nations of her own." Vanier's next posting was to the High Commission in London. At that time he was not an over-zealous Catholic, but his devout wife persuaded him to attend the Good Friday service at Farm Street in Mayfair, conducted by her confessor, the celebrated Jesuit preacher Fr Roy Steuart. Vanier's religious life underwent a transformation, and he became a daily communicant, whenever possible, for the rest of his life.

On the outbreak of hostilities in 1939, Vanier was Canadian minister in Paris. Pauline moved to the wing of a chateau near Le Mans, where she gave catechism classes to the local children, and in the relaxed atmosphere of "phony war" the Vaniers were invited to tour the Maginot Line. They were delighted to see so many Canadian Red Ensigns – though they later discovered that there was in fact only one, which the French had hastily sent ahead of them to each stopping place.

The Germans' sudden advance sent Pauline scurrying with her children and nanny to the English Channel, where they were put on a cargo boat with 300 others, including the president of Poland and a group of English nuns. Bombs dropped all around them, and they had to sleep under tarpaulins with nothing to eat but fishpaste sandwiches in the three days before their landing in Britain. When Pauline discovered that her husband had travelled in the comparative comfort of a British destroyer, where he had dined off chicken, she made a resolution never to be separated from him again. Later she brought a welcome spark to the sombre arrival of official documents from Paris, when she joyfully seized a package crying out, "My hat box! My hat box! I never thought I would see it again."

Pauline made a tour of Quebec drumming up support for the war effort, returned first to London, where her husband was minister to the exiled European governments, and then in 1944 to Algiers, where he was envoy to the Free French. She was deeply disgusted by the flourishing black market, succulent meals and overly made-up women she encountered, but found some satisfaction in keeping open house for members of the Resistance who had come to visit de Gaulle. After the Allied invasion of Europe, Vanier was one of the first civilians to be allowed to return to Paris. Adhering to her resolution to stay at his side, Pauline borrowed a Red Cross uniform from a friend and set off to join him. She was soon busily involved in organizing relief for the starving bargees of Normandy.

The Vaniers returned from Paris in 1953 and were living in retirement in Montreal when Georges was asked to be the second Canadian-born Governor General. It was an appointment to which he and his wife brought a dignity and style that has steadily declined under their successors at Rideau Hall. Mme Vanier tactfully ordered three ball gowns from the English couturier Worth, rather than turning to Paris. Nevertheless, she experienced some difficulty in adjusting to her new position. When a lady was first presented to her, she curtsied so promptly that their kneecaps clashed on the way down. Despite the admonition that she must never embrace a political figure, Mme Vanier threw her arms round her old friend Lester Pearson, the Liberal leader, only to see the Tory prime minister John Diefenbaker glowering at them. Princess Alice – widow of an earlier Governor General, the Earl of Athlone, who had been coaching her in vice-regal proprieties – roundly told her that she had erred grievously and must make public amends by embracing Diefenbaker at the first opportunity.

Shortly after her husband's death Mme Vanier dined with General de Gaulle at the Elysée Palace. This was just before the general's infamous visit to Quebec, and he took advantage of the occasion to tell her that Canada was "an unnatural country," the history of which was of no consequence. Mme Vanier left the room in tears; unfortunately, the Pearson government paid no heed to her warnings.

In her last years at Trosly-Breuil, Mme Vanier's bubbly personality continued to delight in both her work and the steady stream of visits she received from old and new friends. On her 90th birthday, she enthusiastically smoked almost a packet of cigarettes, remarking that doctors had at last stopped telling her that the habit would kill her. When she heard of moves to advance the cause for her husband's canonization, she replied: "Of course Georges was a saint. He was married to me."

A.J. CASSON

A.J. CASSON was the last surviving member of the Group of Seven when he died on February 19, 1992, aged 93.

Painting well into his nineties, Casson was a national institution, enjoying the distinction of having an Ontario lake named after him. The honour was entirely fitting, for Casson was above all the poet of small-town Ontario. He transformed the province's apparently banal vernacular architecture and domestic landscape with a sense of human life that, at its best, invited comparison with his contemporary the American realist Edward Hopper. His love of Ontario, which owed something to his sober Quaker background, made him the odd man out among the Group of Seven, whose reputation was based on their portrayal of the rugged and isolated drama of the northern landscape.

The son of a greengrocer who had emigrated from Yorkshire, Alfred Joseph Casson was born on May 17, 1898, and passed his early childhood in a Toronto tenement. In 1907 his parents moved to Guelph, where young Alfred first experienced the beauties of a rural landscape. "My eyes were opened," he later recalled, "to the shapes, colours and light of nature." He was also delighted to discover the "gingerbread tracery" of the boarded barge houses, which inspired much of his later work. Six years later the family returned to the city, first to Hamilton and then, in 1915, to Toronto. Casson was apprenticed to a commercial graphic designer, who kept him busy retouching withered leaves in seed catalogues.

Commercial art provided Casson, and others of the Group of Seven, with vital financial support at a time when interest in contemporary art in Canada was virtually non-existent. "An artist in Canada," he used to quip, "can teach, starve or go commercial." Casson – who also had the responsibilities of family life after his marriage to Margaret Petry in 1924, which produced a daughter – went on to hold a number of increasingly eminent positions in leading

Canadian graphic design and advertising companies, until he retired in 1958. Retirement finally allowed Casson, now in his sixties, to mount his first significant one-man exhibition.

One consequence of his choice of career was that he never received any formal academic training as a painter. He attended evening classes at the Ontario College of Art and later studied on Saturday mornings with Harry Britton, an associate at the Royal Canadian Academy, who proved a crucial influence in making him see that paintings did not simply entail copying and the accumulation of facts. Casson's style developed with amazing strength, and in 1919 he went to work under Frank Carmichael, the design director of Rous and Mann, who was one of the original members of the Group of Seven and who became a close friend. On weekends, holidays and whenever work was slack, the two took off on painting trips to the countryside. Carmichael also introduced Casson to the other members of the Group, with whom he lunched regularly at the Arts and Letters Club in Toronto, then the artistic focus of the city.

Casson's paintings in the 1920s reflected the dominant style of the Group – dramatic mountain and lake landscapes (no people) conveyed in bold colours and in an emphatic, linear style. In 1923 he sold his *Clearing* to the National Gallery of Canada. This marked a small breakthrough in official tastes, although Casson sold only two or three more works between then and the outbreak of the Second World War.

Throughout the 1920s the Royal Canadian Academy remained hostile to the work of the Group of Seven, and Casson's election to both the Group and the Academy in 1926 was a remarkable diplomatic coup. It was partly explained by the fact that Casson belonged to a slightly younger generation than the other members of the Group and had avoided the fierce in-fighting that had characterized its early clashes with officialdom. (The Group's first efforts had been likened by the art establishment to Hungarian goulash and the inside of a drunkard's stomach.) In that same year Casson also founded, with Carmichael, the Canadian Society of Painters in Water Colour, which did much to revive the medium in Canada.

By the early 1930s Casson's work had begun to change. Carmichael had left the commercial world for teaching, and Casson found himself increasingly drawn to the small villages and communities of his Guelph childhood. The Group disbanded in 1932 after some members became ill and others moved from Toronto. It re-formed the following year as an exhibiting society with a wider membership, calling itself the Canadian Group of Painters. Casson's paintings became pervaded with a sense of humanity for the first time; he also developed a sensuous regard for climatic change.

During the Second World War his gifts as a graphic designer were enlisted for propaganda purposes, and one of his posters for War Bonds won a national prize. He was also involved in setting up the Canadian War Art Programme.

In the late 1940s Casson produced a body of not altogether successful paintings, characterized by flat surfaces with sharp plains of high-pitched colour, which were clearly influenced by his graphic design work. He later reverted to his more typical style, and worked more and more in watercolour. His first proper one-man show in 1959 marked the beginning of a series of exhibitions in Toronto. By the end of the 1960s his paintings were fetching as much as $60,000, though they are now valued at 10 times that amount. Casson viewed his change of fortune with a mixture of amusement and indifference; it was too late to matter.

The last two decades of his life saw Casson showered with honours and exhibitions. In 1978 he was appointed OC, and in 1991 his work *Autumn Evening* (1935) was represented in "The True North" exhibition at the Barbican, co-sponsored by *The Daily Telegraph* and Air Canada.

"Watch your step," the Royal Canadian Academy had said to him in reference to his association with the Group of Seven. It was typical of Casson, both as a man and as an artist, that he refused to do so, and went on to become the most beloved of Canadian painters.

BEATRICE LILLIE

BEATRICE LILLIE, otherwise Lady Peel (who died on January 20, 1989, aged 90), was a theatrical entertainer of genius.

Her credits stretched from revue in the 1920s, when she sang Noel Coward's *Poor Little Rich Girl*, to the musicals *Auntie Mame* and *High Spirits* in the 1950s and 1960s, when she also scored a success as a villainous Chinese madam in the film *Thoroughly Modern Millie* opposite Julie Andrews and Carol Channing. Along the way she toured the world with her brilliant one-woman show, *An Evening with Beatrice Lillie*.

Like the accepted wit who has only to say "Pass the mustard, please" to set the table guffawing, Miss Lillie was never anything but funny on or off stage. She had a reputation as a prankster, and in 1951 ordered a live alligator from Harrods and sent it to Noel Coward with the message "So what else is new?"

But Miss Lillie was no actress. Nature did not intend her to create any character except her eccentric own. If she tried her hand at legitimate drama or indeed any show where the lines were presumed to be sacrosanct, she only caused chaos. Whatever success she had in such circumstances was usually won at the expense of the play and her fellow-players (not to mention the director).

Yet her kind of chaos was apt to be more enjoyable than anybody else's order, and was relished for its disruptive effect in musicals. It was in revue or as a solo turn that "Bea" Lillie won the affection of theatregoers the world over, to the extent of becoming a cult figure owing to her ability to demolish social pretense. An inflected eyebrow, a furtive sniff, a *sotto voce* growl or a steely grimace (the repertoire of grimaces was limitless) were her favourite weapons. Words hardly mattered as she chattered incoherently because the pulling of faces, shooting of glances, under-the-breath murmurs and disdainful corners of the mouth expressed all she had to say. And because she seemed incapable of taking anything or anyone seriously, least of all herself, she enjoyed adulation on both sides of the Atlantic for over half a century.

The cropped hair tightly hidden by a pink fez, the long cigarette holder as something to toy with, the tendency to bang her head inexplicably but repeatedly against the proscenium arch: these were beyond rational explanation, like much of her humour. Her art, though eluding, had something of the amiable air of a game of charades. She had a trick of seeming to ignore the audience so that her private fantasies might be indulged as if unperceived. It was, however, the unexpected and seemingly impromptu side of her fooling that made it so different, summed up perhaps by the story of a pigeon which flew by chance into her apartment. "Any messages?" she asked blandly.

She made many film appearances, including *Around the World in 80 Days*, and something of her garbled, mimic's joking came through, as it did in her work on television. But her off-the-cuff, buttonholing fun required a playhouse or cabaret in which to flourish. Rarely did she need to drag topical events into the spray of light, larky satire. To set the house on a roar she had merely to come up with a warbled complaint about the "wind round my heart," or to muse upon a hostess who had ordered a dozen double-damask dinner-table napkins, or to moralize on a friend called Maud whom she accused of being "rotten to the core."

The daughter of a schoolmaster from Northern Ireland, Beatrice Gladys Lillie was born in Toronto on May 29, 1898. Reputedly expelled, aged eight, from the church choir for making faces while singing hymns, she left St Agnes' School, Belleville, at 15 to move to England with her mother and sister. At 16 she sang in the bill at Chatham music hall and later that year appeared at the London Pavilion in *The Daring of Diane* and at the Alhambra in the revue *Not Likely*.

It was the celebrated Anglo-French producer André Charlot who perceived and encouraged the Canadian girl's unusual style. She worked in shows with titles like *Now's the Time, Samples, Cheep, Tabs,*

Oh Joy, Bran-Pie, Now and Then, Pot Luck and (her first legitimate role) *Up in Mabel's Room.* In 1920 Miss Lillie married Robert Peel, great-grandson of the Victorian prime minister Sir Robert Peel. He was a Guards officer who resigned and became a sheep farmer and racehorse owner. In 1925, when her father-in-law died and her husband succeeded to the baronetcy, Bea Lillie became Lady Peel. "Get me," which was one of her catchwords, was applied on more occasions than that when social posturing needed puncturing. Sometimes, however, the title landed her in difficulties, as when her routine about a suburban snob down on her luck ("I always had my own 'orses") was taken literally by an embarrassed American Midwest audience. Unbeknown to Miss Lillie she had been billed as "Lady Peel."

In 1928 she appeared in Coward's revue *This Year of Grace* in New York and four years later played the nurse in Shaw's *Too True to Be Good,* but she never looked at home off the light musical stage. Nor was she ever off it for long.

During the 1939–45 war she toured the world, entertaining the troops for ENSA. Her husband had died in 1934, and in 1942 their only child, the 6th baronet and an ordinary seaman, lost his life when the destroyer *Tenedos,* in which he was serving, was attacked by Japanese dive-bombers.

After the war she returned to London's West End in the revue *Better Life.* Then came summer shows and tours in North America. Her *An Evening with Beatrice Lillie* proved especially popular on her Canadian tour. She appeared in the *Ziegfeld Follies* in 1957 on Broadway and, in 1958, took over the title part of *Auntie Mame* from Greer Garson.

In the mid-1970s she suffered a stroke in New York and was brought back to England bedridden. During her last years Bea Lillie was largely forgotten by the public, but when the writer Timothy Findley came to London to publicize his novel about Noah, *Not Wanted on the Voyage,* he recalled in a speech at Canada House that the title was inspired by a sketch he had seen her performing almost 40 years earlier.

HUGH KEENLEYSIDE

HUGH KEENLEYSIDE (who died on September 27, 1992, aged 94) was the secret go-between when President Roosevelt sought the prime minister Mackenzie King's help in saving the British Fleet once Britain had been defeated in the Second World War.

In May 1940 Keenleyside was about to depart for Washington on business for the Department of External Affairs when he was called into the Ottawa stationmaster's office to take a telephone call. Employing a cautious circumlocution that made their conversation almost incomprehensible, King told Keenleyside to contact a presidential assistant on arrival so that he could be smuggled into the White House. When Keenleyside later relayed King's urgent plea for planes, Roosevelt turned it down. The president then asked Keenleyside to say the words "British Fleet" to King. The day after Keenleyside's return to Ottawa, King was called out of a cabinet meeting by a telephone call from Cordell Hull, the American secretary of state, who asked him to send someone "in whom he had the fullest confidence" for a talk with himself and "somebody higher up."

Keenleyside duly reappeared in the White House, where Roosevelt told him that within a week annihilation or surrender would be the only military alternatives for Britain. The president suggested that the British Fleet should be sent overseas when the last hope of British resistance had gone. The government could evacuate abroad, say to Ottawa, though in deference to the Monroe Doctrine, King George VI should go to Bermuda instead of mainland North America. While American public opinion would not allow any direct intervention, the Fleet would be permitted port facilities, since (as the president did *not* point out) British tars would then be protecting the United States. Roosevelt felt unable to put this suggestion to Winston Churchill himself, so would King obtain the agreement of the other dominion prime ministers and make representations along these lines?

Keenleyside reported personally to King, who was so badly shaken by the thought of what the Opposition might make of this that he suggested Keenleyside's report refer to Roosevelt as "Roberts," King as "Kirk" and Churchill as "Clark." It did not take the prime minister long to spot a flaw. Was he to tell Churchill at once, or should he get the dominions to make a joint approach? Keenleyside said that the president meant the former; Hull, on the telephone, that he meant the latter. Once again Keenleyside took the overnight train to Washington, where Roosevelt said he hoped that King would tell Churchill at once. The strategy should be: "Keep the Fleet from the Germans. Save the Empire. Win the War." Reluctantly King drafted a message to London, unaware that Roosevelt had now also dropped a hint along the same lines to Lord Lothian, the British ambassador. A few days later Churchill made his celebrated speech promising to fight on the beaches and even from the Empire overseas, which, "armed and guarded by the British Fleet," would carry on the struggle. King smugly noted in his diary, "I recognized that the despatch was helpful." He also recorded that Keenleyside's eyes had been blazing with pleasure.

A couple of days later Keenleyside made a final journey to the White House, where he passed on Churchill's warning to King that, if he (Churchill) fell, a pro-German successor might not agree to such a plan. At last Roosevelt was ruffled, saying that if this represented Churchill's opinion, it was "alarming and distressing." King subsequently communicated with the president through the new American minister to Canada.

The son of an insurance salesman, Hugh Llewellyn Keenleyside was born in Toronto on July 7, 1898, and brought up on the West Coast. He studied at the University of British Columbia and joined the 2nd Canadian Tank Battalion at the end of the First World War, but did not see action. On completing his degree, Keenleyside taught history at a series of American universities, where he took an interest in birth control. He married, in 1924, Katherine Pillsbury, and they had four children.

While working for Macmillan, the publishers, in Toronto, he completed his book *Canada and the United States* (1929), in which he came up with a celebrated definition of the two countries' border as "physically invisible, geographically illogical, militarily indefensible and emotionally inescapable." After joining the new Department of External Affairs, Keenleyside was posted as a secretary to the new legation in Tokyo where he uneasily recognized the rise of the new militant ruling class and co-authored *A History of Japanese Education* (1937).

Back in Ottawa, Keenleyside was appointed secretary of the committee to organize the 1939 tour of King George VI and Queen Elizabeth, now the Queen Mother. This appointment involved every aspect of the royal visit – arranging the itinerary, visiting the stopping points, even ensuring that the royal couple had a sliding wall between their bedrooms on the train. Accompanying the party, he noted the steely determination of the Queen and the tact of the royal party in the United States, though he was amused to hear an equerry assure the King that the strange brown liquid they had been offered was Coca Cola – "it is the folk drink of the lower orders in America."

On the outbreak of war, Keenleyside organized an unusual scheme to beat the American Neutrality Act. Under it Canadian owners of large yachts whose craft had been taken over by the war effort were encouraged to buy substitutes in the United States; these they would then hand over to the Royal Canadian Navy in return for a cheque and a picture of their ship.

Because he had written what proved a perceptive paper arguing that greater continental co-operation would become necessary at the expense of traditional links with Britain, Keenleyside was made secretary of the International Joint Board of Defence set up in 1940. But after the unsympathetic Norman Robertson became his chief at External Affairs, he found himself dispatched to be temporary high commissioner in Newfoundland, whose incorporation into Canada he urged, and then ambassador to Mexico.

Keenleyside came back to Canada as deputy mines minister in 1947, but it was his triumph in a mince-pie baking competition which earned him most publicity. A temporary posting to the United Nations led to the director-generalship of its technical assistance organization.

Keenleyside proved adept at retailing the liberally inclined brand of Americanized goodwill which went down well in the Third World.

In retirement, Keenleyside became chairman of B.C. Hydro, which was involved in a project to tame the Columbia River to reduce serious flooding south of the border and produce saleable electricity. His smoothest diplomatic skills were required to ease relations between federal and provincial governments, as well as on the international fronts, but by the end the project's fiercest opponent, General Andrew McNaughton, refused to speak to him.

Keenleyside continued to take an interest in educational projects. He produced two large volumes of unhurried memoirs and was a stalwart of the Vancouver Round Table.

'PUNCH' DICKINS

"PUNCH" DICKINS (who died on August 3, 1995, aged 96) was the last of the major bush pilots responsible for opening up air routes in northwest Canada.

Until the 1920s, large parts of the dominion's northern regions were inaccessible for much of each year and regarded as little more than a frozen repository for future generations. But Dickins and his fellow airmen created regular links with the south, which made commercial development possible and, in the process, ensured that the aircraft was a familiar sight for Inuit who had never seen a car or a train.

He joined the newly formed Western Canada Airways in 1927, and for the next decade his elegant figure – in goggles, fur jacket, high boots and enormous mittens – was a familiar sight in the North. He was internationally celebrated for a series of pioneering flights over more than one million previously uncharted miles, which earned him such nicknames as "The Snow Eagle" and "Canada's Sky Explorer." He made the first flight across the unmapped Barren Lands of the Northwest Territories and flew the first aircraft on the prairie airmail circuit from Winnipeg to Regina, Calgary and Edmonton and back to Winnipeg. In 1929 he became the first pilot to fly the 2,000-mile length of the Mackenzie River, beginning his flight at Edmonton and touching down at Aklavik near the Beaufort Sea. He also made the first landing at the Great Bear Lake, where his passenger the prospector Gilbert LaBine started the first uranium mine.

Not only did Dickins combine caution and skill with a dislike for the roistering life favoured by some of his colleagues; he was also well endowed with luck. The only time he ran out of petrol in the north, he landed on the banks of the Slave River. He was without a radio and considering building a raft when a steamer pulling into view. The skipper shouted that yes, they had some aircraft fuel aboard. It was for "some chap called Dickins who thinks he is going to fly in here next winter."

In 1930 Dickins became the superintendent, stationed at Edmonton, of the Canadian Airways' Mackenzie River District operations and five years later carried out a successful air survey to photograph blind spots on the Yukon–Northwest Territories border.

After the Battle of Britain in 1940 Lord Beaverbrook, Britain's Canadian minister of aircraft production, called in Dickins, who was then assistant to the president of Canadian Pacific. He became operations manager of Atfero, the air ferry organization which flew desperately needed American-built bombers across the Atlantic.

Dickins's organizational abilities at the international level impressed even the prickly Australian pilot Donald Bennett, who was in charge of the technical and operational fields. He had built up transatlantic deliveries to 150 aircraft a month by the time the organization was turned over to RAF Ferry Command in 1942.

Dickins then became general manager of Canadian Pacific Airlines with a brief to amalgamate a number of small and scattered airlines into one network. At the same time he oversaw the management of six flying schools which produced 12,000 air crew in Canada as part of the British Commonwealth Air Training Plan.

Clennell Haggerston Dickins was born at Portage la Prairie, Manitoba, on January 12, 1899. He was called "Punch" because his elder brother could not manage his first name. The family moved to Edmonton, Alberta, when young Punch was eight, and he attended the local university for a year before enlisting in the 196th Western Universities Infantry Battalion in 1917. After its removal to Bramshott, Surrey, he transferred first to the Royal Flying Corps as a pilot and then to its successor, the RAF, with whom he was in posted to No. 211, a bomber and reconnaissance squadron equipped with DH4s and DH9s and operating over Flanders. Although seven victories were attributed to him in the course of some 79 sorties, he claimed, with characteristic modesty, that this was because his observer was an excellent gunner. Nevertheless, he was awarded the DFC in 1917.

After the war, Dickins worked briefly for General Motors and then joined the Canadian Air Force, becoming one of the Royal Canadian Air Force's first officers on its creation in 1924. He carried out high-altitude experimental fighter flights at Edmonton and flew forest patrols from High River, Alberta, as well as making aerial photographic surveys of northern Saskatchewan and Alberta.

The federal government's creation of the Trans-Canada Airway meant that the growth potential for Canadian Pacific was restricted after the war, and in 1947 Dickins became vice-president in charge of sales for de Havilland of Canada. For 20 years he played an important part in marketing the five-seater Beaver, still a standard plane for northern flying, and the twin-engine Otter to more than 60 countries.

After he had retired, Dickins was named in 1973 a member of Canada's Aviation Hall of Fame with the citation: "Despite adversity, he dramatised to the world the value of the bush pilot and his total contribution to the brilliance of Canada's air age can be measured not only by the regard in which he is held by his peers, but by the nation as a whole."

Dickins was appointed OBE in 1936 and OC in 1968. He had three children with his wife, Connie, who wrote *I Married a Bush Pilot* (1981).

K.C. IRVING

K.C. IRVING (who died on December 12, 1992, aged 93) exercised an economic power in New Brunswick of a kind usually encountered in the Third World.

A publicity-shy tycoon with such an aversion to paying taxes that he resided abroad during his last 20 years, Irving was the founder of one of Canada's largest commercial empires. He owned some 300 companies, which employed one in 12 people in the province and touched every aspect of its life. New Brunswickers cannot hop on a bus, fill up with petrol or even visit a public convenience without adding to the Irving family fortune, which had steadily expanded to an estimated $5.8 billion by 1990.

Superficially devoid of any political interests, Irving once said: "I don't think politics and business mix. New Brunswick is too small for politics." But he identified and wooed – and later fell out with – a succession of provincial premiers. He pointed out that his profits were ploughed back into the province, rather than hived off to end up in New York. But the politicians saw in him a man opposed to anything which clashed with his interests. Irving was a hard taskmaster with the most intimate knowledge of his enterprises. More than one country employee was astonished to find that if the boss happened to be on a visit when a sudden order appeared, he would rally round and make a special delivery or change a tire himself.

"Kenneth, you don't wench, you don't smoke, you don't drink. What do you do for your excitement?" asked Irving's fellow New Brunswicker, Lord Beaverbrook. "I work," was the reply.

The son of a storekeeper and small businessman of Scottish descent, Kenneth Colin Irving was born in the oyster-fishing village of Buctouche, New Brunswick, on March 13, 1899. He opened his first bank account at five (to deposit earnings from a vegetable patch which he worked with his mother) and attended local schools before spending a year each at Dalhousie and Acadia universities.

Young Kenneth joined the Royal Flying Corps during the First World War, but was still learning in a two-seater Camel trainer at Folkestone, Kent, when the Armistice was declared. After considering emigrating to Australia, he worked in the family store before landing the local dealership for Model T Fords, for which he accepted horse-drawn buggies in part exchange. He also took on Imperial Oil's local service station until he lost the agency in 1924 when local rivals put pressure on the company.

Irving responded by going into the business on his own account. After five years he had held his own against the American giant sufficiently to launch Irving Oil as a public company. But he soon bought back all the shares and embarked on a policy of steady expansion. This often involved buying new businesses because he considered they were charging too much for their services. During the Second World War Irving supplied veneer from his forests for Mosquito aircraft. Afterwards he started a shipping line and bought the local railways and the country's only major shipyard – while snapping up every parcel of forestry that came on the market until he owned a quarter of the province's total.

He began to encounter serious criticism because of his ownership of New Brunswick's four major newspapers. When it was disclosed in the Senate that he had secretly acquired a fifth, government agencies embarked on a self-righteous campaign against him. While Irving showed no sign of intervening personally, his editors always kept his picture out of their papers and made a point of playing down, if not suppressing, anything which showed his companies in a bad light. For a time stories about spillages from Irving's ships simply referred to them as belonging to "a local oil company," although criticism later led to adoption of a more open policy. A royal commission on the press roundly declared that the province was a "journalistic disaster area," and a raid on the Irving family's office and homes by RCMP officers led to a formal charge of running an illegal monopoly.

That was enough for Irving. He was already under threat from a proposed inheritance tax. Five weeks after the charge was laid, he announced from the Bahamas that he no longer lived in New Brunswick and that his sons now ran his businesses. "As far as anything else goes," he concluded, "I do not choose to discuss the matter further."

The Irvings and their companies were fined $150,000 by a provincial court, although the decision was quashed on appeal. By then, however, Irving had removed the substance of the complaint by dividing the papers up between members of his family. It was while he was living modestly in Bermuda that the fall of the Shah of Iran gave Irving the chance for his most spectacular success. With his own oil refinery, tanker fleet and reliable supplies from South America, he was able to scoop large profits throughout the early 1980s by entering the volatile "spot" markets with promises to deliver anywhere.

Irving returned regularly to St John, where his tall, bald-headed figure – suggestive in his youth of a bare-knuckle boxer – could be seen staring down from the glass penthouse of his 13-storey headquarters. Some people in the street below wondered whether he had doubts about his single-minded career. Others believed he was musing on his success in passing on the still expanding conglomerate to his three sons – chips off the old block nick-named "Oily," "Gassy" and "Greasy" because of the interests respectively assigned to them.

ROLAND MICHENER

ROLAND MICHENER (who died on August 6, 1991, aged 91) became Governor General in 1967 when the role of the monarchy was being questioned by English Canadians and rejected by French Canadians.

He exuded all the quiet confidence which is necessary in the Queen's personal representative, and his wavy grey hair, trimmed moustache and crisp patrician tones could almost have been plucked from Central Casting. There was one dramatic moment when he was called out of bed at 4 a.m. to sign the War Measures Act in 1970 to deal with the terrorists who had captured James Cross, the British trade commissioner, and Pierre Laporte, the Quebec labour minister.

But Michener's tenure was only a moderate success, as the democratization of the office speeded its decline into a dim reflection of the mystery and splendour of monarchy. This process began when he agreed to eliminate full curtsies and bows at formal receptions, except when the Queen visited the country. Maryon Pearson, wife of the prime minister, Lester Pearson, had objected to the thought of demeaning herself to her old school friend Norah Michener. "Personally, I shall be happier as a Canadian among Canadians," Michener declared the day he was installed, "with such customary Canadian salutations as the handshake or bow."

The son of a Tory senator, Daniel Roland Michener was born at Lacombe, Alberta, on April 19, 1900, and educated at Red Deer High School. He joined the RAF as a pilot in 1918, then studied at the University of Alberta. As a Rhodes Scholar next at Hertford College, Oxford, he won a blue for track and field events and, more important, a half-blue playing hockey against a Cambridge team that included young Pearson. Despite their adherence to different political camps, a close friendship developed between the two students, who even entered as a doubles partnership in the 1923 Canadian Open Tennis Tournament; they were eliminated in the first round.

Michener practised law in Toronto while sitting on the boards of mining companies and contributing to a legal textbook. But in his forties he decided to follow in his father's footsteps and won a seat in the Ontario Provincial Parliament, where he was appointed provincial secretary by George Drew. He was defeated in 1948, but when Drew became national Tory leader, Michener followed him into the House of Commons, where after only four years he was elected Speaker. Michener was so concerned about his atrocious French accent that he asked Louis St Laurent to hear him recite the daily prayer at the start of proceedings, which prompted the former prime minister to remark: "Well, I can understand it, but I doubt if the good Lord can." Nevertheless, his facility improved and he gained a wide respect for impartiality – with one exception. The Tory prime minister, John Diefenbaker, whom Michener had once ruled out of order for questioning his ability to control Question Period, was convinced that Speaker Michener laid too much store by the questionable ideas of his "Liberal friends" and did not rally enough to his own party.

The truth was that Diefenbaker and Michener sprang from very different backgrounds. While Diefenbaker remained a radical outsider, Michener was every inch the civilized, smooth Toronto establishment man. When Michener lost his seat in 1962, he immediately announced that he would not be standing again, which made the beleaguered Diefenbaker so angry that he refused to nominate him to the Senate.

So Michener returned to his law practice, from which he was plucked when Pearson became prime minister, to be high commissioner in India, where he distinguished himself by pointing out all the good works done by his countrymen and wearing a suit and tie all summer. After three years he was recalled to become Governor General in place of Georges Vanier, who had died in office.

A consummate committee man, "Roly" Michener served on Canadian delegations to conferences on Commonwealth relations at Chatham House in London. Married to Norah Willis, who bore him three daughters, he remained an ardent sportsman. He jogged until his last year and appeared on government-sponsored television commercials to promote physical fitness.

JOEY SMALLWOOD

JOEY SMALLWOOD (who died on December 17, 1990, aged 89) had a picaresque career as a journalist, union organizer and pig-breeder until 1949, when he took a reluctant Newfoundland into Confederation; he was the new province's autocratic premier for the next 23 years.

A small, peppery man of large contradictions, he was the island's greatest populist leader: a quondam trade unionist who later rode roughshod over unions; an apostle of instant industrialization who still recognized the danger of destroying the unique character of a people proud to live in England's first colony. Smallwood claimed to be a lifelong socialist, and remained a bitter opponent of the island merchants' power. Yet he realized that "the Rock" was not ready for socialist policies, and in its freebooting democracy – reminiscent at times of *Pickwick Papers'* Eatanswill – he supported the Liberal party. As he campaigned from the back of a large Cadillac, Smallwood would dismiss his more abusive hecklers as "doubtful" supporters. He once insisted that the prime minister, Lester Pearson, should keep on waving to supporters as they passed through a graveyard on the grounds that "some of your most faithful voters are in there." Yet he remained so obsessed with the threat of plots that he bugged his driveway in order to hear what his cabinet ministers were saying to their wives.

Joseph Roberts Smallwood was born at Gambo, Bonavista Bay, on Christmas Eve, 1900, the son of an alcoholic businessman. He led his first strike at Bishop Feild School in St John's, the capital, with the slogan "More Molasses, Less Pudding." At 15 young Joe became a printer's devil; later he switched to reporting. He covered the 1918 Victory Parade in St John's on horseback and the race to fly the Atlantic non-stop, which was won by Alcock and Brown, for the *Evening Telegram.* Anxious for more experience, he then moved to Halifax, Nova Scotia, and Boston, before joining *Call,* the New York socialist daily. In the 1924 presidential campaign he became a speaker for the socialist candidate Robert La Follette, and on one occasion only narrowly escaped being lynched for espousing negro equality.

Smallwood returned to Newfoundland to organize paper-mill workers and railway maintenance staff, and also started a short-lived socialist weekly. Then, in 1926, he came to England, where he stayed for less than a year but developed a deep attachment for the country. He worked as a freelance journalist, campaigned for Labour in the 1927 North Southwark by-election and haunted the British Museum Reading Room, where he wrote his first book, a biography of Sir William Coaker, the leader of the Newfoundland fishermen's union, in three days. Back in St John's, Smallwood became bound up in the fortunes of the Liberal party. He was close to its leader, Sir Richard Squires, who as prime minister from 1928 found himself coping with the Great Depression in an island which had recently been created a dominion yet had known little but recession in peacetime.

After the Liberals were annihilated in the 1932 election, a conservative United Newfoundland party administration applied for financial help from Britain, which suspended the parliamentary system and substituted an efficient, cautious civil service administration that is still regarded by many as the finest government in Newfoundland's history.

With politics in abeyance, Smallwood first promoted a fishermen's co-operative union and ran a co-operative wholesale society, which he left amid accusations of financial mismanagement. No charges were laid, but Smallwood's future political colleague Gordon Bradley, the local magistrate, informed the Commission of Government that Smallwood was not to be relied upon in anything requiring sound judgment or steady work. Kept under surveillance by the police as a troublemaking speaker and journalist, Smallwood next persuaded a local businessman to finance *The Book of Newfoundland,* an eclectic two-volume collection of essays which he edited and then sold from door to door. Smallwood also began a regular series of 15-minute radio talks, *The Barrelman*, in which he praised Newfoundlanders and their history indiscriminately. But by 1943 he was bored with broadcasting and went to Gander to set up a large piggery with the RAF Welfare Fund, using the air base's scraps for feed. It was a vital move, because when the Attlee government decided to call a convention to determine Newfoundland's future. Smallwood won a seat as a Confederate in Gander, which would have been impossible in St John's. A majority favoured a return to independent self-government, but Britain insisted that the convention should continue to sit. Smallwood's superior tactics, the quarrelsomeness of his opponents and his already familiar voice during the broadcast proceedings carried the day after a bitter campaign, in which he more than once had to flee angry mobs. Even now, some suspect the result to have been fixed by the civil servants.

When Newfoundland entered Canada, 73 years after first being invited, Smallwood was asked to form the new province's first Liberal government, and immediately embarrassed Louis St Laurent's federal administration by declaring that a constituency would receive no aid unless it elected a Liberal member. A case of corruption dogged him through his first months in office but was later dropped. While aid in the form of welfare payments and road-building programmes poured in, Smallwood tried to encourage a wide variety of projects, ranging from the crackpot to the Churchillian. Four Icelanders received the first sizeable grant to start a herring business, for which they produced a couple of elderly boats before disappearing. Another plan was to build a replica of the German city of Rothenburg to manufacture toys. To supervise his economic miracle, he first attracted Sir William Stephenson, the wartime British spymaster in America, then Alfred Valdmanis, a former Latvian finance minister and Nazi collaborator. Valdmanis introduced Smallwood to German industrialists, flattered him outrageously and eventually walked off with $200,000 in a suitcase.

Although many industries never got off the ground or lasted only a time, Smallwood successfully appealed in London for an enterprise on the scale of the East India Company: a massive hydro-electric project in Labrador. He interested a consortium headed by Rothschilds after a meeting at 10 Downing Street with Sir Winston Churchill, who described it as "a grand Imperial project, and I don't mean Imperialist." It took 15 years, but eventually, after heroic struggles with the elements and the Quebec government – which claims that it, not Newfoundland, should own Labrador – a plant at Churchill Falls began to supply power to Quebec for resale to New York. The venture differed from many other similar projects in Canada in that it did not require a flood of provincial government cash and was a success; but, as so often in Newfoundland's history Fate intervened, and the value of the fixed-price project was eroded by inflation.

By 1959 Smallwood still had comparatively little to show for 10 years in power, but he scored a notable victory over John Diefenbaker, the prime minister, by getting him to withdraw a threat not to continue federal grants made to Newfoundland under the Terms of Union. He clashed again with the Conservative leader when Diefenbaker refused to send Mountie replacements to deal with a loggers' strike by a newly imported American union. Although a former pulp workers' organizer himself, Smallwood went on to crush the strike after a policeman was killed on a picket line.

To halt the flow of young people to the increasingly familiar mainland, Smallwood developed Memorial University in St John's, which for a time even introduced payments to students. After a long search, he persuaded Lord Taylor, the new town developer, to be its president.

In 1965 Smallwood achieved world headlines when he and Richard Nixon went on from visiting a Helsinki pulp mill to Moscow, where they decided to call on the future U.S. president's "old friend" Nikita Khrushchev. They managed to evade their guides and arrived at the former Soviet leader's flat, only to be refused admittance by a security guard.

When Pierre Trudeau became prime minister in 1968, federal grants were cut, and younger Newfoundlanders, who did not remember the Confederation battles, saw in Smallwood an ancient tyrant with a caustic tongue who seemed to decide economic policy at whim. The 1972 general election left the two parties split with 20 seats each and an independent Irish union leader, elected in Labrador, open to offers. For weeks Smallwood refused to give up because the election of one seat was in doubt, as the returning officer had burnt the ballots. In the end the result was upheld because a judge declared that Canadian law was invalid where it went back before Newfoundland entered Confederation, and Smallwood fell. He resigned his party's leadership, returned briefly as leader of a Liberal Reform party, then resigned again, recognizing, in a favourite expression, that "the tide was out."

In retirement, Smallwood took up authorship again, producing *I Chose Canada* (1973), a characteristically vigorous, if hardly elegant, autobiography that was refreshingly clear of any hint of a ghost writer. He also set about writing and editing two further volumes of *The Book of Newfoundland*. Another project was an *Encyclopedia of Newfoundland*, which brought him to the verge of bankruptcy in 1986. A television camera recorded him being struck dumb with a stroke as he received the writ at his front door.

Almost unique among Canadian leaders Smallwood was not only a real writer himself but a colourful subject for other authors. Richard Gwyn, the *Toronto Star* columnist, wrote *Smallwood, the Unlikely Revolutionary* (1968), one of the finest studies of a still active politician. The satirical novel *Clapp's Rock* (1983) was also a vivid, if hardly flattering, portrait of Smallwood at the height of his power. Its author was William Rowe, who had been a bright young cabinet minister lured into the great little man's circle with the veiled promise of succeeding him.

E.P. TAYLOR

E.P. TAYLOR, the multi-millionaire (who died in the Bahamas on May 14, 1989, aged 88), was celebrated for his vast brewing interests on both sides of the Atlantic and for his ownership of more than 100 racehorses, including the legendary Northern Dancer.

While courting the sober image of a businessman, dedicated to the inviolability of balance sheets, Taylor had an executive jet painted in his turquoise and gold racing colours. His plump figure, impeccably turned out in morning suit and top hat, with pipe clenched in teeth, was a familiar sight on racecourses around the world. Socialists, faced with a capitalist who looked as if he belonged in a cartoon, dubbed him "the Croesus of Big Business" and claimed that his initials stood for "Excess Profits."

Edward Plunket Taylor was born in Ottawa on January 29, 1901, and educated at Ashbury College, the London City and Guilds College, and McGill University. He began his entrepreneurial career with a taxi firm and bus line and invented the first electric toaster to brown on both sides. He then went into a small Ontario brewery owned by his grandfather. Taylor steadily built up what became the giant Canadian Breweries by judicious takeovers and drastic pruning of product ranges, although there were hiccups along the way. At one stage his bank withdrew his credit, and his business would have collapsed without access to British capital.

On the outbreak of war in 1939 Taylor became one of the most successful of the "dollar-a-year" executives who joined the Canadian federal government at Ottawa on a nominal salary. The experience proved anything but a soft option when, with the supply and munitions minister C.D. Howe, he was on board a ship which was torpedoed off Ireland in December 1940. Roused from his bed, Taylor spent several hours shivering in a lifeboat, wearing a pair of silk pyjama trousers, before being picked up by a passing merchant ship and taken to Ireland.

Taylor played a critical part in implementing an agreement – worked out between his prime minister, Mackenzie King, and President Roosevelt – for the United States to supply Canada with parts to replace those the dominion was sending to Britain. In 1941 Lord Beaverbrook persuaded Winston Churchill to appoint him vice-chairman and president of the British Supply Council of North America. When the Americans entered the war, Taylor came up with a figure of 60,000 aircraft and 45,000 tanks a year, which Churchill recommended to Roosevelt and which duly became the official American production target in 1942. Around the same time Taylor also became director-general of the British Purchasing Commission, although he later had to give up for health reasons, returning to work in Ottawa on Allied boards.

Almost immediately Taylor became involved in a personal row with King, who came out in favour of prohibition. Taylor responded in a critical letter to an Ottawa newspaper and, with the aid of workers who threatened to buy no more Victory Bonds if they were deprived of beer, forced King to withdraw. In acting as he had, Taylor earned the undying hatred of the prime minister, who scratched his name from a list of five candidates recommended for appointment as Companions of the Order of St Michael and St George. Taylor eventually received his CMG in 1946 but, thanks to the obtuse opposition of Mackenzie King and the Tory prime minister John Diefenbaker, was never awarded the knighthood or peerage which was his due.

By the end of the war Taylor had the experience and contacts to emerge as a major tycoon, building up his brewery interests south of the border and boldly urging a free-trade area between Britain, Canada and the United States. At the same time he became a founder of the Argus Corporation (now controlled by Conrad Black, owner of *The Daily Telegraph*), took a major shareholding in Massey Ferguson and became developer of the Don Mills industrial estate in northern Toronto.

As a successful racehorse owner with stud farms in Ontario and Maryland, Taylor had more winners than any other breeder in the world. He dominated Canadian racing, helping to raise the prestige of the Queen's Plate in Toronto, for which Queen Elizabeth the Queen Mother stayed at his house on several occasions. He also owned a string of thoroughbreds in Britain and Ireland, employing the great jockey Sir Gordon Richards as his trainer. His greatest horse was Northern Dancer, who won the Kentucky Derby in 1964 before becoming the world's most successful stallion, siring such champions as Nijinsky and The Minstrel.

Taylor's serious business career in Britain began disappointingly in the 1950s when he failed to gain control of George's Bristol brewery, which he said he needed because the local water would be ideal for lager making. British brewers had an ingrained suspicion of predatory North American entrepreneurs. But, with his belief that the industry was destined to be dominated by about nine companies and his advocacy of lager (particularly the Carling Black Label brand, which he owned in Canada), Taylor embarked on a series of mergers that led him to the chairmanship of Bass Charrington a decade later.

By then his Canadian interests were beginning to show signs of being overstretched and he wisely decided to start winding down his interests. He ended his British career fighting, as a matter of principle, a demand from the Inland Revenue for a share of £8,000 travelling expenses he had received as an international company director. Eventually the House of Lords ruled in his favour, Lord Salmon commenting that the reference in the relevant Act to a horse hardly indicated that it bore considerations of the modern world in mind.

On selling out his brewery interests in Britain and North America, Taylor retired to the Bahamas, where he began developing wasteland. He had bought land at Lyford Cay from the developer Sir Harold Christie and turned it into one of the smartest residential clubs in the world, with an entrance fee of $25,000 and a subscription of around $4,000. The Bahamas suffered an economic downturn for a period, but at the time of his death Taylor's New Providence development company, which owns some 5,400 acres, was rapidly providing residential, recreational and commercial property to cope with the expansion of nearby Nassau.

BRUCE HUTCHISON

BRUCE HUTCHISON (who died on September 14, 1992, aged 91) enjoyed such eminence as a journalist that he conducted editorial policy for three months every summer from a wooded retreat on Vancouver Island.

Until the 1960s, Hutchison did not even have a telephone in his cottage at Shawinigan Lake and had to call his office from a local gas station every morning. Yet he was successively co-editor of the *Winnipeg Free Press*, editor of the Victoria *Times* and editorial-page editor of the *Vancouver Sun* – a reflection of his prestige as a classical Liberal pundit. Hutchison's admirers included the prime ministers Mackenzie King, Louis St Laurent and Lester Pearson as well as a readership which relished his homespun prose, redolent of a rural Canada of which they often knew little. He liked to recall that when Japan bombed Pearl Harbor he was pruning cherry trees, and that he was digging an outside privy when offered the editorship of the Victoria *Times*. It was not without significance that one of his best-loved articles was an account of the death of a 500-year-old Douglas fir near his house.

A survivor of an age when journalism was firmly rooted in literature, Hutchison also wrote fiction. In the 1930s he contributed to *Saturday Evening Post* and *Colliers* and even produced the script for a poor Hollywood film, *Park Avenue Logger* (1937). He wrote a novel about journalism during the war, *The Hollow Men* (1944); a collection of sunny tales, *Uncle Percy's Wonderful Town* (1981); and a novella, *The Cub Reporter Learns a Thing or Two* (1991). Some of his funniest stories appeared in his syndicated weekly column "Loose Ends," which portrayed his eccentric *alter ego* Horace Snifkin and the cockney Mrs Alfred Noggins, who was drawn on an ignorant neighbour.

William Bruce Hutchison was born at Prescott, Ontario, on June 5, 1901, and brought up at Merritt in the British Columbia interior when horses were still tied up outside the crowded bar, all Liberals were "swine" and his father was an unsuccessful estate agent. At 16, he went to work for the Victoria *Times*, where his first scoop was the shooting of a visiting Chinese prime minister, which was confined to the back page.

At 20 Hutchison began to cover the B.C. Legislature, and five years later he was sent to Ottawa, where the duel between the incisive Tory Arthur Meighen and the obscurantist Liberal Mackenzie King was reaching its climax. But after a few months he married Dorothy McDiarmid, who was to bear him a son and a daughter, and returned to British Columbia, from which he never moved permanently again. He built a home outside Victoria and maintained a summer camp in the south of the island which, even at the end of his life, a visitor could only reach by a short forest path or by canoe from around the point.

While Hutchison was content to write for local papers, he was also in demand for special assignments in Ottawa, New York and London. The most unusual of these came in 1940 when he was sent, ostensibly, to cover Wendell Wilkie's presidential campaign but really to drop in on local newspaper editors to explain why Canada was involving North America in the war. Hutchison was then asked to aid the war effort by writing *The Unknown Country* (1943), a charming if ill-organized work which endeavoured to show Canada's diversity and independence.

The next year he became one of the three co-editors of the *Winnipeg Free Press*, which entailed supervising the country's most powerful editorial page; but after a few months he escaped back to the West Coast to be a purely writing editor. His postwar assignments included broadcasting for the infant television service, interviewing the actress Zsa Zsa Gabor and covering the 1953 Coronation. He watched the royal procession from Canada House in Trafalgar Square but just before his deadline found that the room with the telephone was locked. In desperation he climbed out onto the parapet and crashed through a window to reach it.

Hutchison wrote an account of the Fraser River, a survey of Canada's prime ministers and an unduly benevolent account of

Canadian-American relations. His most commanding work was *The Incredible Canadian* (1952), a discreetly admiring though unflattering portrait of Mackenzie King. The biography drew on a diary kept by Senator "Chubby" Power, who had resigned from the government during the 1944 conscription crisis. After its publication, Hutchison was given a considerable scoop when St Laurent arranged for him to speak to an anonymous general who said that the government's hand had been forced by the Canadian Army Board's threat of rebellion – a claim later hotly disputed.

While Hutchison raised the standards of editorial comment at the Victoria *Times* and the *Vancouver Sun,* he also attracted strong criticism. The Social Credit premier W.A.C. ("Wacky") Bennett accused him of being "a menace to good government," while readers complained about his failure to follow slavishly the local Liberal line. Younger colleagues muttered about an editor who rarely came near the office, but he was well briefed by a host of visitors who, apart from a host of political luminaries from prime ministers downwards, included the American diplomat George Kennan and the film star James Cagney. The photographer Yousuf Karsh once gave some peremptory instructions to Hutchison's odd-job man and was so embarrassed on discovering that this was the province's chief justice that he plunged into the lake fully clothed.

In *The Unfinished Country* (1985), which took a somewhat darker look at contemporary Canada, Hutchison concluded that he had been right one-third of the time.

SIR ROBERT GUNNING, BT

SIR ROBERT GUNNING, 8th Baronet (who died on December 7, 1989, aged 88), was a sod-busting farmer and the unofficial squire of Peace River, Alberta.

Having set off in 1948 with just one major luxury – a large library, which included the complete works of John Masefield – Gunning arrived at Peace River with his wife and five children to discover that their new home was a draughty log cabin without power or water. Only 14 acres of the 160-acre quarter section had been cleared, the closest neighbour was two miles away, and the nearest paved road 200 miles. But with the help of his children – in particular his 13-year-old boy, who gathered up tree roots after the land was broken, and his 11-year-old daughter, who won admiration for her milking skills – Gunning built the farm up to 2,000 acres and moved into a new house. His success soon led to an invitation to test various new strains of oats for the federal Department of Agriculture. It also enabled him to turn what remained of his prodigious energies towards local public life – he became chairman of the local hospital board, established a native friendship society, and with his wife ran the Peace River Agriculture Society.

Gunning resolutely refused to modify his English accent and eschewed any temptation to ignore his baronetcy, which he inherited in 1950 from a great uncle, one of four brothers who had no sons. Nonetheless he responded as cheerfully to "Mr Gunning" as to "Sir Robert," and made no comment when he and his wife were introduced as "Sir Robert and Mrs Gunning." In 1976 the couple were named Peace River's "Citizens of the Year."

The son of a colonial officer attached to the Sultan of Zanzibar, Robert Charles Gunning was born in East Africa on December 2, 1901, and educated at St Paul's School and Leeds University. He trained as a tanner and was sent out by the African and Eastern

Company – later merged in Lever Brothers – to Nigeria, where his task was to buy hides. Before long Gunning resigned this post but, after another stint in England, returned to Africa to run a bus company in Lagos. He then set out in search of gold, which he found in modest quantities on the River Yelwa, a tributary of the Niger. Fluent in Hausa and Arabic, Gunning directed some 200 Africans as they wielded picks and shovels and drained the gold in pans. Every evening his wife treated the crew for any injuries.

By the time they returned home, they had made enough money to buy back the stables and kitchen garden of Horton, the Adam house in Northamptonshire which had belonged to his ancestor, the Minister Plenipotentiary to the Court of Catherine the Great of Russia, who was created 1st Baronet in 1778. Gunning started a market garden, which was just beginning to show a profit when war was declared. He joined up but was little pleased to find himself considered too old to serve overseas and confined to searchlight duties. On his demob in 1945 he found the market garden had failed. When a local official tried to stop him building a shelter for his car, he went off to see Canadian government officials in London who told him they had just the property he was seeking in Peace River.

Gunning married, in 1934, Helen Nancy Ann, daughter of Vice-Admiral Sir Theodore Hallett; they had 10 children, of whom the eldest, Charles Theodore Gunning, born in 1935, a retired lieutenant-commander in the Royal Canadian Navy, succeeded to the baronetcy.

LOVAT DICKSON

LOVAT DICKSON (who died in Toronto on January 2, 1987, aged 84) made his reputation as the London publisher of the best-selling "Red Indian" author Grey Owl.

After bringing out *Pilgrims of the Wild* in 1935, Dickson brought the buckskin-clad writer to Britain for two highly successful tours, which included a private performance for the Princesses Elizabeth and Margaret Rose at Buckingham Palace, where Grey Owl greeted King George VI as "brother." Grey Owl died in 1938, and Dickson had just broadcast a tribute when he heard that the *Toronto Star* claimed Grey Owl had been born one Archie Belaney in Hastings, Sussex. The newspaper's story – and Dickson's uneasy suspicions – proved all too correct. Two elderly maiden aunts confirmed that they had brought him up. But despite the deception Dickson published an affectionate account of Grey Owl's two visits to England, *The Green Leaf* (1938), and a romantic account of his life, *Half-Breed* (1939). He later produced a perceptive biography, *Wilderness Man* (1973), by which time Canadians, thanks partly to the enthusiasm of John Diefenbaker, who had acted as counsel in a dispute over Belaney's will, were ready to recognize Grey Owl as the advanced guard of the conservation movement.

A mining engineer's son, Horatio Henry Lovat Dickson, known to friends as Rache, was born in Australia on June 30, 1902, and educated in Rhodesia and at Berkhampstead School in Hertfordshire. At 15, he joined his father in Canada and drifted into a series of dead-end jobs. But after editing a weekly newspaper in Blue Diamond Mine, Alberta, he went to the University of Alberta, where he won the Governor General Gold Medal and stayed on to lecture for a year.

Dickson then accepted the offer of a wealthy Canadian to edit the old-established *Fortnightly Review* in London, where he was to spend his professional career. He began his own publishing company, edited the *Review of Reviews* and then started *Lovat Dickson's Magazine* to publicize his imprint. In 1938 he was forced to sell out and went to work for Macmillan, under the future prime minister Harold Macmillan, where he eventually became a director.

Dickson was one of those rare publishers who was also an accomplished writer. His *Radclyffe Hall and the Well of Loneliness* (1975) tackled vividly a best-selling author's lesbian relationship, and *H.G. Wells* (1969) steered a course between Wells's sons and litigious former mistress Rebecca West to win strong admirers. He also wrote *The Museum Makers* (1986), a history of the Royal Ontario Museum. There were two volumes of autobiography, *The Ante-Room* (1959) and *The House of Words* (1963), which combined the writer's buoyancy with introspection and contained some memorable portraits of the London literary world.

In 1944 Dickson published *Out of the West*, a romantic novel full of nostalgia for the Alberta of his youth. On retirement from Macmillan in 1967, Dickson returned to Canada with his wife, the former Marguerite Brodie of Montreal, who bore him a son. He was appointed OC in 1978.

LIONEL CHEVRIER

LIONEL CHEVRIER, former high commissioner for Canada in London (who died, aged 84, on July 8, 1987), was an "old line" French Canadian politician whose major achievement was the creation of the St Lawrence Seaway.

As transport minister in the 1940s, he revitalized the project for the 2,000-mile waterway, linking the Great Lakes and the Atlantic, after it had been in the doldrums since the signing of an agreement between Canada and the United States in 1941. The difficulties involved once prompted President Eisenhower to joke to Chevrier that Canada would be better off as America's 49th state. But Chevrier pressed on and, for the crucial three years of construction, gave up his political career to become the Seaway's first president.

Chevrier's success and, ultimately, failure as a politician sprang from his being born the son of French Canadian parents in predominantly English-speaking Ontario. Fully bilingual, he spoke French in a way that was easily understandable to English ears. He was nicknamed "the Silver Fox" because of his mane of white hair, and was once said to have the immortal air of a minor French official in an old film who, after solving the young couple's romantic difficulties, bursts into song about *amour* and turns out to be Maurice Chevalier.

Lionel Chevrier was born on April 2, 1903, at Cornwall, Ontario, and educated locally and at the University of Ottawa before studying at Osgoode Hall for the Ontario Bar, to which he was called in 1928. He was elected a Liberal MP for the Ontario constituency of Stormont seven years later. During the 1939–45 war, he was the deputy government chief whip, chairman of the parliamentary committee on war expenditure and parliamentary assistant to the minister of munitions before being promoted to transport minister in 1945. As one of Mackenzie King's bright young men for the future, he was sent to the Bretton Woods conference and made chairman of the

57

Canadian delegation to the United Nations General Assembly in Paris in 1948.

In Parliament, he created a precedent by taking advantage of a temporary loophole in procedure which permitted ministers in the Commons to introduce a bill personally into the Senate. As a French Canadian with the right English-speaking connections, Chevrier greatly impressed King's successor as prime minister, the Quebecker Louis St Laurent, who allowed him to take time off for the Seaway project and then return to the cabinet as president of the Privy Council. When the Liberals were defeated after 22 years in office, Chevrier proved himself a doughty combatant in the Commons, becoming known as one of the Four Horsemen who wore down John Diefenbaker's enormous majority. But even though he moved to a Montreal constituency in 1957, Chevrier's seigneurial approach and close identification with old-guard party machine politicians did nothing to stop many younger Quebec politicians regarding him as a carpetbagger.

It was little surprise, therefore, that he failed not only to scent the new nationalistic wind getting up in the province but also to deliver the seats he promised as the French lieutenant of the prime minister Lester Pearson during the elections of the early 1960s. Chevrier made several unfortunate recommendations of political candidates to Pearson, including one who had to resign from the cabinet to stand trial. But by the time a series of corruption scandals began to break, he had resigned as both justice minister and member of Parliament to become Canada's 12th high commissioner to Britain.

Although an unfamiliar figure in London, he demonstrated a natural ability to get on with people. When parties got too heavy at Canada House, his wife, Lucienne, would settle down to play her harp. Chevrier made a strong impact on his fellow Commonwealth representatives, becoming chairman of the committee on Rhodesian sanctions, although he did not hide doubts about their effectiveness. As the first French Canadian high commissioner, he took steps to ensure that Canada House became bilingual, and ordered a statue of Montcalm to match the existing one of Wolfe. But his staff roused the suspicion of the growing British conservation lobby when the High Commission took over the rest of the Trafalgar Square building from the Royal College of Physicians and threatened to remove an imposing staircase until a preservation order was slapped on it. A compromise was only worked out after protesters were invited in from the street to make an inspection.

Chevrier found his three years in the post surprisingly onerous because of the vast number of telegrams from Ottawa and the busy social life, and he was glad to return to Canada as official "greeter" at the dominion's centennial celebrations.

PROFESSOR GERALD GRAHAM

PROFESSOR GERALD GRAHAM (who died on July 8, 1988, aged 85) was an outstanding historian of the British Empire much saddened by the fading of the imperial vision in his lifetime.

The greater part of his career was spent at King's College, London, where he gloried in the title of Rhodes Professor of Imperial History. As the historian of the maritime Empire, Graham had no equal. *The Empire of the North Atlantic* (1950), *The Politics of Naval Supremacy* (1965), *Great Britain in the Indian Ocean* (1967) and *The China Station: War and Diplomacy, 1830–60* (1978) all played a key part in the wider recognition of the key role of sea power in imperial expansion. His breadth of erudition attracted a stream of inquiries from friends, students and colleagues. Why, for example, did the standing orders of the Bombay Station require the survey ships to anchor two cable lengths offshore? The inquirer was rewarded with the information that this distance exceeded the flight of mosquitoes and sandflies; referred to Burton's reference to mosquito bites bringing deadly fevers; and diverted, as a bonus, by a digression on tanghin, a strychnine-like poison used by the queens of Madagascar to kill their husbands. No one asked for Graham's help in vain.

The son of a Nonconformist minister, Gerald Sandford Graham was born at Sudbury, Ontario, on April 27, 1903, and educated at Queen's University (Kingston), Harvard, Cambridge and Berlin. He taught at Harvard from 1930 to 1936 and then had a chair at Queen's for 10 years, though part of this time was spent lecturing at Royal Roads naval college in British Columbia. To induce him to take the latter post, the college promised him the opportunity to cross the Atlantic in a convoy each year, an experience he described in several articles. His early works, which included *British Policy and Canada, 1783–91* (1930) and *Sea Power and British North America* (1941), gave him not only a deep appreciation of the contributions of Empire but the conviction that the wind of change which blew throughout Africa was a destructive hurricane.

Graham had the bluff, salty manner of a retired sailor who seemed more at home on quarterdecks than in archives. He wore his learning so lightly that those who did not know him well were surprised at the range and thoroughness of his scholarship – and at the way he slaughtered many sacred cows of naval history. Married twice, with two sons and two daughters, he used to say, after he had retired to a cottage outside Rye, that – like Kipling – he had made the journey from Empire to Sussex.

PAUL MARTIN

PAUL MARTIN, the former high commissioner in London (who died on September 14, 1992, aged 89), was Canada's most dedicated professional politician even though he failed to win the prime ministership.

An able health minister and a vigorous external affairs secretary, Martin sought the Liberal leadership for 20 years before finally losing it for the last time to Pierre Trudeau in 1968. "A good party man who makes no bones about it," he retained to the end of his days the politician's gift for making friends; he was an acknowledged master of "mainstreeting" – stopping voters as they went about their business to shake their hands. Nevertheless, an enduring part of the Martin mythology was the story of how he asked a man about his mother's health and received the reply, "Same as this morning – dead."

Not the smallest surprise of Martin's long career was his volume of *London Diaries* (1988). While his earlier books effectively buried any pleasure for readers in accounts of endless points made in instantly forgotten speeches, he produced here a uniquely authoritative picture of Anglo-Canadian relations at the moment a left-leaning establishment was being defeated in both countries by a conservatism that had been moribund for almost half a century.

Paul Joseph James Martin was born in Ottawa on June 23, 1903, one of nine children in a working-class bilingual family of French and Irish origin. He studied law at Osgoode Hall, paying for his fees by working on a Ford assembly line at Windsor, Ontario, and went on to do postgraduate research at Harvard; Trinity College, Cambridge; and the School of International Studies at Geneva. Returning home, he set up in practice at Windsor, where his political ambitions – fuelled by reading John Morley's *Life of Gladstone* and attending, as a schoolboy, the funeral of Sir Wilfrid Laurier – led him to be elected MP in 1935. Martin was sent as a delegate to the 19th League of Nations session in

1938, but he was unable to join the Armed Forces the following year because a polio attack at the age of four had left him unable to see out of one eye or lift one arm above his shoulder.

His first appointment, in 1943, was as parliamentary assistant to the minister of labour, a job in which his concern for workers' justice – not least that of his auto-worker constituents – impressed itself on the prime minister, Mackenzie King. When King took the Liberals leftwards in the 1945 election, Martin was brought into the cabinet as secretary of state. One of his first major tasks was to introduce the Canadian Citizenship Act, which legally created a specifically Canadian identity within the old British concept of subjecthood. Moving to the health ministry, where he was to remain for 11 years, Martin took particular satisfaction in championing the Salk polio vaccine. He proved adept at steering cautious improvements in national health, welfare and old age pensions through provincial governments' entrenched rights. "Our task is to starve or discourage Communism – a scorched earth policy – by bettering conditions," he declared grandly.

An initial attempt to become Liberal leader in succession to King in 1948 seemed only to indicate that the promise must be fulfilled later. He continued to interest himself in international affairs, becoming a familiar figure at the United Nations in New York, where he achieved a personal success in breaking a nine-year deadlock which enabled 18 countries to be admitted as members.

When John Diefenbaker's Tories smashed the smooth complacency of a Liberal government that had been in continuous power for 22 years, Martin was one of those who played a key part in restoring the party's shattered confidence on the floor of the House. He was defeated again for the leadership, this time by Lester Pearson, who had won the Nobel Peace Prize for the Canadian compromise at the UN during the Suez crisis. But Pearson seemed to confirm that Martin still had a future by appointing him external affairs secretary. Martin used the job to give foreign affairs a high profile. He launched a series of initiatives on Cyprus, championed the admission of China to the UN and made a peace bid in Vietnam, all of which kept Canada on the front pages of the world's newspapers even if they did not achieve much.

His wealth of experience combined with the hothouse atmosphere of world statesmanship to encourage collections of speeches with such titles as *Paul Martin Speaks for Canada* and *The Quest for Peace*. Although on the floor of the House of Commons he never failed to remember where he stood on domestic issues, his wariness of giving unnecessary offence abroad drove one Opposition MP to exasperated parody:

> *He has the rare ability, or vocabular agility,*
> *With verbiage to drown each point at hand.*
> *And he seems to fear relations,*
> *That we have with other nations,*
> *Will be endangered if we EVER take stand.*

This flaw was well illustrated when General de Gaulle made his 1967 *Québec libre* speech in Montreal, outraging the entire country. Martin suggested delaying any official response until the French leader had explained himself.

Not the least of Martin's claims to have finally earned the prime minister's job when Pearson began to think of stepping down was that he had persuaded Pearson to take seriously "the French Fact" in the political hegemony — a cause which he deemed himself admirably equipped to tackle with his bilingual background. But any advantage he might claim as a senior minister was undermined when the government was defeated on a finance bill in the House, an event which Martin and several other senior ministers missed because they were away campaigning for the leadership. It was left to Pierre Trudeau, the justice minister, to save the Liberal party from catastrophe.

Once the leadership contest was fully under way, Martin was astonished to witness a steady haemorrhaging of promised support until his life's hopes vanished in a tidal wave of a teencult called Trudeaumania. "I didn't know there was a generation gap until it was over," he said in disbelief. On his return to the Commons the day after the leadership election, the whole House rose in respect. But Martin's career received the inevitable *coup de grâce* when Trudeau offered him the justice ministry, which he refused because it would have meant steering through abortion legislation unacceptable to his Roman Catholicism. Instead, Martin became government leader in the Senate, where, like many called to the Lords at Westminster, he brought some badly needed vigour but found himself unable to make any changes of substance.

When Trudeau needed the Senate post for another follower, Martin took up his last appointment as high commissioner in London in 1974. The consummate politician took easily enough to the constant eating, talking and being expensively entertained at the taxpayers' expense, though he had difficulty reassuring himself and others that Trudeau's ill-mannered behaviour towards the Queen was not really intended. Britain had neither the strength nor the energy to win Canada a special relationship with the European Economic Community or to show much interest in Martin's Commonwealth concerns. But Martin used his long-standing personal links with cabinet ministers to lobby effectively for Canada's smaller ambition to keep her place at economic summit tables and for Air Canada to retain landing rights at Heathrow Airport.

He was able to do some service in return, on several occasions advising Harold Wilson and James Callaghan over late-night drinks on how to deal with the threat of federalism posed by Welsh, Scottish and Northern Irish nationalist MPs who held the balance of power. Martin also made a specific contribution towards Canada's continuing warm attachment to Britain by setting up a Canadian Institute of Advanced Legal Studies at Cambridge. It was particularly fitting that as a representative of Canadian Liberalism, which has more in common with Gladstone than the Liberal rump at Westminster has had during the past 60 years, he ended his career at Canada House in Trafalgar Square, only a few minutes' walk from the Reform Club – that Liberal Holy of Holies which once boasted Gladstone as a member.

Martin, who married Nell Adams in 1937, had a daughter and a son, Paul, who became the federal finance minister in Jean Chrétien's government and was strongly tipped as a future prime minister when he was elected an MP at the late age of 50.

HAROLD BALLARD

HAROLD BALLARD (who died on April 11, 1990, aged 86) was celebrated as the owner of the Toronto Maple Leafs hockey team and the Hamilton Tiger-Cats football team and also as a man who never failed to speak his mind.

In the Maple Leafs' brochure, Ballard was described as "one of the most loved and hated men in Canada"; in the words of John Ziegler, head of the National Hockey League, he was "an original, colourful and challenging individual." Ballard's view of Ziegler bore out this description: the man was "a know-nothing shrimp." But then Ballard called his own daughter "a reptile."

However accomplished with invective, Ballard, a big, burly man with bright orange-red hair, sometimes preferred action to words; even in his seventies he was ready to resort to fisticuffs. In 1978 he was with his friend "King" Clancy, a hockey legend, when Clancy accidentally knocked over a fan's beer. The victim remonstrated angrily, whereupon Ballard, as Clancy remembered, "hit him one shot; knocked him kicking. I thought we were both going to get arrested. I was afraid. Harold never gave it another thought. He said it served the guy right, that it would do him some good."

Ballard's philosophy was ably summarized in the Maple Leaf press guide in the year of his death, which described him as "basically just doing whatever he pleases, regardless of what anyone else thinks." One of his first acts after becoming president of the Maple Leafs in 1972 had been to remove a large picture of the Queen from the stadium in order to make room for more seats. "I just booted her out," Ballard recalled. "She never gave me anything. Never paid any taxes for me."

His policies failed to bring the team success; in fact the 1980s proved a lean decade for the Maple Leafs. Nevertheless, Ballard remained a patriot through all disappointments. He sternly opposed any suggestion of hockey games against teams from the Soviet Union. The Russians, he held, were "parasites and barnacles who steal our money." He took pride in having put a Maple Leaf sticker on Lenin's tomb in Moscow. Ballard also remained true to his ideals in the matter of female emancipation. Women sportswriters who wished to enter the Maple Leafs' locker-room were met with his ready response – "if you want to go in there you can – but you've got to take your clothes off too."

Harold Ballard was born on July 30, 1903, and first tasted the limelight when, as an aide to the Canadian hockey team, he carried his country's flag at the opening ceremony of the 1928 Olympic Games. Afterwards, he appropriated it only to suffer the chagrin of having it stolen. An investor when Maple Leaf Gardens was built in 1931, Ballard gradually worked his way up through the organization, though just before he became president there was a hitch when he had to spend a year in prison for fraud after being convicted of diverting the club's moneys into his own account.

Ballard married a clergyman's daughter, Dorothy Higgs, who died in 1969. He never remarried, but befriended one Yolanda MacMillan, who changed her name to Ballard in 1987. The couple took out a marriage licence in early 1990 in the Cayman Islands, but the prospective bridegroom backed out of the ceremony two hours before the wedding and was subsequently declared mentally incompetent. Ballard's last months were devoted to court battles involving his three children. The fortunes of the Maple Leafs, though, began to improve.

MORLEY CALLAGHAN

MORLEY CALLAGHAN (who died on August 25, 1990, aged 86) established a reputation between the wars as Canada's leading writer of fiction – indeed its only author of international standing.

The American critic Edmund Wilson once described Callaghan as "perhaps the most neglected novelist of the English-speaking world." Even with the qualifying "perhaps," this is not a judgment many would assent to, even in Callaghan's native country. His nomination for the Nobel Prize for Literature reflected local pride rather than any real expectation of success.

In a long pair of essays, reprinted in his book *O Canada*, Wilson wondered whether "the primary reason for the current underestimation of Morley Callaghan may not simply be a general incapacity – apparently shared by his compatriots – for believing that a writer whose work may be mentioned without absurdity in association with Chekhov's and Turgenev's can possibly be functioning in Toronto." Others would argue – particularly when discussing the work written by Callaghan after 1964, when Wilson wrote his essay – that the Roman Catholic religious themes which dominated so much of the novelist's work were introduced too patly, and that the bleak endings – a body riddled with bullets lying in the snow, or a girl raped and strangled – too much a judgment on the sinners concerned.

Wilson went so far as to rate Callaghan's work above that of Graham Greene and Evelyn Waugh, but this may just have been an aspect of his anti-British stance. Certainly Callaghan was a more than competent impressionistic short-story writer – indeed, his early stories were generally reckoned to be far better than his novels. Like Ring Lardner, he was good at describing low life – boxing matches, seedy cafés, street-walkers, a drunk who mistakes a confessional for a streetcar. The regular publication of such stories in the *New Yorker*, *Esquire* and *Saturday Evening Post* enabled him to live by his pen alone for much of his life, though some Canadian critics were uneasy that much of his work could be mistakenly assumed to be set south of the border.

Strangely, his popular recognition abroad depends on one bizarre incident in 1929, which has passed into folklore. In a grudge fight in a Paris gymnasium Callaghan, much the smaller and lighter man, knocked out – according to some versions – or just flattened, Ernest Hemingway. A shadow boxer, if ever there was one, Hemingway, was furious: his slightly questionable manhood was affronted. But in the circle of expatriate *literati* in Paris the incident was considered a great joke and duly found its way into the American gossip columns. Scott Fitzgerald claimed that in his role as time-keeper for the bout he had been so absorbed in the fisticuffs that he had allowed the round to last nearly four minutes, instead of the allotted three. The affair still rankled with Hemingway many years later, when in his autobiographical *A Moveable Feast* he poured out his spleen at Callaghan – who also wrote about the affair in his autobiography, *That Summer in Paris*, though with due modesty.

Of Irish descent, Morley Edward Callaghan was born in Toronto on September 22, 1903, and educated at St Michael's College, the University of Toronto and Osgoode Hall Law School. He was called to the Bar in 1928, but never practised law. While a student, he worked during summer vacations as a cub reporter on the *Toronto Daily Star*, where he met Hemingway, who was then on the paper. After reading Callaghan's short stories, Hemingway encouraged him to write and arranged for the publication of his work in one of the numerous small magazines produced in Paris by American expatriates.

In 1929 Callaghan married Lorrete Dee, and Hemingway invited them to take a slightly belated honeymoon in Paris. This trip proved a turning point in Callaghan's life, for it put him on friendly drinking terms not only with Hemingway and Fitzgerald but also with Ezra Pound and James Joyce. Fortunately for Callaghan, his early stories were seen by Maxwell Perkins, the all-powerful American publisher's editor, who issued Callaghan's first novel, *Strange Fugitive* (1928), a somewhat lurid gangster story. It was an immediate success and made him $10,000 – then a great deal of money. After his Paris idyll and a brief sojourn in America, Callaghan returned to Toronto which thereafter was his home. During the 60 years of his writing life, Callaghan published some 15 novels and more than 100 short stories.

The Loved and the Lost (1951) and *The Many Coloured Coat* (1960) are his best sustained work and mark the middle period of his development. Callaghan's novel writing tended to come in bursts. The first of these bursts, which came after *Strange Fugitive,* was secular in tone, but the Catholic influence increased after he had become friends with the French author Jacques Maritain – who had been lecturing at the University of Toronto – and was obvious in his later 1930s writing.

During the Second World War Callaghan took to radio work, performing as anchorman in a current affairs programme and writing plays which, when produced, pleased neither him nor the public. Another flurry of novel writing came in the late 1970s and early 1980s, though most of the titles, which included *No Man's Meat* and *The Enchanted Pimp*, were not published outside Canada. *A Fine and Private Place* (1975), the most autobiographical in tone, was described by one critic as "the story of an unappreciated novelist ... and a contemptuous dismissal of the characters who are blind to the worth of the novelist." This was certainly unfair as far as Callaghan's fellow countrymen were concerned. He was appointed CC in 1983 and over the years won many literary prizes. His long and happy marriage to the bride he took to Paris produced two sons, of whom one is the writer Barry Callaghan.

CARDINAL LÉGER

CARDINAL LÉGER (who died, aged 87, on November 13, 1991) made a heroic gesture after taking part in the Vatican Council when he resigned as Archbishop of Montreal to work with lepers in Africa.

Looking and sounding every inch a Prince of the Church, Léger had been a leading advocate at the council of a new tolerance of contraception and was loud in complaining when Pope Paul VI withdrew "birth control" from the council's competence. This led to suggestions that Léger's liberalism had been assumed rather belatedly and strictly for export. In Montreal, he had been a conventional opponent of contraception, had banned parish bingo, had backed the closure of liquor stores on Sundays and had denounced the pop song "Party Doll." However, he could have argued that in the decade before the Vatican Council opened in 1962, his hands were kept full enough maintaining the Church's independence in a society run by that manipulative son of Holy Mother Church, the premier Maurice Duplessis.

Ironically, Léger returned home from the council to find that a sharp change in the province's political leadership following Duplessis's death had unleashed a liberal spirit which permeated every aspect of power and public morality. As the Church, torn between exhilaration and dismay, withdrew from schools and hospitals while watching its influence in politics and trade unions vanish like the snows of spring, many felt that Léger's archdiocese had become, if not ungovernable, at least in need of a fresh leader.

A storekeeper's son, Paul-Émile Léger was born at Valleyfield, Quebec, on April 24, 1904. He left school at 12 because of poor health and worked as a mechanic and butcher before deciding on Christmas morning, 1923, to become a priest. The Jesuits rejected him because of his tendency to tears while doing the Spiritual Exercises, but he was accepted by the Sulpician Order to study first at Ste-Thérèse Seminary and then at Montreal's Grand Seminary.

Léger undertook further studies in Paris for three years, becoming a Gentleman of St Sulpice, and then was sent to found a seminary at Fukuoka, Japan, where he learned to speak Japanese in six months. After six years he was recalled to Montreal and soon after became vicar-general of Valleyfield diocese. In 1947 Léger was appointed rector of the Canadian College in Rome, a post of considerable importance, since Canada had no official representative at the Vatican. He became one of the young advisers to Pope Pius XII, enjoying a father-son relationship with him, he later recalled, as a result of his work providing food and medicine for the still war-ravaged Italians.

On a visit home for Christmas, Léger could not help noticing the strained relations between Church and State. Archbishop Joseph Charbonneau of Montreal was supporting a bitter strike by asbestos workers. Léger denied that he brought the trouble to the Pope's attention; nevertheless, the next year Charbonneau found it necessary to retire on "health grounds" and Léger replaced him.

Although Léger disliked his predecessor's confrontational style and caused some resentment in the way he crushed a teachers' strike, he was too much Duplessis's rival to be on cordial terms with him for long. *Le Chef*'s suspicion was not assuaged by the fact that the cardinal's younger brother, Jules, the future Canadian Governor General, was then a senior foreign service adviser to the Liberal prime minister Louis St Laurent in Ottawa. Through a programme of administrative reforms, nightly radio broadcasts and fund-raising for the needy, Léger gradually established himself as the last in the line of great bishops who had been the unquestioned leaders of the French Canadian community ever since Quebec fell to Wolfe in 1759.

When he was named as Canada's sixth cardinal in 1952, he arrived in his see in suitably triumphal style, riding from New York in a special train. Among the crowd waiting at the station was Léger's father, who reminded him that he had always wanted to drive a train as a boy – "Now you have got your train."

Léger lectured Duplessis in ornate ecclesiastical periods on the principles governing the Church's social doctrine in the temporal field, with emphasis on workers' rights as outlined in Pope Pius XI's encyclical *Quadragesimo Anno*. Duplessis was exasperated by what he saw as Léger's demagogy, and took great pleasure in his friends' imitations of the cardinal which made much of his darting eyes and expressively thin lips.

Duplessis's preference for Archbishop Maurice Roy of Quebec led to a celebrated pun: *Mieux un Archevêque Roy qu'un Cardinal Léger* (Better a royal archbishop than a lightweight cardinal). When Duplessis died in 1959, Léger smoothly declared at the funeral that the deceased had passed into history, where his place was unclear but would certainly be prominent.

Léger was spoken of, if not very convincingly, as *papabile* – a potential candidate for the papacy. His speeches denouncing casuistry and a juridical approach exercised noticeable influence in the Vatican Council's debates. He opposed the application of the word *mediatrix* to the Virgin Mary, for instance, and fought proposals for seminary theology to consist wholly of St Thomas Aquinas's work. But it was in his role as leader of the party bent on achieving the Church's sanction for contraception that he made his greatest impact, although the encyclical *Humanae Vitae* came down in favour of traditional doctrine.

In 1967 he spent three weeks in prayer before being allowed by Pope Paul VI to tender his resignation in order to work in Cameroon. Although only 63, some 12 years short of his official retirement, Léger explained: "I have reached the age where a certain sclerosis of soul and body might set in. The spur must be used to get out of the rut." Unfortunately, this dramatic gesture did not turn out quite as expected. Léger lived at a leprosarium at first, but he was painfully conscious of not being a member of a religious order working in the country. He prayed for the lepers, complained a French bishop, conducted services and said Mass, but he did no medical work and this confused the Africans.

Léger later moved to the country's capital, Yaoundé, where he posed a protocol problem, since as a cardinal he outranked every official diplomat in the country. In justification, he said that he was engaged in "symbolic action," and his example certainly accounted for an increase in aid.

When, years later, Léger returned to Montreal, he took up ordinary parish work and left his successors alone. He returned briefly to the mission field in 1979 when, on being appointed co-chairman of the Canadian Foundation for Refugees, he flew to camps on the Thailand-Cambodia border. But although he returned to Canada with 331 refugees, he had to spend three weeks in hospital afterwards, suffering from exhaustion.

As the pace of secularization increased during his last years, many visitors to the cathedral in Montreal felt that the most reassuring thing about the place was the presence of Cardinal Léger praying next door.

EUGENE FORSEY

EUGENE FORSEY (who died on February 20, 1991, aged 86) was the leading authority on the reserve powers of the Crown to dismiss a government or refuse to dissolve a legislature. His book *The Royal Power of Dissolution of Parliament in the British Commonwealth* (1943) exasperates progressive spirits, not least for its willingness to accept that the monarch or her representative retains power to disallow legislation. But it remains an invaluable guide to political circumstances which are periodically the subject of nervous debate in Britain and the cause of full-blown crises in the dominions and remaining colonies.

The Australian Governor General Sir John Kerr, who dismissed the Labour prime minister Gough Whitlam in 1975, was only one of those who have had reason to be grateful for Forsey's advice. When the Australian crisis broke, Forsey wrote to offer Kerr his support, which led to a close epistolary friendship. This was cemented when Kerr visited Canada in 1979 and devoted a chapter of his autobiography, *Matters for Judgment,* to lauding the Canadian.

Forsey also published a collection of vigorous essays, *Freedom and Order* (1974), and a mammoth history, *Trade Unions in Canada, 1812–1902* (1962). But *The Royal Power* remained his major work, largely because his energies were devoted to opposing the watering down of Canada's institutional British heritage for the sake of a spurious independence which threatened eventual absorption into the United States.

Forsey's contradictory character never ceased to baffle his countrymen, who nonetheless remained addicted to his perceptive magazine articles, frequent letters to newspapers and witty comments on radio and television. A legal authority who had never passed a law exam, he was a royalist and a socialist, an elder of a French-speaking congregation of the United Church, and a significant figure in the academic world long after he had given up his only, very minor, full-time post at McGill University.

Eugene Alfred Forsey was born of English West Country and Protestant Irish stock at Grand Bank, Newfoundland, on May 29, 1904. He was brought up at the Ottawa home of his grandfather, the chief clerk of votes at the House of Commons and, from an early age, preferred attending debates to playing games. As a result he could claim to have heard speeches by every Canadian prime minister since 1894 bar one, Sir Charles Tupper, who spent his last years in England. Forsey was a superb mimic of this *galère*, able to produce the platform style of Sir Wilfrid Laurier, the Ulster-shaded ponderousness of Sir Robert Borden and the peevishness of Mackenzie King.

He was educated at Ottawa Collegiate and then McGill, where his Conservative loyalties were severely shaken when he was accused of Bolshevism for writing an essay in defence of the progressive policies of the Tory prime minister Arthur Meighen. On taking up a Rhodes scholarship at Balliol College, Oxford, Forsey became a socialist and joined the Oxford Labour Club – a decision which drove the humorist Stephen Leacock, McGill's professor of economics, to threaten to shoot him when he returned to take up a lectureship. Forsey's truculent demeanour ensured that he was never promoted during his 12 years at McGill. But he produced an influential monograph advocating nationalization of the Nova Scotia coal mines in 1926 and helped to draft the Regina Manifesto, the constitution of the Co-operative Commonwealth Federation, Canada's first major socialist party. In 1941 he became a research director of the Canadian Labour Congress, to spend much of his time defending workers' rights against the threat of legislation.

Two years later Forsey achieved national prominence when he challenged a sneering review of *The Royal Power* by John Dafoe, the influential editor of the *Winnipeg Free Press*. Dafoe was inflamed by Forsey's criticism of Mackenzie King's role in the 1926 constitutional crisis, which had led to the humiliation of the Governor General, Lord Byng. For more than two months he conducted a series of vitriolic attacks on Forsey, who ran rings round him in letters of reply before eventually descending to Dafoe's level and demanding, "Would it not have saved time if you had simply announced at the outset that the *Winnipeg Free Press*, speaking *ex cathedra* on a constitutional question, is infallible?"

Forsey unsuccessfully stood as a CCF candidate for Parliament three times but formally broke with the socialists in 1961 when the CCF's successor, the New Democratic Party, enshrined the concept of a separate status for Quebec in its platform. He had considerable sympathies for John Diefenbaker's government, and voted Tory in the rapid series of elections in the early 1960s. But while little pleased with the Liberals' determination to ignore the past in favour of the short-term demands of the present, he gladly took the Liberal whip when his friend Pierre Trudeau offered him a senatorship in 1970. He did this, he maintained, because in constitutional matters he was a Conservative in the great tradition of Sir John A. Macdonald. By way of thanks, he bombarded Trudeau's private office with returned government press releases, underlining grammatical errors or noting significant precedents in the margin.

Forsey, who was appointed OC in 1967, enjoyed the opportunity to display his erudition and wit during his nine years in the Upper House. He did not hesitate to use distinctly unsenatorial language, as when he denounced one bill as "a roaring farce and a resounding fake." He also took pride in the fact that in 24 divisions on government measures he only voted nine times for the Liberals. He was deprived by compulsory retirement at 75 of the opportunity to vote against Trudeau's "patriated" constitution, but finally parted company with the Liberal party over a decision to cut rail services in eastern Canada and the government's attempt to ignore an unfavourable report on the Royal Canadian Mounted Police.

In his last decade, the perceptiveness of Forsey's warnings that the new constitution would not work made him constantly sought after for comment, which he delivered with witty pessimism in a distinctive Upper Canadian lilt. Forsey published a crisp volume of memoirs, *A Life on the Fringe,* in Toronto during his final year; he also wrote a 30,000-word introduction to a special edition of *The Royal Power,* which was published in Sydney in one volume with the other great work on the subject, the Australian H.V. Evatt's *The King and His Dominion Governors* (1936). Injudicious Australian editors tried to correct his copy. "But I have my *Oxford Dictionary* and my *Fowler* by me," he boasted, "and I don't let them off lightly."

THE REVEREND JOHN FOOTE, VC

THE REVEREND JOHN FOOTE (who died on May 2, 1988, aged 83) was awarded the Victoria Cross for his work helping the wounded under heavy fire on the beach during the ill-fated Dieppe Raid.

In eight hours of action on August 19, 1942, he assisted the medical officer in the first-aid post, exposing himself to "an inferno of fire," according to his citation, as he repeatedly went out onto the beach to give first aid, inject morphine and carry men down the shore to be picked up. While the tide went out, he calmly helped to move the post to a beached landing craft, from which he later removed the wounded when its ammunition was set alight by gunfire. Foote saved at least 30 lives. As the boats came in, he lifted the first man onto his back, walked down the beach into the sea and waded out to the nearest boat. Despite the jam around it, he then persuaded others to help him transfer the wounded man on board before returning to the beach to pick up another. For more than an hour the padre sought out boats, calling to all who could hear: "Every man carry a man!" When only one boat remained, two men grabbed his arms and pulled him into it. But as the boat moved away from the shore, Foote leapt into the water and returned to the beach because, as he said, "The men ashore would in all likelihood need me far more in the months of captivity ahead than any of those going home."

The commander of the Royal Hamilton Light Infantry, to which he was attached, had been concerned about the chaplain taking part in the raid, but Foote had reassured him, saying, "I know what's in the wind, I want to go." When Lieutenant-Colonel Robert Labatt jibbed, Foote replied, "Well, I'll make my own arrangements, and if you see me on the beach you can order me off." Somewhere in the columns of dark silhouettes that night the stowaway Foote sat on a hard bench among the men.

John Weir Foote was born at Madoc, Ontario, on May 5, 1904, and educated at the University of Western Ontario, Queen's University and McGill, where he studied to become a Presbyterian minister. He served congregations at Coulonge, Quebec, and Port Hope, Ontario, before enlisting at the beginning of the war in the Chaplain Services.

After Dieppe Captain Foote spent three years in a prisoner-of-war camp and did not gain his VC until 1946. When he first received the news, he thought it was a mistake. He stayed on with the army until 1948 before going to work briefly for the Ontario Liquor Control Board and then entering local politics as a Conservative member of the provincial parliament for Durham. For seven years until his retirement from politics in 1957 he was minister for reform institutions. He then served as sheriff of Northumberland County from 1960 to 1979.

Foote said that he rarely thought of the raid. "I don't like dwelling on unpleasant things. If I did something of value it was in the prison camp. The action at Dieppe was the easy part of it." His fellow prisoners in Stalag Luft 8b at Lambsdorf in Lower Silesia attested to the truth of his statement. The Canadians spent three months tied at the wrist with rope from Red Cross parcels, then 14 months shackled with slightly freer chains. It was possible to slip the shackles, but the Germans would make offenders stand head and toes to a wall for a minimum of one hour with the threat of rifle butt between the shoulders if they moved.

As the only clergyman in the camp, Foote conducted services attended by all denominations and told everyone to call him just John instead of Padre. He organized baseball, bridge and cribbage tournaments, and encouraged men to take study courses for their return to civilian life. His leadership came to the fore during the fortnight when three prisoners killed themselves by slitting their wrists or throats with razor-blades. The dead men had taken the easy way out, he pointed out in a strongly worded sermon at a special service. They had acted selfishly in failing to show consideration for the loved ones who were waiting for them at home. No further suicides followed.

Foote died just before a meeting of the VC and GC Association in London, whose vice-chairman was Major-General H.R.B. Foote, who was born in India during the same year as John Foote and won his VC in the Western Desert in 1944. They were not related.

BUCK CRUMP

BUCK CRUMP (who died on December 26, 1989, aged 85) rose from track labourer to president of the Canadian Pacific Railway before overseeing the company's evolution into an international conglomerate.

Although his story was not quite the progress from rags to riches that he liked to proclaim – his father was superintendent of the company's Kettle Valley Division in British Columbia – he made no disguise of his personal devotion to the railroad. Crump's private carriage was fitted with lights so that he could inspect the track when travelling by night, and his annual reports were largely concerned with rolling stock, freight and passenger revenues. In 1964 he was able to boast to shareholders that the volume of freight transport was at a record high. But a scheme to attract more passengers with reduced fares failed, and under his leadership company policy, steered by his deputy and successor Ian Sinclair, was increasingly devoted to the development of Canadian Pacific Investments. Set up two years earlier, this freed the declining, subsidy-seeking services from the non-transport operations.

As head of an operation which represented the largest British investment in Canada – since City of London capital had cemented the new dominion by financing the railway – he had no hesitation in making his voice heard in Britain. He encouraged the transfer of shareholdings to Canada, and he publicly disagreed with John Diefenbaker's Conservative government by supporting Britain's application to join the Common Market. By the time of Crump's retirement as chairman in 1972, some financial analysts were criticizing his caution, but considerable problems followed diversification.

Norris Roy Crump – known as "Buck" to all behind his back, but as "Mr Crump" to his face – was born at Revelstoke, British Columbia, on July 30, 1904. As a boy he narrowly escaped with his life when he was seized by a bear, which only agreed to drop him after a bucket of slops from a nearby hotel kitchen was hastily offered as an alternative. After starting work as a labourer, he became an apprentice machinist in Winnipeg then took leave of absence to study engineering at Purdue University, Indiana, where he wrote a thesis on dieselization. While working his way up the company, one of his toughest jobs was to supervise a section of track in Northern Ontario where accidents were so frequent that drivers used to notch them up inside their cabs. He was given the prestigious responsibility for the company's coast-to-coast flagship train, *The Canadian* – though it eventually lost millions of dollars.

When Crump became president in 1955, the company had been without firm leadership since the death of the great imperial railwayman Sir Edward Beatty more than 20 years earlier, and was teetering on the edge of bankruptcy. Nevertheless, Crump, the rough and ready westerner, was hardly welcome when he arrived at the CPR headquarters in Montreal. "We are accustomed to wise men from the East," he was told. "This company is a tankful of sharks, and I'm just going to have to learn to swim with them," Crump replied. His determination became clear when a dieselization programme was rammed through in the face of a three-day firemen's strike. A small, thickset man who liked to wear his hat on the side of his head and keep a fat cigar in his mouth, Crump was more than a match for the toughest union negotiators. He would begin by unbuttoning his jacket, snapping his braces and saying: "I was working before you were born. Now what is it you want to say?"

Crump, who was appointed CC in 1971, was proud of his collection of antique guns and also claimed an interest in pre-17th-century history. But when some employees wanted to give him a gift, he insisted on golf clubs rather than the picture suggested by his wife, Stella, with whom he had two children. A year after retiring to a bungalow in Calgary he admitted to being perfectly happy, except for an attempt by some people to introduce culture into the city.

ROLAND WILD

ROLAND WILD (who died in Vancouver on December 29, 1989, aged 85) was an author and journalist whose legendary scoop was a report on the ill-fated attempt to westernize Afghanistan in 1928.

Reporters were officially forbidden to enter the country, but the 24-year-old Wild simply took a taxi through the Khyber Pass and arrived in Kabul as the country's first "parliament" met to embark on the ambitious reform programme launched by King Amanullah. The Afghanis – who like quarrelling among themselves next to repelling foreigners – were hardly reassured by a royal edict that they should sit on chairs and benches rather than their hunkers. Gingerly holding hands, the fiercest tribesmen entered a barbed-wire enclosure more than a little cowed by the order declaring that the proper dress for liberalizing MPs was morning coats and Homburg hats worn, preferably, with trimmed hair and shaved faces. But it only took a hint in the King's address that the veil for women was to be abolished for resentment to bubble. Within a few months, Amanullah had abolished and restored the veil before being driven from the throne, on which he was eventually replaced by the bandit son of a water-carrier.

Wild's widely syndicated story and photograph for the *Daily Mail* and his coverage of the world's first airlift – in which the RAF evacuated 308 people from the British legation in Kabul – gave him the first major break in a career that seemed to develop like a story in *Boys' Own Paper*.

The son of a paper manufacturer, Roland Gibson Wild was born at Manchester on July 30, 1904, and educated at Radley College, Oxfordshire, where he distinguished himself as a fives player, before starting work with the *Bolton Evening News*. On moving to the *Leicester Mail*, he received the most succinct rebuff of his career from Winston Churchill. Standing as a Liberal during the 1923 general election, Churchill was less than pleased by the attentions of the Tory journal's bright young reporter: "You, your editor and your goddam paper can go to Hell!"

Wild's adventurous disposition took him instead to the *Allhalabad Pioneer*, where he reported on the ceremonial bathing in the Ganges and the growing rioting, which brought him into contact with Gandhi, whose journey to London for the 1930 Round Table Conference on India he covered. Back in England, Wild worked as a leader-writer on the *Bristol Evening World*, where his knowledge of the world and tall, elegant figure earned him the admiring label of "lounge-lizard" from colleagues, who were astonished to see him communicating with his deaf first wife in sign language. Already his reputation was sufficient for him to be asked to produce a biography of the unfortunate Amanullah, which appeared in 1932, written with all the hot breath of a newspaperman's immediacy.

An even larger subject followed, the official life of K.S. Ranjitsinjhi, the great cricketer and Jam Sahib of Nawanagar. "Ranji" had insisted that his biography be written by someone who would also cover his role as a ruler, so Wild duly set off to shoot tigers and gather materials in Ranji's kingdom in Gurat, India. Published in 1934, the book, which remained the standard work on Ranji for almost 50 years, ensured that Wild was able to do much as he liked from then on. He made an expedition to Liberia to investigate the slave trade, drove in the Monte Carlo Rally and reported on the Spanish Civil War – of which his most vivid memory was knocking shut the open doors of a line of taxis lined up in Madrid. A then novel idea of going from one side of the United States to another in a caravan led to his *Double-Crossing America* (1938).

At home, he wrote a biography of the 19th-century chief of the Clan Macnab, but concentrated mostly on crime stories. He compiled *Cases and Crimes of 1933 and 1934* and was co-author of a life of the criminal counsel Sir Henry Curtis Bennett. He also wrote a book on Norman Birkett, which was withdrawn at the last moment because the subject was still practising at the Bar.

On joining up with the East Yorkshire Regiment in 1939 he was involved in running training camps in Scotland and Cornwall, which led to his book *The Rest of the Day Is Yours* (1943). At the end of the war he was sent to run a newspaper in Germany; he covered the trial of William Joyce ("Lord Haw-Haw"), and wrote about Germany for the *New Statesman* and *Manchester Guardian*. But postwar London did not have the old flavour, and in 1947 he set off with his photographer second wife, Barrie, for Vancouver, which was to remain his base. He soon began a series of books on Canadian subjects – including an account of Arctic travel, a history of Vancouver and a biography of the British Columbian premier Amor de Cosmos. For a time he went down to Hollywood to cover film stars and do a series of features on California's black population, then totally ignored by journalists.

In 1954 Wild decided to welcome middle age with a round-the-world journey. But this was memorable less for his articles than for his wife's photograph of him – by now completely bald – talking to the hirsute Archbishop Makarios in Cyprus. It was widely syndicated with the caption "The Lord giveth and the Lord taketh away."

Returning to Vancouver, he worked for local newspapers and started to file for *The Daily Telegraph* a series of lively dispatches showing appropriate scepticism about British Columbia's Social Credit administration and suitable awe for the province's vast interior. Although he travelled little in his later years, Wild wrote a book about his abiding passion, *Golf: The Loneliest Game* (1969), and was a familiar figure in Vancouver, where he displayed a liking for cowboy hats and for issuing orders to his black Labrador in English, French and German.

MAJOR-GENERAL 'JOHNNIE' PLOW

MAJOR-GENERAL "JOHNNIE" PLOW (who died on April 25, 1988, aged 83) commanded the artillery of the First Canadian Army in the crucial battles of early 1945 which smashed the last German hopes of halting the Allies west of the Rhine.

For the attack on the Reichswald front on February 7, with almost all of Montgomery's 21st Army Group guns under his control, Plow put down the largest concentration of fire ever seen on such a narrow front in the war in Western Europe. Nine tons of shells burst on each of 268 targets held by the hapless German 81st Division, completely breaking its will to resist. Later, when the Germans brought the full strength of their heavy guns to bear from across the Rhine on the Canadians attacking through the Hochwald, Plow engaged them so effectively that they were unable to halt the advance.

Ten months earlier, during the battles for Rome, he handled a mass of artillery with impressive skill. When the attacking Canadian infantry were caught in a deadly hail of fire from enemy tanks and guns, Plow silenced the worst of the opposition by firing a "William" target – a concentration of a full army artillery – on the town of Aquino. Within 33 minutes of the target being identified, it was hit simultaneously by 19 field, nine medium and two heavy regiments firing 92 tons of ammunition. It marked the first time in the war that a "William" target – previously only held to be theoretically possible – had been fired by an Allied army.

The formidable reputation for speed, accuracy and technical innovation earned by the Royal Canadian Artillery during the war owed much to Plow's leadership, which brought out the best in men through his sympathetic, good-humoured approach to problems. A brother officer remarked that "unlike some of the noisier, or more charismatic, members of his profession, he was inclined to let his guns do his talking."

Edward Chester Plow was born at St Albans, Vermont, on September 28, 1904, and educated at Lower Canada College, Montreal, before attending the Royal Military College, Kingston. He was commissioned into the Royal Canadian Horse Artillery and was serving in an exchange appointment with the British Army when war broke out in 1939. He remained in England with the Canadians until, in December 1943, he went to Italy as commander of 1st Corps's Artillery.

At the end of the war he was posted to Vancouver as district commander, then two years later promoted to Eastern Command in Halifax. In 1958, while he was still a serving officer, John Diefenbaker, the prime minister, appointed him Lieutenant-Governor of Nova Scotia, bringing down the wrath of the Opposition, who alleged that Plow took nine months' leave so he could retire on a full pension. For Plow, the most modest and upright of men, it was a painful period, mercifully followed by five years of distinguished service as the Queen's representative. Later, as a civilian, he became a director of the Imperial Bank of Commerce. He was awarded the DSO in 1944 and was appointed CBE the following year. In 1933 he married Mary Nichols, who survives him with their daughter.

AIR MARSHAL ROY SLEMON

AIR MARSHAL ROY SLEMON (who died on February 12, 1992, aged 87) was in the "hot seat" at the North American Air Defence Headquarters in Colorado Springs when the first major alert of a Soviet attack occurred at 3:15 p.m. on October 5, 1960.

With the alarms ringing and the status board showing 40 missiles approaching from the North Atlantic, Slemon coolly asked, "Where is Khrushchev?" "In New York," came the reply. He called his American chief, who was flying over South Dakota, and Strategic Air Command, but not the Chiefs of Staff. The other early-warning stations reported nothing untoward, and the computers resolutely refused to calculate any target areas. Then, after three minutes, there was a message saying that a newly installed scanner at Thule, Greenland, had picked up the rising sun. As relief spread round the system, the arrival afterwards of a crate of electronic equipment labelled "Moon reject kit" only seemed appropriate.

Slemon's unflappability was the fruit of 35 years' service in the Royal Canadian Air Force: he had been one of the first university engineering graduates, a senior Canadian officer in Bomber Command during the Second World War and chief of the Canadian Air Staff in the early 1950s.

Charles Roy Slemon was born at Winnipeg on November 7, 1904, and educated at the University of Manitoba before being accepted in 1923 for flying training in the Canadian Air Force. He began on Avro 504 Ks before moving to Sopwith Camels for advanced training. He was the first student to fly solo and, in December 1924, was one of four to pass out in the fledgling RCAF's first wings parade at Camp Borden, Ontario. Flying was still hazardous. When Slemon and another pilot flew the 1,500 miles from Ottawa to Winnipeg in two Vickers Vedette flying boats, they had 11 forced landings, seven of them because of stone-cold engines.

The military content of most RCAF operations was minimal, with the result that officers found themselves so involved in a curious blend of agricultural, fishery, forestry and photographic duties that some called themselves "bush pilots in uniform." Slemon was commended for his work in command of No. 9 Photographic Detachment, which worked in Orient Bay and Northern Alberta. But by 1938, the approaching war concentrated priorities, and Slemon was sent to RAF Staff College.

The following year he returned to Canada as senior air staff officer, Western Air Command, and in 1941 he was appointed director of operations at RCAF HQ in Ottawa. Crossing the Atlantic again, Slemon was posted SASO of Bomber Command's No. 6 Group, whose all-Canadian personnel were known for their high spirits and lack of enthusiasm for discipline. He swiftly took over as deputy commander from the First World War ace "Black Mike" McEwen as No. 6 joined the German campaign and then, in 1945, became deputy air officer commander-in-chief of the RCAF Overseas. The appointment involved responsibility for the large Canadian air contingent preparing for the attack on Japan. But when the Pacific war ended after the atomic bombings, Slemon became air member for supply and organization at the Air Ministry in London, then returned to Canada to take charge of RCAF operations and training.

His vigorous public advocacy of an integrated North American air response to the growing Soviet nuclear threat earned the irritation of the Liberal government in Ottawa. However, when the post of deputy commander of Norad was allotted to Canada at the formation of that organization in 1957, Slemon was the obvious choice.

Never given to thinking much about politics, Slemon threw himself into the project, inviting groups of Canadian businessmen to Colorado Springs and dismissing nationality as immaterial. He was, therefore, incensed when Norad was told to go on alert in the 1963 Cuban missile crisis, and the prime minister John Diefenbaker prevaricated instead of giving the immediate order. Sending a flood of messages to Ottawa, pointing out that Canada was bound by treaty to respond, he did all he could to ensure that obligations were fulfilled as far as possible, even without official orders.

Shortly after his retirement in 1964, Slemon was involved in a serious accident when his RCAF Cosmo transport had a mid-air explosion in the port engine at 20,000 feet and crashed into a ravine at Wiarton, Ontario. All emerged unscathed. Slemon was appointed CBE in 1943, CB in 1946, received the U.S. Legion of Merit the same year and the French Legion d'Honneur and Croix de Guerre with Palm in 1947. He retired to Colorado Springs, where he enjoyed a sinecure post at the local air museum.

DR ROSS TILLEY

DR ROSS TILLEY (who died on April 19, 1988, aged 83) was the Canadian plastic surgeon immortalized in "We Are McIndoe's Army," the anthem of the Guinea Pig Club of former patients at the Queen Victoria Hospital's burns unit in East Grinstead, Sussex.

The first four lines – rendered feelingly to the tune of "The Church's One Foundation" – recall the work of Tilley alongside the anaesthetist John Hunter under Sir Archibald McIndoe in repairing and rehabilitating badly burned airmen in the Second World War:

> *John Hunter runs the gas works,*
> *Ross Tilley wields a knife –*
> *And if they are not careful,*
> *They'll have your flaming life.*

The anthem's ribaldry says everything about the Guinea Pig spirit which McIndoe inspired and Tilley bolstered to maintain the morale of aircrew facing a long series of operations and painful treatment as their disfigured faces and shattered bodies were rebuilt with skin grafts from burn-free areas. A quiet, reflective and chubby counter to Archie McIndoe's more extrovert personality, "the Wingco," as Tilley was known (though he was later promoted group captain) brought Canadian Guinea Pigs the reassurance of a softly spoken Canadian accent and a touch of home in East Grinstead. Because of McIndoe's insistence on an absence of service "bull" in his wards, he was often in conflict with authority. Tilley's steadfast support was the armour which saw McIndoe through many a clash with the red tape brigade.

Of 650 Guinea Pigs, 170 were Canadians, and to treat their ever-increasing number Tilley persuaded Ottawa to finance the building of a wing to accommodate them, a lead which was followed by the gift of a further wing from the United States. And so another verse was duly added to the anthem:

> *We've had some mad Australians,*
> *Some French, some Czechs, some Poles.*
> *We've even had some Yankees,*
> *God bless their precious souls.*
> *While as for the Canadians –*
> *Ah! That's a different thing,*
> *They couldn't stand our accent*
> *And built a separate wing.*

A doctor's son, Albert Ross Tilley was born on November 24, 1904, at Bowmanville, Ontario, and gave his first anaesthetic at the age of 12 while accompanying his father on his rounds. He graduated in medicine from the University of Toronto and trained in surgery at the Toronto Western Hospital, Bellevue Hospital in New York and Edinburgh Royal Infirmary. He took up plastic surgery with Fulton Risdon, one of Canada's only four plastic surgeons who had been students of Sir Harold Gillies, a pioneer in the field during the First World War. He practised in Toronto and also in the Canadian Army reserve as war came in 1939; in 1941 he transferred to the RCAF as principal medical officer and the next year was transferred to East Grinstead.

After the war Tilley became professor of surgery at Queen's University, Kingston, the first plastic surgeon to teach and practise there. Later he held appointments in Toronto at Sunnybrook Hospital, specializing in war veterans' cases, and the Wellesley Hospital.

A keen and accomplished golfer, he and his Australian wife, Jean, made many trips abroad. When she grew tired of taking the clubs everywhere, he retained sets in Canada, England, Australia, Monserrat and Honolulu. Tilley was appointed OBE in 1944.

G.P. PURCELL

G.P. PURCELL (who died on November 16, 1987, aged 82) was the tough, irascible journalist responsible for building up the Canadian Press news agency. As its general manager for almost 25 years Purcell was a perfectionist who believed there was "no room and no time for mistakes in CP."

Under his overlordship Canadian Press – a co-operative owned by the country's daily newspapers – grew to serve almost 400 radio and television stations. He guided development of a wire-photo service, a coast-to-coast tele-typesetter circuit and parallel services for French-language papers in Quebec. In the agency's style book, which he wrote himself, Purcell defined CP's job as the "unbiased, fearless recording of demonstrable fact." The book added, "Accuracy is fundamental, good taste a dominant factor. Being reliable is more important than being fast." "If you talk to a guy named Macdonald," Purcell liked to admonish reporters, "tell him: Spell it!" His employees found him at once autocratic, impatient, demanding, witty, concerned for their personal problems and always ready to pitch in and handle the news desk himself for a 12-hour stint on a fast-breaking story.

A local newspaper editor's son, Gillis Philip Purcell was born at Brandon, Manitoba, on November 25, 1904. He got his first job on the *Hanna Herald* in Alberta and joined Canadian Press in 1928. He was watching an air-supply exercise on Salisbury Plain as a public-relations officer with 1st Canadian Corps in 1941 when a canister hit him after bouncing on the ground. Next morning, General Andrew McNaughton, the Canadian commander, found him sitting up in bed chewing a cigar and dictating memos. His left leg had been so badly mangled that it had to be amputated above the knee; as a result the CP style book later admonished: "Specify whether amputations are above or below the knee – it makes a considerable difference." Invalided out the following year, Purcell, who in peacetime always wore a blue polka-dot bow-tie, became general manager of CP in 1945. He took a particular interest in election coverage. The agency's reports on federal general election nights became so fast that a law had to be rewritten to ensure that results from eastern provinces could not be broadcast while there was a chance of influencing voters before the close of polls in the West.

Purcell retired in 1969 when he was appointed OC. By then the hard-driving, abrasive news executive had finally begun to mellow, as a friend expressed it, "like an old chain-saw." His lifelong dictum, invoked when he lost his leg and on other trying occasions, was "I never worry about things I can't do anything about."

BOB FURLONG

BOB FURLONG, the former chief justice of Newfoundland (who died on February 9, 1996, aged 91) was one of the last leading opponents of the island's decision to join Canada in 1949.

Despite absorption into Canada's legal élite, "the Old Justice," as he was known, insisted – privately and sometimes not so privately – that he was a Newfoundlander first and foremost. "I became a Canadian by Act of Parliament," he would say evenly in a soft Irish accent that was uncontaminated by any North American intonation.

Furlong never visited the Ireland of his ancestors, and he last saw England in 1938. His law partner then died; the war intervened; afterwards there were always commitments. But he remained largely indifferent to New World values. He kept up membership of his London club, the Naval, and continued to have his suits made in Savile Row and to read the *Weekly Telegraph*, the *Spectator* and *Times Literary Supplement* every week.

The son of a lawyer, Robert Stafford Furlong was born in St John's, the capital of England's first overseas colony, on December 4, 1904. He was educated at St Bonaventure's College and called to the Newfoundland Bar in 1926.

During the Second World War he served with the Royal Naval Volunteer Reserve as an intelligence officer and censor on the island – a period about which he spoke little except to admit to once dining aboard the *Prince of Wales* with the writer H.V. Morton during the Atlantic Charter Meeting between Winston Churchill and Franklin Roosevelt.

When peace returned, Furlong had no doubt that the British attempt to drive the island into Canadian arms should be resisted. One of the resulting campaign's more unusual elements concerned the court case stemming from an allegation by the pro-responsible government champion Peter Cashin that three High Court judges had only

94

supported the Commission of Government after being promised jobs. Cashin forgot the charge minutes after making it at the constitutional convention on the island's future. But the judges, represented by Furlong, sued for libel – much to Whitehall's dismay.

In the farcical one-day hearing which ended with a hung jury, Cashin, though no lawyer, conducted a rousing defence; while Furlong, who was also legal adviser to the government radio station, found himself called into the witness box by the defence to give evidence about responsibility for the broadcasting of the speech.

On reluctantly accepting appointment as chief justice in 1959, Furlong had no delusions about why the offer had been made to him: it was because he had the three Cs after his name – QC (Queen's Counsel), PC (Progressive Conservative) and RC (Roman Catholic). "And you know," he would continue, "it wasn't such a bad system as all that."

His 20 years in the post were an important period of integration of Canadian and Newfoundland law. He passed the last death sentence in Newfoundland on a man who had shot a Mountie; the man was later reprieved. Furlong kept up with case law throughout Canada, but he was so slow on occasion with judgments that the House of Assembly passed a law to ensure none were delayed more than six months.

He enjoyed a generally friendly relationship with Joey Small-wood, the Liberal premier who had led the island into Confederation, though he had firmly rebuffed an offer to be attorney general in the new province's first government: "You know, Joe, I wouldn't sit in the same room as you."

But 21 years later, when Smallwood's parliamentary majority hung on the outcome of a disputed constituency result, Furlong's judgment dealt him the final blow. In upholding the result Furlong declared *obiter dicta* from the bench that he did not recognize precedents of the Supreme Court of Canada before Newfoundland entered Canada.

Furlong's influence extended far beyond legal circles. He was president of the Newfoundland Historical Society and Drama Festival and served on the Rhodes Scholarship Selection Committee.

An avid bibliophile, he inherited a large library from his father which included a second-edition Kelmscott Chaucer and a Book of Common Prayer that had belonged to the 18th-century explorer Captain John Cartwright: it always fell open at the burial service. When an American scholar came to St John's to talk about the definitive monograph he had just completed on the 15 surviving copies of a 16th-century Latin account of the Newfoundland fisheries, he was astonished to receive an invitation from Furlong to come home after the meeting to look at a 16th over a drink.

Furlong's books were stacked in teetering piles throughout his long, weatherboarded house – an old coaching inn where he lived all his life and in which he died when it burned down.

A man of great kindness beneath a crusty exterior, Furlong was a bachelor who had the same girlfriend for almost 60 years until she died. He was appointed MBE in 1946 but never to the Order of Canada.

DR GEORGE LAURENCE

DR GEORGE LAURENCE (who died on November 6, 1987, aged 82) played an important part in the study and development of the Canadian nuclear reactor Candu, which is regarded as one of the most successful in the world.

While the Candu (Canadian Deuterium Uranium) faces competition from the American pressurized-water reactors, it remains a remarkable achievement for a country with such a small scientific base. Its reputation for reliability and economy in producing electricity is a reflection of Laurence's work on the safety of reactors.

George Craig Laurence was born at Charlottetown, Prince Edward Island, on January 21, 1905, and gained a M.Sc. at Dalhousie University before studying for his doctorate under Lord Rutherford, who had already done much to unravel the structure of the atom at the Cavendish Laboratory in Cambridge. Rutherford's students were relatively unsupervised and had to build their own equipment. As a result Laurence came up with a cloud chamber in which vapour was produced by the use of a bicycle pedal.

On returning to Canada in 1930, Laurence joined the National Research Council in Ottawa, where he helped in the standardization of radium, the radioactive element found in pitchblende. He was head of the council's X-ray section. As one of the pioneers seeking self-sustained fission reaction, he therefore contributed to the decision to set up a large nuclear establishment in Canada. When the joint British-Canadian-American atomic energy project was started in Montreal in 1942, he was its senior Canadian scientist. He moved with the project to Chalk River, Ontario, and was also an adviser in New York to General Andrew MacNaughton, the Canadian representative to the United Nations Commission concerned with the peaceful use of atomic energy. As director of technical physics at the Crown corporation Atomic Energy of Canada, Laurence oversaw the development of the Nuclear Research Universal reactor (NRU).

In 1961 he became president of the Atomic Energy Control Board of Canada, which regulates all aspects of nuclear energy in Canada. Laurence, who was married with two children, was elected a Fellow of the Royal Society of Canada in 1941 and appointed MBE in 1945.

DONALD FLEMING

DONALD FLEMING (who died on December 31, 1986, aged 81) was a finance minister with strict economic instincts at a time when Tory governments, in Ottawa as in London, failed to take the threat of inflation seriously.

He was dedicated to balanced budgets. But his careful plans — aimed to produce neither a deficit not a surplus — seemed to be always blown off course by the sudden and expensive decisions of John Diefenbaker's administration from 1957 to 1963. As a minister fervently behind the promise to switch 15 per cent of Canada's trade to Britain from the United States, he felt free to lecture the Macmillan government on the need to end the sterling area's discrimination against dollar goods. When he protested against Britain's intention to seek membership of the European Economic Community, he was outmanoeuvred by a sudden British proposal for a free-trade area, which he could never have accepted. But realizing that Britain was determined, he played some part in reconciling differences between Britain and the United States, holding talks with George Ball, under-secretary of state, in Paris. He also became the first chairman of the Organization for Economic Co-operation and Development.

The son of a mathematics teacher, Donald Methuen Fleming was born on May 23, 1905, and went to the Collegiate Institute at Galt, Ontario. He studied at the University of Toronto and Osgoode Hall Law School before setting up in practice as a lawyer. Fleming became a Toronto MP in 1945, and ran for the federal Progressive Conservative leadership in 1948 and 1956. During the acrimonious Pipeline Debate, he was suspended from the House for refusing to sit down. As he left, Diefenbaker called out, "Farewell, John Hampden," and his seat was draped in the Canadian Red Ensign. Landing at Toronto airport from Ottawa, Fleming was greeted by a roaring crowd to whom he made a 20-minute speech and gave a Churchillian V-sign.

The incident helped to bring 22 years of unbroken Liberal rule to an end.

By 1962, Fleming's failure to cope with the economic slump, which began when the Tories came into power, prompted Diefenbaker to move him to the justice ministry, and the following year he resigned his seat after the fall of the government. In 1967, however, Fleming offered himself for the leadership one last time – "Only Fleming Is Ready Now" proclaimed his campaign badges – but was defeated again. In his last years he settled in the Bahamas as a financial adviser.

Although his friends claimed that he had a sense of humour, Fleming was more memorable for his dogged determination. He took grave exception to a colleague's suggestion after the devaluation of the Canadian dollar to 92.5 cents American, that the decision was a compromise between Diefenbaker's demand for 95 cents and other cabinet ministers' for 90 cents.

A member of a businessmen's Bible study group in Toronto, Fleming was a non-smoking, teetotal workaholic. He once told the House of Commons that "17 or 18 hours work per day and 100 hours per week are an insignificant price to pay for the privilege of serving Canada."

ALISTAIR CAMPBELL

ALISTAIR CAMPBELL (who died in Ottawa on July 20, 1994, aged 89) was the Scots-born chairman of the Sun Life Assurance Company of Canada when it announced the removal of its head office to Toronto in 1978.

The company, whose imposing granite headquarters on Dominion Square symbolized the economic might of the English Montreal, had good reasons for the decision. The Parti Québécois government had passed a law making French the mandatory language of work in the province. Sun Life was failing to attract the best actuarial students, and there was a growing fear that if the province became independent, the company might never be able to leave. But the announcement caused an uproar. The premier, René Lévesque, attacked Sun Life's "cowardice" and refusal to accept "the normal evolution of Quebec which had nourished it for just over a century." His finance minister, Jacques Parizeau, accused the company of being "one of the worst exploiters of the Quebec economy" and threatened to make it relinquish $400 million in policies held in the province. Campbell and his president, Tom Galt, were summoned to Ottawa to meet the prime minister, Pierre Trudeau, and the finance minister, Jean Chrétien, but they remained adamant, only agreeing to postpone a policyholders' meeting for three months. The decision – made openly and followed surreptitiously by some other companies who preferred to move their headquarters by night in unmarked lorries – was duly endorsed by the policyholders.

Nevertheless, it was also a personal tragedy for the reserved Campbell. He had to leave the city which had been his home for four decades knowing that he was the last in a long line of Highland emigrants who had risen by hard work and determination to the heights of what had been the dominion's largest life insurance company.

A schoolmaster's son, Alistair Matheson Campbell was born at Strachur, Argyll, on July 3, 1905, and educated at Inverness Royal Academy and Aberdeen University, where he took a first in mathematics. He was doing postgraduate research when Sun Life's personnel officer, on a recruiting tour of universities, offered him a job at the generous salary of $1,500 a year. Making it his business to know every name and face in English Montreal, Campbell rose steadily within the company's ranks as it coped first with heady boom and then with the gruelling Depression. He became a Fellow of the American Society of Actuaries and of the Institute of Actuaries of Great Britain. In 1939, while the vaults of the Dominion Square headquarters were specially prepared to lodge the British gold reserves, Campbell set up a special insurance branch of the Foreign Exchange Board in Ottawa. The following year he managed to join the Canadian Forestry Corps, from which he transferred to the Royal Canadian Artillery, with whom he served in Italy and Holland. Always readiest to relax completely in London, he was surprised during one leave to find that the Bank of Montreal branch had given his savings to another man with the same name.

On returning to Sun Life, Campbell continued his steady rise, becoming actuary in 1946, executive vice-president in 1956, president in 1962 and chairman in 1970. He played a vital part in fending off an ever-present threat of foreign takeover by pushing through the "mutualization" of the company by which ownership was transferred from the shareholders to the policyholders. In 1948 he added another dimension to his life by marrying Barbara Hampson, who bore him three daughters; there was also a stepson.

A keen skier and golfer in his younger days, who took great interest in reforesting 100 acres at his home in rural Quebec, Campbell always stressed the need for vigilance in business. "Without problems," he would drily observe in his always perceptible Scots accent, "there would be no need for senior executives."

WALTER GORDON

WALTER GORDON (who died on May 4, 1987, aged 81) was the Liberal finance minister whose attempt in his 1963 Budget to check the flow of American investment into Canada launched a heated debate over the country's economic dependence that would last for the next 20 years.

The measure, placing a 30 per cent tax on foreign purchases of Canadian companies' stock, had to be withdrawn in the face of widespread protest and sharp stock market falls. But Gordon had no doubt that he had identified a crucial threat to the continuance of an independent Canada.

Walter Lockhart Gordon was born into a Toronto family on January 27, 1906, and educated at Upper Canada College and the Royal Military College, Kingston, before taking a job in the family accountancy firm. For all the "establishment" background which went with money, a military moustache and a serious public demeanour, Gordon had a strong radical streak. He was already so concerned about the number of American takeovers in 1938 that he went to London and gained promises of £5 million for a holding company that would buy shares in Canadian firms. Only Bank of England discouragement because of the approaching war prevented what he believed could have been a big operation.

The following year Gordon moved to Ottawa to help set up the Foreign Exchange Control Board. He spent some time after the Fall of France discussing the implications of a possible British defeat, then was involved in the wartime tax agreement between the federal and provincial governments before returning to spend much time with the family business management consultancy.

Gordon's years in and out of government began in the 1930s when he worked on an investigation into price spreads, where he became friends with Lester Pearson, and included chairing an inquiry into Canada's economic prospects in the mid-1950s. Gordon managed

Pearson's leadership campaign and outlined his beliefs in his book *Troubled Canada* (1961). On standing for a seat in the 1962 election, he was attacked by John Diefenbaker as "the Toronto taxidermist who fills Mr Pearson with flossy economic ideas."

Like many who enter the parliamentary arena after the age of 50, Gordon did not find life on the Front Bench easy. His offer to resign after his disastrous Budget was rejected, and he had to produce another. But Pearson, whose internationalist creed was fundamentally at odds with Gordon's aims, accepted it two years later after his friend had urged him to call an election which left him still leading a minority government.

Gordon wrote another book, *A Choice for Canada* (1966), which ensured that he remained a powerful influence in the land, then returned to the cabinet as minister without portfolio. Gordon challenged a takeover of a bank, set up the inquiry into national ownership under Professor Melville Watkins but caused more of a flurry by making a speech denouncing American policy in Vietnam, which was immediately repudiated by Pearson, though several speeches on a similar theme by other cabinet members followed. After supporting Pierre Trudeau's successful bid for the leadership on Pearson's retirement, Gordon left the House.

In his later years, Gordon espoused both nuclear disarmament and lower bank rates while continuing to write books that outlined ideas with which many Canadians agreed but were unwilling to face.

COLONEL FRED TILSTON, VC

COLONEL FRED TILSTON (who died on September 23, 1992, aged 86) won the Victoria Cross in March 1, 1945, for his part in an epic battle with German paratroops in the Rhineland.

For two days, the 2nd Canadian Corps had been battling to break through a gap near the southern end of the Hochwald Forest to launch their armour towards the last bridge over the Rhine. Lieutenant-General Guy Simonds, determined to outflank the Germans holding the "gap," ordered his 2nd Division to clear the enemy from their immensely strong defences in the northern half of the forest. In the misty sunshine of early morning, Tilston, with his company of the Essex Scottish Regiment, led the attack. Advancing across 500 yards of open country towards the wood, he kept dangerously close to the bursting shells of his supporting artillery to gain the maximum cover from its barrage. By the time he reached the enemy's dense belt of barbed wire, he had been wounded in the head. Having forced his way through in front of his men, he silenced a machine gun, which was holding up his left platoon, and was the first into the German position and the first to take a prisoner.

He then ordered his reserve platoon to mop up, and advanced with the remainder of his company towards the enemy's main defences, which lined the western edge of the Hochwald. As he approached, he was severely wounded in the hip and fell. Shouting to his men to keep going, he struggled to his feet and rejoined them as they reached their objective. Despite his wounds, Tilston then led an assault on an elaborate trench system, and succeeded in clearing out the near-fanatical paratroops who defended it. The enemy put up a savage resistance, and the company was reduced to only 26 men, a quarter of its original strength. Before he could organize a defence, the enemy counter-attacked repeatedly, supported by a hail of mortar and machine-gun fire from the flank. Moving in the open from platoon to platoon, Tilston positioned his men and directed fire against the attacking Germans, who penetrated close enough to throw grenades into the trenches, now held by the Canadians.

Soon ammunition began to run low; the only source was the company on their right. Six times Tilston crossed the open, bullet-swept ground which separated the two companies to fetch bandoliers and grenades to his troops and to replace a damaged radio, essential to communications with battalion headquarters. On his last trip, he was hit again, so badly that he could not move. He was found in a shell crater. Although in great pain, he refused a morphine injection until he had given orders for the defence of the position to his one surviving officer and had made sure that the need to hold it was clearly understood.

For his gallantry in securing a base from which to clear the Hochwald, Tilston was awarded the Victoria Cross, but the action cost him the loss of his legs.

Frederick Albert Tilston was born in Toronto on June 11, 1906, and educated at the De La Salle College and the University of Toronto, where he studied pharmacy. Although he was rather too amiable a man to take games seriously, Tilston was a successful player of both ice hockey and rugby. His size – he was 6 feet 3 inches tall and weighed more than 200 pounds – made him a formidable forward.

During his childhood he conceived a passion for music, and his first purchase after joining Sterling Drug, the pharmaceutical company, was a piano. He covered Alberta and British Columbia for the firm before being promoted sales manager at Windsor, Ontario.

On the outbreak of war, Tilston was commissioned into the Essex Scottish, the local regiment, and joined his battalion in England in 1941. Within a month of his arrival, his military career, and his life, nearly ended when, during a battle "inoculation," a bullet pierced his lung and lodged near his heart. He recovered after a series of operations and rejoined the regiment in 1942, but he was too late for the rehearsal of their first active operation and, to his chagrin, was left behind when they embarked on August 19 for the disastrous raid on Dieppe.

During the bitter fighting in Normandy in 1944, Tilston was wounded a second time when his jeep struck a mine. He had just been promoted to the rank of major and was commanding a rifle company for the first time when he led the attack on the Hochwald.

Tilston refused to allow the loss of his legs to interfere with his work or his enjoyment of life. With peace he married and, exactly one year after being wounded in the Hochwald, returned to Sterling Drug as vice-president in charge of sales. He subsequently became its chief executive and chairman.

COLONEL CHARLES STACEY

COLONEL CHARLES STACEY (who died on November 17, 1989, aged 83) was already Canada's most respected military historian when he achieved celebrity, verging on notoriety in some eyes, by publishing a revelatory account of the prime minister Mackenzie King in 1976.

No breath of personal scandal had touched King during his long years of power. His fuss-budgety manner and ruthless political skill had earned him the unloving awe of his countrymen, which a four-volume edition of his diary, produced by a disciple, had done nothing to dispel. But Stacey's biography, *A Very Double Life*, showed that, for all his humbug, King was an astonishingly colourful figure in that journal's recesses. His admiration for Gladstone led to the same night-time forays to save prostitutes as the 19th-century British prime minister's, only they induced significant outpourings of self-disgust at his own weakness. The diary also contained accounts of King's contacts with the spirit world, which included his predecessor as Liberal prime minister, Sir Wilfrid Laurier, King George V and Leonardo da Vinci. As the Germans invaded Poland in 1939, his deeply missed mother assured him that all would be well because Hitler had been shot. This error led him to swear off spiritualism for the duration, though afterwards he passed on a message to Churchill from the dead Roosevelt which, among other things, said that King had the wisdom the British leader lacked.

With the book's publication, Stacey found that his lectures were front-page news. He was accused of muckraking, and calls were made for his resignation as professor of history at the University of Toronto – a demand easily denied since he was already retired. Ironically, the book was his first to earn any decent sum. Even now, a few of those who remember King question whether the bland ambiguities in the diary amount to all that Stacey implies. But Stacey's official history of the Canadian Army, written with clarity, reliability and a sense of authenticity due to his own personal experience of the events described, remains an unquestionable achievement.

Charles Perry Stacey was born of Protestant Irish stock in Toronto on July 30, 1906. He was educated at the University of Toronto, where he was also commissioned in the Signals Corps of the Canadian militia and used the money from his first academic prize to pay for his officer's sword. He went on to Corpus Christi College, Oxford, and then Princeton, where he became a junior lecturer and produced his first book, *Canada and the British Army* (1936).

On the outbreak of the 1939–45 war the official account of the Canadians in the 1914–18 war had still hardly been begun, so Stacey was invited to become historical officer at Canadian Military HQ in London to ensure matters would be better organized the second time. He was ideally suited for the task, being a professional historian who enjoyed the support of the future Canadian commander Harry Crerar. Stacey organized historical officers and war artists to accompany every division on operations in the field, and began a series of preliminary narratives for his history. Their full value became clear after he wrote the first official account of the Dieppe Raid, all 4,000 words of which appeared in *The Daily Telegraph*. By the Normandy invasion, his department was circulating unofficial accounts of operations for planning officers to draw lessons from them.

When peace came, Stacey made his first acquaintance with Mackenzie King, whom he showed around the Falaise battlefield. The prime minister had no military understanding but a strong political instinct which, Stacey noted, led him to make unnecessary and often highly inappropriate speeches whenever he saw a group of Frenchmen. Years later, Stacey discovered that the antipathy was not one-sided. "It interested me to see how Stacey, the historian, seemed to pick out each class of tank by name," King confided to his diary. "One felt it was almost a sort of worship of these various instruments of destruction. Horrible looking things. All rusted. Piled up."

Stacey returned to Ottawa as director of the General Staff's historical section, only to find that he had to fight for its survival. The British and Canadian cabinet secretaries tried to deny him access to documents, while a new Canadian defence minister, Brooke Claxton, decided that any public interest would have been exhausted once the first volume of his official history was published in 1948. This was the summary, *The Canadian Army 1939–45*, which won a Governor General's Award for Literature. Thanks to some skilful lobbying, Stacey was able to get *Six Years of War* (1955) and *The Victory Campaign* (1960) published. These were highly valuable, reliable traditional histories, but it was the policy volume, covering all three services, *Army, Men and Governments* (1970), that proved his greatest triumph.

On retiring from the army in 1959, Stacey went to the University of Toronto. In 1965 he was lured back to Ottawa for a year to reorganize the Directorate of History following the unification of the Armed Forces – a decision about which he had considerable, caustically expressed reservations. Stacey's other works included an authoritative account of the capture of Quebec in 1759, a two-volume study of Canadian foreign policy and a volume of tart memoirs, *A Date with History* (1983), which left readers regretting that he had not permitted his prose style greater freedom earlier.

His last book, *The Half-Million* (1987), written with Barbara Wilson, was an account of the now almost forgotten wartime presence of Canadian troops in Britain. In it Stacey, who was appointed OBE in 1945 and OC in 1969, reflected that he had heard claims that nobody in Britain had been interested in Canada for more than 60 years. However, he went on to say that it would be strange if the affinity between the countries, which had survived so many vicissitudes, did not endure into the foreseeable future.

CHARLES RITCHIE

CHARLES RITCHIE, the former Canadian high commissioner in London (who died on June 8, 1995, aged 88), was a diarist with a power of witty observation and elegant evocation which promised at times to place him near Pepys and Boswell in the eyes of posterity.

In *The Siren Years* (1975), one of four slim volumes of "undiplomatic diaries" published in his lifetime, Ritchie brilliantly captures the changing moods of wartime London. As third secretary at the High Commission after the outbreak of war in 1939, he found himself by day organizing the passages of those claiming urgent business in Canada, while by night enjoying the patronage of Mayfair and at weekends sharing the enfeebled efforts to keep alive great country-house life. At the same time he enjoyed entrés to intellectual society through the novelist Elizabeth Bowen, who made their love story the basis of her moving war novel *The Heat of the Day*.

Eschewing any temptation to record his official work, which nevertheless peeps through, Ritchie savours the mood at each stage of the war. He is at Boodle's Club when it decides to permit members to dine without evening dress for the duration. He watches London in flames at night, and wakes next morning to the sound of shovelling glass. When he, too, is bombed out, he relishes the oneness with Londoners and, later, manages to board a boat to Normandy in the wake of the invasion. As an "insider-outsider" of the London he always loved, Ritchie was aware of the contrary pulls of affection and duty as his country emerged from its colonial chrysalis after the 1914–18 war to steer an increasingly independent course. He sustained himself by a good-humoured reflection that little in the diplomat's life is really significant, particularly after a few drinks.

Charles Stewart Almon Ritchie was a member of an old-established Nova Scotia family which had produced a father of Confederation and a chief justice of Canada. The son of a lawyer who died young, he was born at Halifax on September 23, 1906, and went to preparatory schools in England and Ontario before entering King's College, Halifax. *An Appetite for Life* (1981) opens with him making his first entry sitting in his bedroom at 17 as he describes his home, family and the girls he takes to dances. While the book shows signs of considerable rewriting, the apprentice diarist goes on to record his move to Pembroke College, Oxford, where his rooms house Dr Johnson's teapot and he embarks on the conventional pursuits of gambling, drinking and chasing women.

Study at Paris and Harvard followed as well as brief spells as a French teacher in Ontario and a journalist on the *Londoner's Diary* of the *Evening Standard*. The latter experience was not a happy one. He owed his appointment to his mother's friendship with Lord Beaverbrook, and ever afterwards he claimed to be gnawed by the suspicion that journalism was harder than diplomacy.

In 1934 Ritchie joined the Department of External Affairs, which had been his ambition ever since his father's old law partner, the Conservative prime minister Sir Robert Borden, made the suggestion in a letter to him at school. When Ritchie was given his first foreign posting to Washington in 1938, the United States was still unconcerned about the approach of war. But by his return in 1945, it had woken up to its superpower status, and was playing host to the San Francisco conference which set up the United Nations – an occasion of heavy comedy which he vividly captures.

After that the more conventional treaty making in Paris seemed tame, though he enjoyed liaising with the Australian delegation, whose foreign minister, H.V. Evatt, made a point of undercutting any position taken by the Canadians. A chance remark about his feeling ignored at a lunch party prompted Lady Diana Cooper, wife of the British ambassador, to launch a "Ritchie Week." With the help of the novelist Nancy Mitford, she organized a series of parties, dinners and even a ball in his honour. Walls were daubed with giant letters proclaiming "Remember Ritchie." Five hundred balloons were let loose from the British Embassy's courtyard, one of which was recovered by a mystified inhabitant of Boulogne. On the last night the bemused

Ritchie asked Duff Cooper, the ambassador: "You don't think, do you, that you can have an *embarras de Ritchies?*"

Returning to Canada, Ritchie married his cousin Sylvia Smellie and soon found himself running the Department of External Affairs. But small-town Ottawa's atmosphere of relentless overwork and political ambition began to cloy. Soon, he set off again, accompanying Louis St Laurent on an official visit to India. At Delhi he witnessed that dignified prime minister discovering he had lost his dress trousers just before a banquet, and having to send out for an extremely greasy pair hastily purchased from a nearby bazaar. Ritchie progressed from being Canadian ambassador in Bonn to the United Nations, where he characteristically coped with severe outbreaks of the ludicrous by settling down to read the 18th-century writer Horace Walpole's letters.

On being moved to Washington, he was made to feel John Kennedy's dislike of professional diplomats. But when recalled to Ottawa during the 1963 Cuban missile crisis to discuss Canada's refusal of the American summons to nuclear arms, his most caustic published comments were reserved for the prime minister, John Diefenbaker. A clash between another prime minister and another president led to even greater humiliation. Ritchie accompanied his old friend Lester Pearson, who had replaced Diefenbaker, to Camp David the day after Pearson had made a speech in Philadelphia calling for a halt to the bombing in Vietnam. First, Lyndon Johnson failed to greet them on arrival, then he spent much of lunch on the telephone. Afterwards, Ritchie watched him harangue the hapless Pearson on the terrace, catching only the occasional presidential expletive through the window. Ritchie was taken for a walk by Johnson's special assistant McGeorge Bundy, on which he was given a similar dressing-down for Canada's ineptitude. They then returned in time to witness the climax of Johnson's anger in which the president seized the sitting prime minister's lapel while raising his other hand to heaven in imprecation. Later, Johnson saw them off from the airport with some show of geniality.

Ritchie's appointment as high commissioner in London in 1967 should have been the natural and untroubled climax of his career.

No great issues existed between Canada and Britain. He was delighted to be in London, though conscious that his young diarist self had a sharp eye for the peculiarities and pomposities of those in senior positions. The following year Ritchie found himself representing Pierre Trudeau, the prime minister least well disposed to the old links. As a professional envoy he had no difficulty relaying his new master's opinions, whatever he might have thought privately about the much-trumpeted threat to withdraw Canada from NATO. But he made no secret in Whitehall of his exasperation with the new style of Ottawa bureaucracy. "Don't ask me," he said after presenting some changes in immigration and trade regulations. "My government never tells me anything."

At the High Commission, it was not unknown for an air of mild chaos to attach itself to him. Once, the Russian ambassador was unexpectedly announced, and afterwards a top secret document which Ritchie had been reading was missing. Panic rapidly mounted among the staff until a cleaner asked if they were talking about the folder she had found under a cushion. To the annoyance of his staff, Ritchie claimed that his head looked like a pin sticking up in the back of his limousine. As a result he liked to walk to his engagements whenever possible, often calling in at the National Gallery or a Charing Cross Road bookshop on the way back, thereby making him late for his next appointment. Yet Ritchie was not only the best-known Commonwealth high commissioner of his time, whose droll wit made invitations to his lunch table sought after, he was a man of wide contacts. When the Department of External Affairs was having difficulties extracting British policy on Rhodesia from Whitehall, he went out for a walk and returned with the information: he had met Sir Alec Douglas-Home, the foreign secretary, by the pond in St James's Park.

After four years, Ritchie was brought back to Canada and briefly given the job of special adviser to the Canadian Privy Council. Appointed CC in 1972, he then retired to edit his diaries and enjoy a leisured life rotating between London in the spring, Chester, Nova Scotia, in the summer and Ottawa in the winter.

Revelation of his unpublished manuscripts will determine whether Ritchie is one of the great diarists. What is certain is that, as a frustrated novelist, he had the ability to create vivid scenes, a sense of wonder and that keen awareness of human life around him which is usually found in great diaries. A tall, pencil-slim man, he would appear in his middle eighties, elegantly groomed, for a lunch in a darkened wine bar off Fleet Street, or even a boat in Docklands, at which he would launch into a stream of gossip and worldly anecdote in a slightly high-pitched voice that combined prewar Mayfair, mandarin Ottawa and old colonial Nova Scotia. While neither the first nor the last to feel the conflicting tugs of his new nation and the Old Country, Ritchie knew that his transformation from the assured "junior colonial status" of his youth made him a rarity. "But *that's* what makes me so interesting," he would say.

HUGH MACLENNAN

HUGH MACLENNAN, the novelist (who died on November 9, 1990, aged 83), employed the expression "two solitudes" to sum up the uncomprehending divisions between Canada's English- and French-speaking peoples.

MacLennan used the phrase – which he took from the German poet Rilke's description of those elements of love that "protect and greet and touch each other" – for the title of his second novel. But for all the acclaim it received on publication in 1945, *Two Solitudes*, notwithstanding some lush descriptions of rural Quebec and witty vignettes of English Montreal, is an uneven love story. *Barometer Rising* (1941) is much more impressive. A brilliant evocation of the great Halifax munitions ship explosion of 1917 – which, witnessed by the young MacLennan, flattened one-third of the Atlantic seaport – it illuminates the emergence of Canada's nationhood from the sufferings of the First World War.

As the first major Canadian novelist to explore his country's national character, MacLennan brought a concern for geography, weather and tradition to his fiction, at times risking descent into didacticism. The combination of his richly cultured background and transplanted Scottish Highlander's mystic vision usually saved him from sinking too deeply into commercialism and over-preaching. MacLennan's need to give free rein to his views found fulfilment in the essay form; he published several collections of charm and perception. His essays ranged over the decline of classics, the destruction of the English character by Suez and the lovable, if sometimes corrupt, French of Montreal.

His most significant discussion of Canada's search for its own identity was an account of being summoned to New York by a movie mogul who had bought an option on *Barometer Rising*. Over lunch the mogul explained how he had tried a "switcheroo" that would transfer the story to the Johnstown Floods – before grasping that the essential Canadian element made a film impossible. MacLennan went on, with broad satire, to describe how his next novel would open in London during the American Civil War and show the hero, Lord Peter Sandwich, sailing aboard HMS *Atrocious* for the southern states where he would fall for a clutch of glamorous women before losing a leg at Gettysburg. The essay is entitled "Boy Meets Girl in Winnipeg, and Who Cares?"

John Hugh MacLennan was born the son of a Gaelic-speaking doctor in the mining town of Glace Bay, Nova Scotia, on January 20, 1907. He went to Dalhousie University before winning a Rhodes scholarship to Oriel College, Oxford, where he read Mods and Greats. On being rejected for a teaching post at Dalhousie in favour of an Englishman with identical qualifications, he did postgraduate work at Princeton University. This became his first book *Oxyrhynchus* (1935), the study of a Roman colony in Egypt cut off from its roots. A trip to Russia cured him of any leftist sympathies and he returned home to teach Latin and history at Lower Canada College, the British-style public school in Montreal. After being rejected by the Armed Forces in 1940, he settled down as a writer and teacher, and rose to become professor of English literature at McGill University.

MacLennan's deep-seated Calvinism gave him a strong awareness of the guilt inherent in both the individual and the community, though an element of hope acted as balance. *The Precipice* (1950) describes a Canadian girl whose marriage to a thrusting American executive breaks up, while *Each Man's Son* (1951) is a hymn of postwar confidence in which the hero escapes a crippling life in the Cape Breton coal mines. The strongly autobiographical *Watch That Ends the Night* (1959), which tells the story of a couple coming to terms with the wife's approaching death, is generally regarded as his best book. But like *The Return of the Sphinx* (1967), which deals with the continuing hostility between French- and English-speakers, it reflects concern that control of the nation's future is slipping into the hands of others. The last novel, *Voices in Time* (1980), was too close to George Orwell's *Nineteen Eighty-four* to command much attention abroad. Yet its picture of Montreal 50 years after a nuclear holocaust has a sense of the human ability to wrest some form of happiness, even in a civilization clearly decaying, which is more convincing than Orwell's picture of unmitigated despair.

MacLennan was suitably loaded with honours, being appointed CC in 1967 and winning five Governor General's Awards for Literature. But while he was listened to with respect, he was little heeded as he criticized Canada's drift during the past 30 years. Although ashamed of his poor spoken French, he became increasingly critical of the way English Canada's traditional values were ignored – either to enforce the standing of a French oligarchy in Ottawa or the free-trade agreement with the United States.

When *Two Solitudes* was finally filmed on location in Montreal in 1978, MacLennan wryly noted that its director (Lionel Chetwynd) was British born while the two main parts went to an American (Stacy Keach) and a Parisian (Jean-Pierre Aumont).

BRIGADIER JIM ROBERTS

BRIGADIER JIM ROBERTS, the first Canadian deputy secretary-general of NATO (who died on February 17, 1990, aged 82), marketed some of the first soft ice cream in Britain before becoming a successful brigade commander in the Second World War.

On his arrival in 1938 from Toronto, where he had been an insurance clerk, Roberts helped his brother Stewart launch a novel delicacy called Snow Cream at Empire Exhibition in Glasgow. Although the product was sold in specially imported crisp cones at four pence each, it easily held its own against cheaper custard creams. The following summer the brothers opened shops in the seaside towns of Scarborough, Blackpool and Douglas. Then, with the approach of war, supplies became uncertain, and the public was urged not to go on holiday. The business quickly collapsed.

Roberts went home to join the Royal Canadian Dragoons, a regular regiment, and returned to Britain to establish his reputation as a promising officer by writing a pamphlet on armoured-car warfare. Given command of the 12th Manitoba Dragoons, he got a chance to demonstrate his qualities in the operation to capture Falaise. Protecting the left flank of 2nd Corps as it drove southeast to link up with the Americans, his Dragoons prevented the enemy reinforcing their crumbling defence. With the battle at its height, he found a way through the turmoil of the Falaise Gap to bring supplies to the beleaguered Polish Armoured Division. Later, when the trap closed around the encircled German army, his cars wreaked terrible execution as the enemy attempted to escape.

The last shots had not been fired before his squadrons began probing northwards towards the Seine. That waterway crossed, his regiment took the van of the Canadian advance through the enemy defensive belt along the Channel coast. Operating as much as 40 miles ahead of the leading armoured division, they led the way into Belgium, capturing Nieuport and Ostend. His courage and initiative were rewarded with a DSO. For a month during the Canadians' sacrificial battle to open the port of Antwerp, Roberts held the front along the canal from Zeebrugge to Bruges. Then, on October 29, two days before the fighting ended south of the Scheldt, he was summoned to replace the commander of the 8th Infantry Brigade who had been killed in action. Roberts's men were so devoted to him and taken with his uncompromising standards, warm personality and courage that it was said that "there were real tears and much cursing of fate" when he was taken away.

Almost immediately the 8th Brigade moved to the Nijmegen Salient to relieve part of the American 82nd Airborne Division facing the Reichswald Forest. Three cold months later Roberts launched them into the opening assault on the German defences of the Rhineland. His task was to capture two of the last enemy-held Dutch villages in the frozen flood plains of the Rhine. He had intended to attack with tanks and armoured personnel carriers but a last-minute thaw resulted in a switch to boats and amphibians. It was a brilliant success.

Two weeks of bitter and costly fighting against German paratroopers followed for Roberts and his brigade before the immensely strong defences of the Hochwald Forest were broken and the Rhineland battles ended. To his mystification and delight, Roberts was then selected to attend a two-week course in England. He returned to find his men clearing the enemy from northern Holland. That task complete, they were ordered eastward into Germany, where they found that the line of the Ems-Jade Canal across the base of the Wilhelmshaven-Emden peninsula strongly defended by an enemy offering to parley. Accompanied by only two officers, Roberts drove through the German positions and convinced them to surrender. Afterwards, General Erich von Straube, a German commander of the old school, sought to salvage his pride by asking if Roberts had been a professional soldier before the war. "No," Roberts replied in one of the war's classic put-downs, "in civilian life I made ice-cream."

James Alan Roberts was born on August 17, 1907, the son of a Toronto surgeon who returned home from the First World War disabled and unable to perform operations. Young James was educated at Jarvis Collegiate Institute, then went into the Sun Insurance

Company. He remained with them for 13 years in Toronto and New York until he received his brother's call.

One of Roberts's last duties as a soldier was to sit on the court martial of Major-General Kurt Meyer, commander of the notorious 12th Panzer Division, accused of murdering Canadian soldiers in Normandy; a death sentence was imposed but later commuted to life imprisonment. Roberts would have liked to stay on after the war, but left after a row about an unauthorized leave. He first became president of an Ontario knitting firm, which failed in the face of foreign competition, then served as an investment counsellor. He next made the unprecedented move to the post of associate deputy minister under his former commanding officer, Gordon Churchill, minister of trade and commerce in the Tory administration of 1957.

Roberts was never entirely at ease in the mandarin milieu of the Ottawa civil service, but his quiet determination proved particularly useful to Churchill during the negotiations to sell Canadian wheat to China.

After the Liberal victory of 1963, Roberts was the only professional head of a department appointed from outside by the Tories, and there were rumours that his days were numbered. To clarify his position he called on Lester Pearson, the new prime minister, who greeted him warmly with a story of how Roberts's father had interviewed him during the First World War and had approved his transfer from the Medical to the Flying Corps. Roberts gladly took the job of deputy secretary-general of NATO, a post which gave him ample opportunity to demonstrate his skill in handling people during the troubled period when General de Gaulle withdrew France from membership. Roberts had his differences with Pearson's successor, Pierre Trudeau, but was appointed Canadian ambassador to Switzerland and Algeria. The job involved spending a couple of weeks every three months in an Algiers hotel, which was a marked contrast to his pristine residence in Berne.

On retiring first in Switzerland and then in Britain, Roberts wrote a frank autobiography, *The Canadian Summer*. He also continued to take an interest in the Canadian Association for Retarded Children, which he had helped to found after a son of the second of his three marriages was born with Down's syndrome.

ANDREW TAYLOR

ANDREW TAYLOR, the polar explorer (who died in Winnipeg on October 8, 1993, aged 85), played an important part in the wartime operation that laid the foundation of the present British Antarctic Survey.

In 1943 it was decided, at the highest level, to mount a secret naval operation, code-named "Tabarin," for the purpose of safeguarding British sovereignty in the sector of the Antarctic that lies south of the Falkland Islands. As a surveyor with cold-weather experience, Captain Taylor was seconded from the Canadian Army in England to take part in the operation. He joined "Naval Party 475" under the command of Lieutenant-Commander J.W.S. Marr, a veteran of Shackleton's last expedition. In December 1943 the party sailed from England in *Highland Monarch* for the South Atlantic. Bases were established at Deception Island, South Shetland Islands and Port Lockroy, off the west coast of the Antarctic Peninsula.

But Marr was no longer a fit man, and Taylor took over the organization and execution of field surveys from the base, for which man-hauling was the order of the day. At the end of the year Marr was invalided home, and Taylor was given command of the operation. He received no detailed briefing on the purpose of the operation, but merely ordered to establish a third base at Hope Bay, near the northeastern tip of the Antarctic Peninsula, while maintaining the other two bases. Taylor performed this task with conspicuous success. At Hope Bay two dog teams, landed by the relief ship, were available for extended travel in the second season, but deficiency in field equipment necessitated improvisation.

Nevertheless, on sledge journeys totalling nearly 1,000 miles, Taylor and his party made valuable contributions to mapping and scientific collections. In their travels they visited the hut on Snow Hill Island where members of the Swedish South Polar Expedition had wintered in 1903. Taylor greatly extended the Swedish survey and, in the words of Sir Vivian Fuchs, "laid the foundations of the highly efficient sledging for which Hope Bay was to be become renowned during the next 19 years." Before his men left the Antarctic, Taylor insisted that each complete a preliminary report on their year's work.

In January 1946, when the relief ship arrived, Taylor handed over his command to Surgeon-Captain Edward Bingham. On the journey to Britain he was assigned to keep an eye on the much-decorated but unpredictable Lieutenant-Colonel "Paddy" Mayne of the SAS, who was being invalided home.

Although Taylor had held at least a major's command for more than a year, the Canadian Army authorities were never apprised of this fact – something that rankled with him for the rest of his life. He saw it as a further slight that, although he was awarded the Polar Medal with Antarctic clasp (1944–45), he was not officially informed of the award and only learned about it through a chance encounter with a friend. He was also disappointed in not finding a publisher for his Antarctic memoirs, which were written with style and humour.

Andrew Taylor was born in Edinburgh on November 2, 1907. His parents settled in Winnipeg when he was three. He studied civil engineering at the University of Manitoba, and qualified as a dominion land surveyor. He worked for four years in northern Manitoba in temperatures far lower than any he would later experience in Antarctica. At the outbreak of the war he was municipal engineer in the mining town of Flin Flon, and was commissioned into the Royal Canadian Engineers.

After his Antarctic service Taylor returned to Canada to pursue an army career as an Arctic specialist. In 1947 he took part in the establishment of two weather stations in the Queen Elizabeth Islands as Canadian observer with a U.S. icebreaker task force. The experience aroused his interest in those northern islands and led him to take a degree in geography at the University of Montreal. His subsequent army service included periods on loan to the U.S. Army Corps of Engineers to write manuals on land navigation and on Arctic construction. Finally, he was responsible for investigations into snow-compacted air runways in Northern Ontario.

On his retirement from the Canadian Army in 1952, Taylor was employed as a research associate by the American Geographical Society in New York to write *The Physiography of the Queen Elizabeth Islands* (1955). He also produced a doctoral thesis on *Geographical Discovery and Exploration in the Queen Elizabeth Islands* (1955), which remains a standard reference work. In 1956 he was employed as an assistant chief engineer on the siting of the Distant Early Warning Line in the Arctic. Then, under the auspices of the Department of Northern Affairs, he tackled the monumental task of indexing the British Parliamentary Papers on 19th-century exploration in the Canadian Arctic. Next Taylor returned to survey work before running an antiquarian bookshop.

A big man with a soft prairie drawl, Andy Taylor had a dogged determination and took a just, if over-sensitive, pride in his achievements. In 1986 his pleasure at being appointed OC was tinged with disappointment that the citation made no reference to his service in the Antarctic, where he is commemorated by Mount Taylor, near Hope Bay.

On his last visit to England in 1987 he was at the Naval Club in London for a reunion of surviving members of Operation Tabarin, but the dinner fell on the night of the "Great Storm" which struck southern England on October 16, 1987, and he was the only person to turn up. He bore this blow philosophically, remarking on the 1:100,000 chance of such an event, an assessment based on the number of days since the last "great storm" of 1703.

Taylor was twice widowed, and had two sons and a daughter by his first marriage.

BRIGADIER-GENERAL 'BEN' CUNNINGHAM

BRIGADIER-GENERAL "BEN" CUNNINGHAM (who died on July 18, 1992, aged 84) served with distinction in the disastrous Dieppe Raid and later commanded a brigade of the 3rd Canadian Division in the D-Day landings in Normandy.

Cunningham was brigade major of the 4th Brigade when its battalions landed on the fire-swept beaches of Dieppe on August 19, 1942. As the senior staff officer, his duty was to co-ordinate their operations, obtain fire support and keep Divisional HQ informed. To do this, he was positioned with his radios in a tank-landing craft circling close offshore. For eight hours, during which the vessel was heavily damaged by enemy fire, his brigadier was wounded and casualties mounted alarmingly, Cunningham set an inspiring example of cool courage. His voice gave no hint of the bloody shambles on his vulnerable craft as he maintained the link with the inferno on the beach. He was awarded an immediate DSO.

On the day after the raid, Cunningham was appointed to command the Queen's Own Cameron Highlanders of Canada, whose CO had been killed on the beach at Pourville. He remained with them for only six months, for early in 1943 General Harry Crerar chose him as his GSO1 Operations at 1 Corps HQ. Ten months later, Cunningham was promoted to command the 9th Infantry Brigade. Its three Highland battalions from eastern Canada formed part of the 3rd Canadian Division, which had been selected for the assault on Normandy.

Before noon on June 6, 1944, the 9th landed behind its sister brigades at Bernières with the task of pushing southward towards Caen. Congestion on the beaches and uncleared pockets of the enemy caused delays, restricting the advance of Cunningham's leading battalion group to a single road. He halted them near Villons-les-Buissons when it became clear they could not reach their objective before dark. Next day, as they advanced towards Carpiquet on the outskirts of William the Conqueror's city, they were viciously counter-attacked on their left flank by Kurt Meyer's 12th SS Panzer Division. In the ensuing battle, the North Nova Scotia Highlanders suffered more than 240 casualties and lost 21 of their supporting tanks. Of those captured, at least 23 were later found to have been murdered by the SS – an incident the Canadians never forgot.

In its first action, Cunningham's brigade had come off second-best against an efficient German force, but there had been extenuating circumstances. At the outset, they had been beyond the range of their artillery, and communications with the supporting ships of the navy had broken down. And on their eastern flank, for very good reasons, the 3rd British Division had not kept pace, leaving the way open to Meyer. It was from that same area a month later that Cunningham launched his brigade as part of a three-division attack to take Caen. In two days of furious fighting against SS Panzer troops, they drove through the villages north of the city. When the Stormont, Dundas and Glengarry Highlanders fought their way into its centre, Cunningham was with them. Weeks of intense fighting followed as British and Canadians attacked south of the city to hold the German armour on their front.

Cunningham's brigade had been in the line without relief since D-Day when on July 25 they attempted to take the village of Tilly-la-Campagne, east of the Caen-Falaise road. The attack was a costly failure. The hard-driving commander of the 2nd Corps, Lieutenant-General Guy Simonds, brooked no excuses. Cunningham and two of his battalion commanders were relieved. There was almost universal resentment in the 9th Brigade at what they saw as an injustice done to their trusted brigadier. Certainly, Cunningham was not disgraced, for he was immediately given command of the Royal Military College at Kingston. At the end of the war he was appointed CBE.

Douglas Gordon Cunningham was born in Kingston, Ontario, on March 22, 1908, and educated at Upper Canada College before earning a place at the Royal Military College. In 1929 there were few vacancies for officers in Canada's tiny Permanent Force, and like most graduates he opted for a civilian career and service in the local militia. He was called to the Ontario Bar in 1933, and joined a practice at Kingston, having already been commissioned in the Princess of Wales' Own Regiment.

In July 1940 Cunningham was a captain on the staff of the 2nd Canadian Infantry Division when it arrived in Britain. After attending the first Canadian War Staff Course in England, he was appointed staff captain of the 6th Infantry Brigade. Six months later he joined the 4th as its brigade major.

After the war Cunningham resumed his law practice in Kingston. He remained a keen supporter of the militia and became president of the Canadian Infantry Association and honorary colonel of the Princess of Wales' Own Regiment. With the integration of the Canadian forces, he was translated to the rank of brigadier-general.

Cunningham was a keen yachtsman and golfer. He married, in 1939, Isabelle Simpson; they had three children.

ERNEST MANNING

ERNEST MANNING, the former premier of Alberta (who died on February 19, 1996, aged 87), ran his province with exemplary fiscal rectitude for 25 years in the name of the "funny money" theories of the Social Credit party.

A tall, quietly spoken man, whose only hint of secular flamboyance in his youth was a liking for spats, he exuded an air of trust that lost nothing from being inextricably linked with the strong Baptist faith which he preached each Sunday morning on the radio.

Manning never renounced the eccentric doctrine of social credit, which his depressed Prairie province embraced wholeheartedly in the 1930s. However, his commitment slackened as one Act of the province's legislature after another foundered on its inability to control the federally supervised financial system.

From 1947 onwards, he was amply rewarded for his careful stewardship of the Alberta treasury with the discovery of first vast reserves of oil and then natural gas. Acting as both premier and provincial treasurer, Manning made Alberta virtually a debt-free province and set up a board to supervise orderly development and plan investment in tertiary industries. Albertans became as reluctant to upset the political boat during his leadership as outside entrepreneurs, who believed the province a fine place to invest, whatever the strange beliefs claimed by its government.

Ernest Charles Manning was born at Carnduff, Saskatchewan, on September 20, 1908, the son of a farmer and a lady's maid who had emigrated from England. He went to local schools before experiencing a turning point at 17, when he heard the Calgary teacher William ("Bible Bill") Aberhart preach on the *Back to the Bible Hour* radio programme. Young Ernest went to Calgary, moved in with Aberhart and his wife and became the first student at Aberhart's Prophetic Bible Institute. On graduating he became the preacher's right-hand man, running the school and taking the radio service, in which the favourite hymns were "O God, Our Help in Ages Past" and "Onward Christian Soldiers." On the air, he aped Aberhart's manner so effectively that he was popularly known as "The Echo."

Aberhart had no interest in politics until he read a book expounding the complicated political doctrine of social credit, developed after the First World War by the Scottish engineer Major C.H. Douglas. Its message that modern industrial society suffered from a lack of consumer credit which the State should help to alleviate by paying out a "national dividend" attracted a few candidates in the 1935 British general election and the 1961 New South Wales election. It had more success in New Zealand, where it won the occasional seat, and in British Columbia, where W.A.C. Bennett's government, under the Social Credit banner, held power for 20 years.

However, when mixed with a fundamentalist Christianity which avoided offending different denominations in Alberta in the early 1930s, the social credit philosophy took on a near-messianic power for drought-wracked, credit-starved westerners who blamed all their troubles on the eastern-dominated Conservative and Liberal parties. Aberhart began to include social credit in his broadcasts in 1932, and two years later he and Douglas – who considered the preacher's interpretation of his ideas defective – gave evidence before the provincial legislature. When the United Farmers of Alberta government rejected a social credit programme, Aberhart launched his own party, though he claimed it was not a party but a movement and that, anyway, no other party began its meetings with a hymn.

With the aid of Manning's considerable organizational skills and a ready-made constituency base in the churches, Social Credit put up candidates in all 63 seats and, promising to pay every adult Albertan $25 a month, won 56 in the province's election of August 1935. Manning became provincial secretary and, at 26, the Empire's youngest cabinet minister. Although handicapped by a bout of tuberculosis, he was responsible for control of the legislature, since Aberhart had not stood in the election and, when he won a seat in a by-election, preferred to speak in caucus rather than on the floor of the House.

Reducing Douglas's five-year programme to 18 months for Albertan purposes, the new government ignored Foreign Office disapproval by becoming the first in the Empire to fail to meet obligations on an external debt when it defaulted on bonds totalling $3.2 million. It halved the interest paid on others and also introduced a system of deferred payments with the issue of "prosperity certificates." Yet like other measures aimed at reforming the financial system, this latter move was struck down in the courts.

Stung by constant jeering from the press at the spectacle of 13 acts being either disallowed by the federal government or declared *ultra vires* by the courts, the government passed the Accurate News and Information Act. This sought to compel newspapers to carry unedited corrections to erroneous stories about the government, but in the end it too failed, while the government's leading opponent, the *Edmonton Journal*, was awarded a Pulitzer Prize.

Visiting Britain in 1938 in search of capital for oil exploration, Manning found himself turned down because of the approaching war, but he had more luck when he turned south to the United States. By the 1940 provincial election, the government's mandate had not been fulfilled. Nevertheless, its small successes, sound administration and enthusiastic endorsement of the war enabled it to retain power.

When Manning, who had been turned down by the army because of the tuberculosis scars on his lungs, became premier on Aberhart's death three years later, the religious element was as strong as ever. The cabinet included a Mormon bishop, and the Speaker of the legislature was a United Church minister.

Manning quickly took advantage of wartime prosperity to win another general election victory by vigorously attacking the growth of socialism in the West. He then embarked on one last attempt to introduce social credit. The Alberta Bill of Rights Act guaranteed Albertans a $600-a-year pension and provided for the licensing and controlling of banks, but it was eventually struck down by the Judicial Committee of the Privy Council.

While continuing to condemn orthodox banking, Manning began cleansing the government of unorthodoxy by abolishing the

Social Credit Board, which was supposed to produce expert advice for the introduction of policies. He also sacked the British deputy minister L.D. Byrne, who, like Major Douglas, had come to blame social credit's failure on an international Jewish conspiracy.

In 1949 he recalled $113 million of the province's debt and initiated a programme for building roads, schools and libraries. For 20 years until his voluntary retirement in 1969, Manning maintained his smooth administration with little difficulty. Government accounts were set out with the old-fashioned aim of showing that taxes collected for various purposes were specifically being used for them. He was hardly a burning enthusiast for parliamentary traditions, however. On one occasion he declared that an opposition was "just a hindrance – you don't hire a man to do a job and then hire another man to hinder him." The electorate showed no more objection to this than it did to his taking on the post of attorney general, although not a lawyer.

Nevertheless, while he remained easy about his province – though it rejected the Social Credit party at the first election after his departure – Manning was distinctly uneasy about Canada as a whole. Recognizing the constant failure of the right wing in the federal Parliament, he proposed a new "social conservative" party, made up of Social Crediters and Tories, which would champion free-market policies with a humanitarian concern for the truly needy. His last major speech was a rejection of the arrogant Pierre Trudeau's proposals for coast-to-coast bilingualism, which he perceptively predicted would be seen as "a constitutional Munich."

On retirement, Manning continued with his radio evangelism and co-operated in setting up a series of government-related agencies with the second of his two sons, Preston, who was to emerge on the public stage two decades later as one the best-trained political sons since the Younger Pitt; an older boy, Keith, suffered from cerebral palsy.

In 1970 Manning was appointed to the Senate, where he was considered a dour loner though proved a perceptive critic of ambiguities in legislation that came before the banking, trade and commerce committee. At home, some old Social Crediters claimed to be scandalized when he accepted a seat on the board of the Canadian

Imperial Bank of Commerce, saying that he could now qualify as one of the "50 Big Shots" – the men controlling and manipulating the wealth of Canada who had played an important part in Aberhart's eastern demonology.

Since social credit has had its day, Manning's most significant contribution may turn out to have been his encouragement of Preston. Ignoring the attractions of provincial politics, Preston Manning leads the western-based federal Reform party, which captured 52 seats and 19 per cent of the vote in the 1993 general election to become the right-wing champion in Parliament.

PROFESSOR TUZO WILSON

PROFESSOR TUZO WILSON (who died on April 15, 1993, aged 84) enjoyed an international reputation as an earth scientist.

He was best known for his contribution to the theory of plate tectonics, which describes the dynamics of the outer crust of the earth. This revolutionized the thinking of geologists and geophysicists about how mountain ranges are built and ocean deeps produced. Wilson's name will remain linked with the theory through his recognition of the cyclical nature of continental drift, and through his suggestions about the origins of oceanic islands such as Hawaii.

His interest in mountains was not only academic. At heart an adventurer, he undertook a number of exciting climbing expeditions. From boyhood he had known the leading Arctic explorers through his father, who had the task of equipping the Canadian Arctic Expedition of 1913–18. Before the Second World War he carried out fieldwork in the Northwest Territories, and became well acquainted with the ice-scored terrain of the "barren lands" west of Hudson Bay.

In 1944, after overseas war service with the Royal Canadian Engineers, Wilson became director of Army Operational Research in Ottawa with the rank of colonel. In this capacity, early in 1946, he organized and directed "Operation Musk-Ox," designed to test tracked vehicles on a winter journey of nearly 3,000 miles from Churchill on Hudson Bay northwards to Cambridge Bay on Victoria Island and thence southwards to Grande Prairie in northern Alberta. Ten years later he organized the University of Toronto expedition to the Salmon Glacier in northern British Columbia, which made valuable measurements of ice depth and movement on that glacier. Its members then played a key role in the Canadian International Geophysical Year (1957–58) expedition to northern Ellesmere Island in the next two seasons.

The Antarctic also claimed a share of Wilson's interest in the Geophysical Year. He visited the American stations of McMurdo, on the shore of the Ross Sea, and Amundsen-Scott, at the South Pole itself. In 1980 Wilson was commemorated in the British Antarctic Territory in the place-name Wilson Mountains, one of a group on the Black Coast named after distinguished contributors to the theory of continental drift. "This is indeed exciting," he wrote, "and follows a family tradition." Mount Tuzo, a peak in the Canadian Rockies near Banff, is named after his mother (*née* Tuzo), who made the first ascent with a guide at the first Canadian Alpine Club meet in 1906.

John Tuzo Wilson was born in Ottawa on October 24, 1908, and educated at the University of Toronto, where he read physics and geology before going to Trinity College, Cambridge, on a Massey Fellowship. On returning to North America he took a doctorate at Princeton University, and began work with the Geological Survey of Canada. He then was professor of geophysics at the University of Toronto from 1946 to 1974.

An original and enthusiastic thinker, Wilson delighted in confronting orthodoxy, and was an inspiring lecturer to his students and indeed wider audiences. He was a stimulating leader in every undertaking in which he was involved. In 1959 he was appointed president of the International Union of Geodesy and Geophysics. This led to many invitations to visit foreign countries, including China, to build links with scientific academies. Seven years before his retirement, the university recognized Wilson's ability as an administrator by appointing him to the additional post of principal of Erindale College, a fledgling campus situated on the outskirts of Toronto.

When he finally left the university, Wilson took on the directorship of the Ontario Science Centre, which was the world's largest public museum of science. Under his leadership, the centre became a model for "hands-on" science exhibitions and developed the concept of mobile science exhibits, under which selected displays were taken on tour across the province. Then, after three years as chancellor of York University, Toronto, Wilson was able to return to scientific research.

With undiminished energy he began a study of the dynamics of mountain building and had completed several scientific papers on that subject shortly before he died. His publications included *One Chinese Moon* (1959), *Continents Adrift* (1972) and *Unglazed China* (1973).

Appointed OBE in 1946, OC in 1970 and CC in 1974, Tuzo Wilson was a Fellow of the Royal Society of Canada, serving as its president in 1972–73. He was elected a Fellow of the Royal Society (of Britain) in 1986. Wilson married, in 1938, Isabel Dickson; they had two daughters.

STEWART MACPHERSON

STEWART MACPHERSON (who died on April 16, 1995, aged 86) had one of the most familiar voices on the wireless in Britain when he decided to return to the comparative obscurity of North American radio in 1949.

At the height of his popularity MacPherson was question-master of the quiz programmes *Twenty Questions* and *Ignorance Is Bliss*. He was chosen to compère three Royal Variety Performances, and in 1947 beat Winston Churchill to become the *Daily Mail* Voice of the Year. His success was all the more remarkable for the fact that he had arrived in London, aged 28, with £2 10s. in his pocket.

Stewart Myles MacPherson was born in Winnipeg on October 28, 1908, and dropped out of high school early. He was living at home – largely off his widowed mother – doing occasional refereeing and newspaper match reports when he met Alex Archer, captain of the British Olympic hockey team, who urged him to try his luck in England. To get there MacPherson had to work his passage on a livestock train. He suffered the humiliation of having his smelly presence ordered off the platform at Haileybury, Ontario, because he was not a first-class passenger and then a further 23 days purgatory on a tiny cattle boat.

Any hopes of a job in Fleet Street were quickly dashed. He was selling shoes in a Kensington store, which was to fire him for chewing gum on duty, when he was asked to write programmes for hockey matches at Wemley Arena. MacPherson was thus strategically placed when the BBC decided to hold an audition for a commentator. The other applicants – two South Africans, an Australian, an Irishman and an Englishman – were all experienced broadcasters but knew little of the game. When the Canadian took his place behind the microphone – for the first time and without notes – the BBC executive Michael Standing was immediately impressed by his high-speed commentary and colourful summing-up of play. "That was quite a *tour de force,*" said Standing, "but how do we know that you were getting the names right?" "Well, you had the programme in your hand, " replied MacPherson, omitting to mention that he had written it and had known most of the players in Winnipeg.

The day he joined the BBC in 1937, the wisecracking, cocksure MacPherson's racy delivery brought an immediate gust of fresh air to sports coverage in Britain. He soon branched out to cover first bicycling and boxing and then such events as the Lord Mayor of London's Show and the royal tour of Canada – when he made a point of seeking out the policeman who had ordered him off the platform at Haileybury to buy him a drink. A key element in MacPherson's success was his willingness to go a little beyond the BBC's rules of decorum, as when he announced during a boxing commentary from Prague that his wife had just had a boy.

War at first dealt MacPherson a severe blow when the BBC abandoned outside broadcasting. Too old to join up, he despondently returned to Winnipeg to become sports editor of a local radio station. But a few months later he received a cable inviting him to join the BBC's war reporting unit. Arriving back in London just in time for the Blitz, he was assigned to the RAF. He sent a notable account of a bombing raid over Cologne, and was later switched to the ground with the invasion of Europe.

MacPherson was sent home by General Montgomery for filing a report too soon, though he was allowed to return 24 hours later when it emerged that the culprit was the Australian Chester Wilmot. Colleagues noted that his lack of news training meant that he was less concerned with being first with the big story, but he more than made up for this with his ability to find offbeat features behind the front line. His compatriots in the CBC received a memorable rocket when they pressed on to Paris and found that they had left him to cover the Canadians' return to Dieppe for the BBC.

By the end of the war MacPherson was a star, able to abandon his £635 annual salary to increase his income twenty-fold as a freelance. He covered the Oxford and Cambridge boat race, the maiden voyage of the *Queen Elizabeth* and the 1947 royal tour of South Africa. At the same time he took the *Twenty Questions* team – usually compromising Anona Winn, Jack Train and Richard Dimbleby – to theatres around the country. But his celebrity, wealth and Bentley car had to be enjoyed without his family. MacPherson let it be known that his old friend Ed Murrow had dangled an attractive offer, which meant that he would earn less money but keep more in the United States than in Britain under a Labour government. The real reason for his moving was that his wife, Emily, who had been rescued from a ship sunk at the beginning of the war, refused to live in England with their son and daughter. In the end MacPherson accepted that family life came first.

After making a final broadcast of *Twenty Questions* from Buckingham Palace (the young Princess Margaret was a fan), he accepted Murrow's invitation to join the Minneapolis station WCCO. From the moment of his arrival in the Midwest he started to build a new career, covering floods, sports fixtures and particularly Adlai Stevenson's presidential election bid, although one of his bulletins earned a sharp rebuke by telegram: "Stop speculating, start reporting. No regards. Murrow."

When CBS decided to sell WCCO, MacPherson declined to move to Los Angeles or New York and returned to Winnipeg to run a sports stadium. In 1960 he started up CJAY, a small commercial television station, which gave him all the work he wanted – conducting a chat show, covering political conventions, reading the late-night news and recording a daily editorial, *Stew's View*, in which he used that rapid-fire delivery long abandoned by all but sports commentators to give his opinion of the world and its ways. Yet despite the work, his family and old friends, MacPherson could never quite conceal the cost of this new life. In the comparatively narrow horizons of Winnipeg, he was one broadcaster who sounded like many. To any young journalist newly arrived from England, he would admit how he woke at 4:30 a.m. to hear the BBC report great state occasions, and irritate studio staff by delaying shooting to recall some anecdote of Churchill, Murrow or Dimbleby.

MacPherson had continued at first to visit Britain to make programmes, and in the 1950s he had successfully fought a court action for lost fees brought by his former agent, the bandleader Maurice Winneck. During his last years, he maintained contact through occasional letters to *The Daily Telegraph*. In one during the Gulf War, he pointed out that the much-criticized CNN reporters, unlike those of his generation, broadcast direct and had no time for second thoughts. On the 50th anniversary of the Normandy invasion, he recalled how he had landed on D-Day Plus One with a job to be done. He found it unbelievable that BBC staff covering the anniversary celebrations now needed a psychotherapist's help to overcome the stress involved.

MacPherson claimed he had only two regrets: he had reported boxing and he had not moved to Britain earlier and stayed longer.

CAPTAIN TOM FULLER

CAPTAIN TOM FULLER (who died on May 9, 1994, aged 85) was the multi-millionaire chairman of the Fuller construction group of companies and a much-decorated gunboat officer.

The grandson of the chief architect of Canada who built the Houses of Parliament and the son of another chief architect, Thomas George Fuller was born on December 13, 1908, and grew up at Britannia Bay, Ontario, where he acquired his love of ships and sailing. He worked as a draughtsman and dug sewers in Toronto during the Depression. His father advised that there was more money in contracting than architecture, and Fuller had just founded Fuller Construction with a partner when war was declared.

Fuller was a member of the Ottawa Flying Club, and immediately tried to join the Royal Canadian Air Force. But he was told that at 30 he was too old (he was known as "Gramps" from then on) and, anyway, he was in a reserved occupation. At once Fuller sold his share in the business for $1, instructed his partner to fire him and returned. Again he was turned down for flying duties, though the RCAF were keen to offer him a commission in the Works and Bricks Department.

Eventually, Fuller joined the Royal Canadian Naval Volunteer Reserve as an acting lieutenant and left for England. After completing his training course at HMS *King Alfred* at Hove, Sussex, he applied to join submarines, but was told that submarine captains were being retired as too old at his age.

Fuller found his true metier in the Coastal Forces. He won his first Distinguished Service Cross in command of a motor gunboat (MGB) for an action off Dover on May 12, 1942, when some motor torpedo-boats and MGBs intercepted the heavily escorted armed raider *Stier*, which was attempting to escape down the Channel. *Stier* got away, but two German torpedo-boats were sunk. Operating from

Ramsgate, Kent, Fuller's MGB flotilla trained for the specialized fighting in the Dover Strait and took part in dozens of hectic actions against enemy coastal convoys and E-boats. In 1943 he went out to the Mediterranean where, based at HMS *Mosquito* in Alexandria, he won a Bar to his DSC for operations in the Aegean.

Fuller had a distinctive way of operating. On one occasion a British officer who outranked him went to sea with him and, when the action began, tried to take over, ordering disengagement. "I hit the bugger over the head with a number six Pyrex fire extinguisher," Fuller said, "ordered re-engagement and stood on him throughout the whole action. Of course when I got back to base I had to report myself for mutiny." In 1944 Fuller took command of the 61st MGB flotilla, operating from the island of Vis on the Dalmatian coast of Yugoslavia, where he supplied Marshal Tito's underground army of partisans by pirating German supply ships. He would roar up to his target, all guns blazing, and run alongside so that commandos could board.

He was lucky as well as daring. A 30-ton schooner he seized had a cargo of sausage, cheese, wine, cigarettes, cigars and eight bags of mail intended for a German garrison. Fuller attributed a good part of his success to the blood-curdling threats uttered by the Yugoslav partisan who manned the MGB's loud hailer. One evening they captured a 400-ton schooner with a valuable cargo of food, whose crew gave up without a struggle because of the explanation of what would be done to them personally, with knives, if they disobeyed.

Fuller had three courts martial and 13 boats written off or sunk under him, and – though the longest time he was ever in action was nine and a half minutes – he was involved in 105 fire fights and another 30 operations where there was no gunfire. Asked how he survived, he said: "Tracer. You can see the bullets coming. You learn to duck." In 1944 he was awarded a second Bar to his DSC, and was also mentioned in dispatches for his command of the 61st MGB flotilla. The following year, he was appointed in command of HMCS *Naden*, the naval barracks in Esquimalt, B.C. He served as commanding officer of HMCS *Carleton*, the naval reserve division in Ottawa, from 1949 to 1952, and was promoted captain RCN(R) in 1951.

He returned to his construction business in 1946 and, as a pioneer in pre-cast concrete construction, specialized in complex hospital projects. In 1949 he built the Metcalfe Building, the first modern air-conditioned high-rise building in downtown Ottawa, with walls of glass and aluminum spandrel. The Fuller Group, the largest locally owned construction company in the city, has completed over 500 major projects in eastern Canada in the last 55 years.

Fuller helped to preserve and restore Christ Church Cathedral and established the electro-physiology and pacemaker laboratory in the Ottawa University Heart Institute. He founded Bytown Brigantine Inc., "to build character through adventure" for underprivileged young Canadians. For more than 70 years he supported the Britannia Yacht Club, which produced Olympic gold medallists in sailing and canoeing. He also built his own sailing boats throughout his life. When he was 70, his doctor told him the pace he was keeping was killing him and he should stop drinking. He went home at once and laid the keel for an ocean-going brigantine, *Fair Jeanne*, named after his second wife Jeanne McDonald. She bore him four sons; there were a son and a daughter by his first marriage to Penelope Sherwood.

BRIGADIER-GENERAL 'SWATTY' WOTHERSPOON

BRIGADIER-GENERAL "SWATTY" WOTHERSPOON (who died on November 28, 1988, aged 79) won a reputation for boldness and tactical skill during the Second World War as a commander of the armoured reconnaissance regiment which blocked the last escape route of the Germans in Normandy.

In action for the first time at the end of July 1944, his South Alberta Regiment avoided the worst of the disaster which befell their division, the Canadian 4th Armoured, on the Caen-Falaise road. Two weeks later they were launched with supporting infantry, to close the gap through which the nearly encircled German armies were streaming eastwards between Trun and Chambois. At St Lambert-sur-Dives, Wotherspoon fought his way across the last roads open to the enemy. From the hills above the village, his tanks engaged the long columns of German armour and other vehicles as they approached down the roads from the west.

The slaughter was terrible as his gunners picked off the lead and tail vehicles, then systematically destroyed the convoys. For three days the desperate enemy mounted attack after attack to break through. The battle ended for the South Alberta Regiment with the capture of thousands of prisoners and the award of a DSO to Wotherspoon and a VC to the leader of the squadron which "corked the bottle" in the village itself, Major David Currie. After the miserable campaign to open Antwerp – and a cold winter on the Maas – Wotherspoon led his regiment into the Rhineland, where the five-day battle of the Hochwald Forest provided his severest test as a commander.

For the first three days he supported the infantry brigade of his division as they broke through the German Schlieffen defences and forced their way into the infamous Falaise Gap under what

Montgomery described as the heaviest enemy fire faced by British troops in the European campaign. As the 4th Canadian Armoured Brigade took up the battle, its brigadier fell ill and Wotherspoon was given temporary command. Two days of costly and bitter fighting followed before the well-sited enemy panzers and paratroops were forced to withdraw.

Wotherspoon continued to lead the brigade for another 10 days of constant action, which ended with the destruction of the last German bridgehead west of the Rhine. In the final weeks of the war in Europe, Wotherspoon and his South Albertas drove deep into northern Germany, where VE Day found them near Oldenburg. By that time he was the only armoured or infantry regimental commander in his division to have remained in command unwounded since their first battles in Normandy.

Gordon Dorward de Salaberry Wotherspoon was born on January 12, 1909, at Port Hope, Ontario, where he began his education at Trinity College School. Later, at the Royal Military College in Kingston, he achieved the unique distinction of becoming the senior cadet and winning the Sword of Honour and the Governor General's Gold Medal. When he graduated in 1930, a career in the Permanent Force held little appeal for him. Instead, he joined the Governor General's Horse Guards, a Toronto militia regiment, and earned a law degree at Osgoode Hall. He was called to the Bar in 1933.

Early in the war he came to England with the Horse Guards but before D-Day was transferred to the South Alberta Regiment. Recognizing the potential of these independent-minded westerners, he threw his considerable energies and powers of leadership into their training. He was rewarded by their successes in battle and by their reputation for skill and durability.

After the war he was promoted brigadier to command a militia armoured brigade and was colonel commandant of the Royal Canadian Armoured Corps from 1968 to 1973. Wotherspoon first practised law, then in his early fifties embarked upon another career, on the board of Eaton's department store. In 1935 he married Margaret Trumbull Warren; there were three sons and a daughter.

THE MARQUESS OF EXETER

THE 7TH MARQUESS OF EXETER (who died on January 12, 1988, aged 78) emigrated to British Columbia in 1930 where he did "a job of work" on the Cecil family ranch and later devoted himself to leading a religious movement called the Emissaries of Divine Light.

Although registered in the United States as a church, the Emissaries are non-sectarian and concerned that "people should find peace within themselves." Six-month courses were given in Practical Living and Finding Peace and "Bishop Cecil" (as he was sometimes known) would tour North America giving lectures. The sect, dedicated to ontology (the principle of "real being"), was founded in the 1930s by the bearded American prophet Lloyd "Uranda" Meeker. He in turn was succeeded by the cattle-ranching Lord Martin Cecil, as he was styled before succeeding to the marquessate in 1981. There are some 200 Emissaries living at 100 Mile House, Lord Exeter's ranch on the old Cariboo Road in south-central British Columbia, and several hundred centres throughout the world.

Lord Exeter's English relatives strongly resented the wagging tongues who described the Emissaries as an eccentric cult, denying that he and his family were concerned with anything other than Christianity. His brother, the 6th Marquess, an Olympic gold medallist, was once asked whether he too might become an Emissary. "There's no question of it," he replied. "I'm Church of England, you know."

Lord (William) Martin Alleyne Cecil was born on April 27, 1909, the second son of the 5th Marquess of Exeter. The marquessate was created in 1801 for Henry Cecil, 10th Earl of Exeter, who achieved immortality in Tennyson's poem "The Lord of Burleigh" through his romantic marriage to the peasant girl Sarah Hoggins. But he also rejoiced in the quixotic titles of Hereditary Grand Almoner and Lord Paramount of the Soke of Peterborough. Lord Martin was educated at the Royal Naval College, Dartmouth, and after serving in the Royal Navy as a sub-lieutenant started work on his father's Bridge Creek Ranch, British Columbia, where the "shack" contrasted with the family seat of Burghley House at Stamford – the great palace built by Elizabeth I's minister William Cecil.

In 1932 he built 100 Mile House on the site of a watering hole dating back to the gold rush. A piercingly blue-eyed pioneer, Lord Martin developed the ranch into a flourishing community and group of property companies. He inherited the 12,000-acre property on the death of his father in 1956, but the 20,000-acre Burghley estate eventually passed to a charitable trust. Besides leading the Emissaries and being a prominent cattle baron, he was also an accomplished horseman, cross-country skier and sportsman in keeping with the sect's belief of "living life to the full." He was the author of *Being Where You Are, On Eagles Wings* and *Beyond Belief.*

Exeter married first in 1934 Edith Lilian Csanady de Telegd, a Hungarian, who died in 1954, and secondly in 1954, Lillian Jane Johnson from Milwaukee. He is survived by a son of the first marriage and a daughter of the second. The son, Lord Burghley, (William) Michael Anthony Cecil, also an Emissary, born in 1935, succeeded to the title.

Major-General Bruce Matthews

Major-General Bruce Matthews (who died on September 12, 1991, aged 82) was one of the youngest divisional commanders in the last six months of the Second World War and later a senior member of the Toronto business community.

Matthews took over the battered 2nd Canadian Infantry Division after its bloody battles on the Scheldt and soon brought it to a high state of efficiency. In the Rhineland, the division fought with great skill through what Montgomery called "the heaviest German artillery fire seen in the campaign" to defeat enemy parachute and panzer divisions. Matthews's advance from Calcar through the Hochwald and Xanten ended when the Rhine bridge at Wesel was blown almost in the face of a force he had organized to "bounce" it. Across the Rhine, Matthews set his division a blistering pace as they struck north to liberate Holland. They were mopping up beyond Groningen when, on April 18, 1945, he was ordered to move with all speed to cover the right flank of the British 30th Corps near the Weser River. Despite a critical shortage of transport, by next evening his leading troops were in action 150 miles to the east. Having taken Oldenburg, he was advancing on Wilhelmshaven when operations came to an end on May 4.

Albert Bruce Matthews was born in Ottawa on August 12, 1909, the son of a stockbroker who became Ontario's 16th lieutenant-governor. He was educated at Upper Canada College and Geneva University before becoming a partner in the family firm. He was initially turned down by the Royal Canadian Naval Reserve because of colour-blindness. But at the outbreak of war he was in command of a battery of militia artillery, and later raised the new 5th Medium Regiment.

Matthews's first action came with the landings in Sicily where, as artillery commander of the 1st Canadian Division, he controlled their fire support from the monitor ship *Roberts*. Two weeks later, he demonstrated the cool courage for which he was to be noted by deliberately spending hours under direct enemy fire finding deployment areas for which his guns could engage the defences of Agira.

In the nine months of campaigning which followed – ending after the bitter struggle for Ortona on the Italian mainland – his guns won a reputation with the infantry for accuracy and reliability. Matthews was awarded the DSO for his part in the campaign. On his appointment to command the artillery of the 2nd Canadian Corps in the Normandy invasion, Matthews showed himself, in operations of increasing complexity, a master of the gunner's art. His co-ordination of the massive fire support for the invasion of Walcheren Island, involving 314 guns, was a triumphant climax to his artillery career.

After the war Matthews slipped easily back into the Toronto business network, where he held tepid views on the value of publicity but demonstrated a straightforward efficiency which was immediately appreciated. He held a large number of directorships, including Excelsior Life, Dome Mines and Standard Broadcasting, and he was also chairman of Massey-Ferguson and president of the Argus Corporation for a time. Regarded as the archetypal English Canadian, with his ramrod-straight back and impeccable dress, Matthews worked in a room containing signed photographs of King George VI and Queen Elizabeth, silver cigarette boxes and silk lampshades. On suitable occasions a piper would play him in with "The Bruce Matthews March," composed by a Calgary Highlander in his honour in 1945.

He continued to support the militia and from 1964 to 1969 was colonel commandant of the Royal Regiment of Canadian Artillery. Only the fact that he had recently been president of the Liberal Party of Canada prevented the prime minister, Lester Pearson, offering him the post of Governor General in succession to Major-General Georges Vanier. But Matthews was able to render invaluable service when he wrote an important memorandum to Pearson which led to the partial abandonment of Mackenzie King's ban on honours in the 1920s with the establishment of the Order of Canada. He was appointed CBE in 1944.

OMOND SOLANDT

OMOND SOLANDT (who died on May 12, 1993, aged 83) was one of the pioneers of operational research – the application of scientific knowledge and methods to practical problems in battle – during the Second World War.

A Canadian doctor working in Britain in 1939, Solandt was turned down by the Canadian Army Medical Corps and found alternative work organizing blood supplies in southwest London to cope with the expected large numbers of bombing casualties. He proved so flexible that the Medical Research Council sent him to take charge of a unit at Lulworth, Dorset, to investigate why soldiers were passing out after firing guns in their tanks: cordite fumes from the charges and lack of ventilation was the answer. Solandt was then given the problem of examining how much the tanks' inaccurate shooting was due to human error and how much to the guns themselves, a task that led to studies of fumes, physiology and vibrations.

He was next commissioned into the Canadian Army to become deputy superintendent and then superintendent of the Army Operational Research Group, an organization of some 60 scientists from a wide variety of disciplines at West Byfleet, Surrey. It was a job that took all Solandt's good-humoured tact at first, since hard-pressed officers in North Africa, particularly, were exasperated to find that they had to provide protection and food for mysterious boffins whom they suspected of spying on them from Whitehall. However, eventually Solandt's 10 groups proved their worth both in the field and at home.

One of their more unusual discoveries stemmed from tracking of the V2 rockets in order to give Londoners a four-minute warning of where they might land. They were able to do this because although the Germans had taken over a new telephone link between England and Holland installed just before the war, they did not realize that the old system was still in place. The Dutch Resistance was therefore able to ring up to announce the latest launch. In the course of trying to measure the trajectory, the unit was surprised to find interference from the stars, which led to the birth of radio astronomy.

In later life, Solandt enjoyed recalling how he was called to a police station where one of his men was held after being spotted standing on his head and writing in a notebook. After being given permission to speak by his superior, the man explained that he had been studying bumps in the ground to calculate how they would hinder the fragments of an exploding shell.

The son of a United Church minister of Austrian ancestry, Omond McKillop Solandt was born in Winnipeg on September 2, 1909, and studied biological and medical science at the University of Toronto before doing postgraduate work in physiology under the Nobel Prize winner C.H. Best. In 1933 he contracted polio, which left him only with a weakness in his hands. Nevertheless, he graduated as a doctor three years later to take house jobs at Toronto General Hospital and the London Hospital in England, where he became a member of the Royal College of Physicians. In the six months before the outbreak of war, he was a Fellow of Trinity Hall, Cambridge, doing physiological research under Sir Joseph Barcroft and the 1st Lord Adrian.

The war with Japan ended in 1945 before Solandt could take up his post of scientific adviser with Lord Louis Mountbatten's South East Asia Command, but he was part of the Joint Military Mission which was sent to evaluate the effects of the atomic bomb dropped on Hiroshima and Nagasaki. On his way back to Cambridge, he was offered the chairmanship of the Canadian Defence Research Board, where he restarted Canada's small operational research organization and thrust forward the development of electronic technology and studies of warfare in extreme cold. While concentrating on continuing Canada's wartime partnership with Britain and the United States – a matter of importance in the Cold War and the Korean conflict – he encouraged collaboration between government, universities and industry. But this now fashionable policy contained the seeds of destruction, since a committee was dissatisfied, after he had left, with the necessary large involvement in civilian projects.

It was in this postwar period that Solandt, a powerfully built man with a love of the outdoors, decided with some friends that foreign diplomats, generals and others should be given a chance to see a different Canada from that encountered on the Ottawa cocktail circuit. They organized canoe trips deep into the Ontario and Manitoba bush to retrace the journeys of the early *voyageurs*. Solandt's interest in the North led to the establishment of the defence board's laboratory at Churchill on Hudson Bay. It came naturally to Solandt to take a close interest in the Canadian Arctic, not only "because it is there" to be mapped and studied, but also because Canada among her allies was uniquely placed for Arctic research. Thus, he gave his full support to the field leaders of such projects as the 1951 Beaufort Sea Expedition, the Banks Island expeditions of 1952–53 and the Northern Ellesmere Island expeditions, 1953–54. When a chance came up for a Canadian to join an American expedition to the South Pole, he volunteered and proudly became the first of his countrymen to stand at the bottom of the world.

By now firmly established as a member of Canada's "good and great," Solandt went on to become vice-president of Canadian National Railways and de Havilland Aircraft of Canada, then chancellor of the University of Toronto and founding chairman of the Science Council of Canada. Appointed OBE in 1946 and CC in 1970, he was a member of the International Development and Research Centre in later life, which led him back to medical interests. His host of appointments included advising on cold water engineering in Newfoundland, wheat and maize development in Mexico, insect physiology in Kenya and livestock in Ethiopia.

ROBERT BEATTY

ROBERT BEATTY (who died on March 3, 1992, aged 82) made a name for himself in the British theatre and cinema as "a tough guy."

Dark-haired, velvet-voiced and craggy-jawed, "Bob" Beatty had a genial, lopsided grin and a gift for looking relaxed. He could always be counted on in manly, especially military, roles to do the right thing, but it had, on the whole, to be legal. He himself was apt to blame the frequency of his marriages on his tendency to "rest" between acting engagements for longer than necessary, but if his career was held back by his likeable temperament he was always a pleasure to watch.

This was especially so in 1987 when he brilliantly evoked President Reagan in Granada Television's documentary-drama *Breakthrough in Reykjavik*. As one television critic remarked: "Robert Beatty *was* President Reagan: every gesture, every breath almost, a tribute – the greatest tribute one actor can pay to another."

Robert Beatty was born at Hamilton, Ontario, on October 19, 1909, and educated at Delta Collegiate School, Hamilton, and the University of Toronto. After working as a cashier in a gas and fuel company, with plenty of amateur acting, he began making radio broadcasts. A well-intentioned New York aunt sought advice on his behalf from the English actor Leslie Howard as to where her nephew should train for the stage – New York or London? The answer was abrupt and obeyed.

Beatty, nearly 30, crossed the Atlantic to attend the Royal Academy of Dramatic Art. For his first London appearance, in 1938, he walked on at the Apollo in Robert Sherwood's *Idiot's Delight* and (with a Canadian accent which he would never discard) understudied Raymond Massey in the lead. Groomed by Ealing Studios in the 1940s as an orthodox symbol of muscular masculinity, he also acquired, on the West End stage, a reputation as a reliable member of that small group of wartime actors who could sound authentically American.

After three more plays – including *The Petrified Forest* at the Globe – he was the eponymous, and utterly charming, *Soldier for Christmas* (Wyndham's, 1944) in Reginald Beckwith's warm comedy. This was a break with his tough guy image, and it led to other good parts in not-so-good plays like *Laura* and *A Bell for Adano*. Beatty's subsequent appearances in the theatre included *The Aspern Papers, Breaking Point, Difference of Opinion* and *Man and Superman*, with Peter O'Toole.

But it was to films and broadcasting that Beatty was increasingly drawn. He had begun as an extra, and after smallish parts in good wartime pictures – *Dangerous Moonlight, 49th Parallel, One of Our Aircraft Is Missing* – he made a particularly fine impression as the drunken deckhand "Yank" in Charles Frend's *San Demetrio London* (1944). He won acclaim, too, in Carol Reed's masterly *film noir, Odd Man Out* (1946), in which he played a friend of the wounded IRA fugitive (James Mason). Beatty had to brave much miscasting. In films such as *The Gentle Gunman* (as an IRA activist) and *The Square Ring* (as a washed-up boxer) he proved nicer than was needed. He enjoyed more success, opposite Jack Warner, as an RCAF prisoner-of-war in *Albert RN* (1953). He was also emotionally expressive in *Time Lock* (1957) as an anxious father whose small son was trapped in a bank vault.

If Beatty had fewer chances in comedy than his talent deserved, he was effective enough as a womanizing American in *The Amorous Prawn* (1962), giving chase to the croaky Joan Greenwood around a Scotch baronial pile. He was also one of the few actors in *2001: A Space Odyssey* (1968) who refused to be upstaged by the "sci-fi" hardware. As a nonentity mistaken by the Nazis (and everybody else) for an American brass-hat in *Where Eagles Dare*, he kept amusingly mum. Among other films in which he took a vigorous if sporadic hand were *The Pink Panther Strikes Again, The Spaceman and King Arthur* and *Superman III* and *IV*.

Beatty's voice was regularly heard on radio and as a narrator on television, but his first important role on the box – that of the Mountie detective Mike Maguire in the cops and robbers series *Dial 999* – went down so well that he believed it put him out of work for a decade. His face, he reflected ruefully, had grown too familiar. It grew more familiar still when he began to advertise on television a hair-care product, which his own luxuriant locks seemed to endorse.

Beatty had a gift for impersonation – he gave, for example, an effective imitation of Humphrey Bogart. In *Walk with Destiny* (1974), a BBC centenary television tribute to Winston Churchill, he played Lord Beaverbrook with extraordinary plausibility. His numerous other credits on the small screen include *Jesus of Nazareth, Suez, Minder on the Orient Express* and such popular series as *The New Avengers*. One of his last appearances, in *The Return of Sam McCloud*, ranked among his best work; he gave a delightful account of the hard-nosed Manhattan detective, outwitted by Dennis Weaver's cowboy turned "green" senator. Beatty was married four times, and had a son.

JOAN MILLER

JOAN MILLER, the actress (who died on September 1, 1988, aged 78), became a celebrity as the "Picture Page Girl" in the first television broadcasts in 1936 and went on to become one of the most powerful and sensitive players of her time.

Among the earliest "TV personalities," she appeared as a telephone switchboard operator in Cecil Madden's pioneering magazine programme *Picture Page*, the first British television "entertainment" broadcast from Alexandra Palace in 1936. Discovered at a desk answering a telephone, the personable Miss Miller would be seen saying: "You want to see so and so? I'll put you through." Then a famous face would appear. A year or two later she made broadcasting history when a BBC transmission from Alexandra Palace was picked up inadvertently in Long Island and Miss Miller's face appeared on American screens.

But it was as an actress of unusual emotional force that she stood out in the postwar British theatre. In Shakespeare, Euripides, Shaw, Ibsen, Strindberg, Priestley and a host of modern plays, Miss Miller could be trusted to be compelling without any apparent desire to upstage her fellow-players. Her acting won wide respect for its authority and finesse in all kinds of roles. But it seemed at its best in the expression of turbulent feelings which could no longer be denied. The dramatic authority she brought to a role gave even to the shrillest writing a touching sincerity. Hence her notable success as *Miss Julie* (1949) and in Lillian Hellman's *The Children's Hour* (1950).

Joan Miller was born at Nelson, British Columbia, on January 6, 1910, and educated at the King Edward High School, Vancouver. She made her first stage appearance at the Empress Theatre in *When Knights Were Bold* and went on to run an amateur company. In 1934 she won the Bessborough Trophy for the best Canadian actress at the Dominion Drama Festival, held in Ottawa, which led J.T. Grein, the influential British drama critic, to introduce her to London where she made her

West End début as a walk-on at His Majesty's Theatre. As understudy to Lady Tree in *Henry IV (Part 1)*, Miss Miller played Mistress Quickly. After a season with another great Shakespearean, Robert Atkins, at the Open-Air Theatre, Regent's Park, came the stint in *Picture Page*, but she never doubted that she was destined for the theatre.

She first won general critical acclaim in 1945–46 at the Torch and the New Lindsey, two of London's pocket theatres, in Ibsen's *Rosmersholm* and in two J.B. Priestley plays, *The Long Mirror* and *For Services Rendered*. She also played the mother in *Pick-Up Girl*, a study of sexually abused adolescents.

All these productions were directed by Miss Miller's husband, Peter Cotes, who managed the New Lindsey and who later ran the Library Theatre, Manchester, where Miss Miller appeared in *John Gabriel Borkman* and as Shaw's *Candida*, a performance she was to repeat at the Boltons in London – another of the small houses where Cotes was making his name as an adventurous director. He found her some very satisfying roles in modern pieces which he presented, such as *A Pin to See the Peepshow* (1951), based on a recent murder case, and *The Man* (1952). The latter included Bernard Braden and Neil MacCallum because, although she never returned to Canada, she liked to help young Canadians.

While her acting could cast an almost hypnotic spell over an audience in a role filled with fearful imaginings (admirers longed in vain to see her Lady Macbeth), she could play high comedy with a surprising ease, as she showed in *Hay Fever* towards the end of her career. Although she was to work frequently in the cinema and on television – most notably in *Jane Clegg* and *Woman in a Dressing Gown* – it was as a stage actress that her art mostly flourished. After an admired Medea at the Oxford Playhouse in 1957, she spent a season at Stratford-on-Avon where, among other roles, her Queen in *Cymbeline* reigned supreme; and in 1958 her grief in Ted Willis's *Hot Summer Night* showed her powers at their peak. In many subsequent roles – such as Nora Melody in *A Touch of the Poet* or Lucy Amorest in *The Old Ladies* or Madame Raquin in *Therese Raquin* – Joan Miller ensured that, whatever the quality of the play or of the acting around her, the evening would be worthwhile for her emotional integrity and controlled authority.

THE DOWAGER LADY BEAVERBROOK

THE DOWAGER LADY BEAVERBROOK (who died on October 28, 1994, aged 84) was a leading racehorse owner and the widow of two Canadian millionaires, Sir James Dunn, Bt, and Lord Beaverbrook.

After devotedly nursing her husbands through their last illnesses she flamboyantly plunged into the racing world that they had both disliked. "Lady B's" colours – beaver brown with maple-leaf green crossbelts – were carried to victory in three Classic races; the St Leger by Bustino in 1974 and Minster Son in 1988 and the 2,000 Guineas by Mystiko in 1991. Bustino's narrow defeat after a gruelling finish in the King George VI and Queen Elizabeth Diamond Stakes in 1975 became known as one of the great races of the century. He retired to stud afterwards, but his defeat was avenged when Petoski, a 12-1 long shot, won the race 10 years later, beating one of the best ever fields.

One of Lady Beaverbrook's trademarks was that all her horses had seven-letter names. There was Petoski, by her own horse Niniski, Relkino, Boldboy, Biskrah, Charmer and Terimon, who was second in the 1989 Derby to Nashwan at incredible odds of 500-1. Bookmakers have been wary ever since of letting another Derby runner, however poor its chances, start at that price. She was also notable for the large sums invested in her horses, though they did not always bring her success.

For all her strong desire to win, Lady Beaverbrook loved her animals dearly. Though her great wish was to win the Derby, she declared: "I don't mind about the jockeys. They are paid and want to be there. But no one asked the horses." She carried a photograph of each of them all the time, and always put their well-being and happiness before their careers. As a result she never liked them to travel far in horse boxes; when Rampage died in the 1971 New Stakes at Royal Ascot she insisted on walking down the course in floods of tears with her trainer Dick Hern to bid him farewell. In 1990 she moved the majority of her horses from Hern, with whom she had enjoyed great success, to Clive Brittan, who had a special equine pool.

A Greek tobacco merchant's daughter, Marcia Anastasia Christoforides was born on July 27, 1910, at Sutton in Surrey and educated at Roedean School. As a 19-year-old believer in Empire Free Trade, she wrote a strongly worded letter to S.W. Alexander, a *Sunday Express* financial journalist, in the hope of winning a job. He had nothing to offer but asked if she had ever heard of Sir James Dunn, who was looking for somebody. "Who is that?" she asked. "Is it Dunn the hatter?" "No, he's as mad as a hatter all right," replied Alexander, "but he's also a prominent financier."

On becoming a secretary in Dunn's London office, Christofor, as she was known to friends, was fired by him after two months for making a mistake over a message and then reinstated after sending a sharply worded letter of protest. From then on the slim, olive-skinned beauty became Dunn's indispensable aide and companion. With his guidance she successfully invested in the stock market, though on one occasion she cashed in her holdings to put them on a horse at the advice of the owner to reap winnings at 8–1. "It was her first day of betting, and her last," Beaverbrook boasted years later.

When Dunn returned to Canada to take over the direction of the ailing Algoma Steel Corporation at Sault Ste Marie, Ontario, Christofor followed to become its assistant secretary. Early in the war, she helped him to keep control of Algoma by liquidating her own assets to invest in the company when a bank tried to call in a loan and the Canadian government threatened nationalization. She then nursed him through severe illness and, in 1942, became his third wife. This was not the easiest of tasks. The irascible Dunn insisted on having his shoelaces ironed and would not permit electric razors in his house for fear of cancer. He also had food fads, which she catered for by transporting food and cooking implements in hat boxes wherever they went.

To protect Dunn's comfort, she furnished a large home in St Andrews, New Brunswick, around which was constructed a nine-foot fence and where they entertained the few old friends he was glad to see.

On Dunn's death in 1956, leaving $65 million, his widow inherited half his fortune; with this money she donated a science block and set up law scholarships at Dalhousie University in Nova Scotia. But she was so desolate that she talked of entering a convent. Then Lord Beaverbrook, Dunn's friend since boyhood, gallantly came to the rescue. He explained that he needed loving care, demanded her constant companionship and used her diary in writing *Courage* (1961), his highly coloured memoir of her late husband which she disliked and Dunn's children hated so much they threatened to sue. In 1961 she and Beaverbrook went through the old Scottish custom of plighting their troth at Torpichen church, outside Glasgow. Two years later, when Beaverbrook was approaching his end, he married her at Epsom register office. It was exactly 21 years after her first marriage.

She openly acknowledged that Dunn's memory held the warmest place in her affection, and Beaverbrook, though clearly very fond of her, was a widower of 36 years and therefore temperamentally incapable of paying a wife attention all the time. When questioned about the marriage, he pointed out that his spouse was richer than him; it was suspected that he hoped that she might divert some of her fortune into his Beaverbrook Foundation at Dalhousie's rival, the University of New Brunswick.

On becoming a widow for the second time in 1964, Lady Beaverbrook received no money because her husband declared in his will that she was adequately provided for, but she was emotionally better able to cope. In addition to taking up racing through her friendship with the Earl of Rosebery, she took a renewed interest in Dalhousie, to which she had paid little attention during her marriage to Beaverbrook. In 1968 she became chancellor of Dalhousie, where staff soon learned always to have Bollinger champagne ready and to expect her close interest in plans and appointments, which led to many expensive changes of mind.

In 1976 Lady Beaverbrook demonstrated that she deserved her place in the pantheon of the super-rich when she hired a private jet to fly her sister and herself to Canada at $26 per minute. She did not want her two puppies to travel with the freight on a regular plane, she explained.

LIEUTENANT-COLONEL JACK MAHONY, VC

LIEUTENANT-COLONEL JACK MAHONY (who died on December 20, 1990, aged 79) won the Victoria Cross in a desperate bridgehead battle on the Melfa River in Italy on May 23 and 24, 1944.

Leading the 5th Canadian Armoured Division's breakout from the Hitler Line, Lord Strathcona's Horse lost 17 tanks and were halted short of the Melfa River by German Panther tanks and 88 mm guns positioned on both sides of the river. Three of their light tanks, armed only with heavy machine guns, succeeded in crossing the Melfa and went to ground around a farmhouse. At the height of the battle, Mahony, who was following the armour, ordered his motor company of the Westminster Regiment to dismount. Under heavy artillery fire he led them in extended line over open ground to the river, where they slid down the steep bank and waded across the shallow stream. As Mahony positioned his platoons to defend the crossing site, the weight of enemy fire increased: the little bridgehead was obviously ringed by enemy tanks, infantry and self-propelled guns. It was 3:30 p.m., and until dark there could be no hope of buttressing the defence with anti-tanks guns, which would have to cross an open bullet-swept approach to the Melfa. First blood went to the Westminsters when their left-flank platoon stalked and destroyed a self-propelled 88 mm gun which was firing at the Strathconas beyond the river. Almost at once the enemy's artillery fire intensified, and four enemy tanks were seen advancing across the stubble fields towards the centre of the bridge-head, followed by a company of infantry.

With no regard for his own safety, Mahony moved about his position, encouraging his men. Well aware of his lack of anti-tank guns, Mahony sent an effective message to the German armour by having his PIATs (light anti-tank weapons) engage them at long range

160

with high-angle fire. As they drew near, his company met the enemy with such a fusillade from every rifle and machine gun that their infantry went to ground. The tanks continued to work forward but, without infantry support and wary of the PIATs, turned and withdrew when they were only 200 yards away. The Westminsters' casualties had been heavy. Their strength was only 60 men, and all but one of the platoon officers were wounded when, an hour later, a second and more determined enemy attack ground towards their position.

On the right a section was pinned down in the open by accurate and intense machine-gun fire. One tank which penetrated the position was destroyed by a soldier, who killed its commander in the turret then lobbed a grenade into the open hatch. Mahony crawled forward and by throwing smoke grenades extricated the section with the loss of only one man. Soon he himself was wounded in the head, then twice more in a leg. Despite intense pain he refused medical aid. Having lost three self-propelled guns as well as the tank to the Westminsters' aggressive defence, the Germans withdrew. Mahony now directed his left platoon to clear a group of farm buildings, which sheltered another enemy tank, but the attempt failed.

As darkness fell, he ordered his sadly depleted company to draw in close to his headquarters and so make the bridgehead more compact. There they dug in, loosening the rock-hard soil by exploding anti-tank grenades, and grimly awaited the next enemy attack. Mahony was everywhere – cheerful and confident, exhorting those who were feeling the strain and infusing his men with determination. The enemy could see that he was the soul of the defence and fired at him constantly with all weapons from rifles to 88 mm guns. Shortly after nine o'clock the first reinforcement from his regiment arrived; Mahony allowed his wounds to be dressed but refused to leave his men.

All night heavy artillery and mortar fire harassed the Westminsters, inflicting heavy casualties. The long ordeal ended in the morning when fresh Canadian troops attacked and broke the enemy resistance. The bridgehead had been vital to the Canadian Corps' success. Failure there would have meant delay, a repetition of the attack with heavy losses in men and material – and would have given the

Germans a breathing space in which to gather enough strength to break the impetus of the advance. Mahony was invested with the VC by King George VI on July 31, when His Majesty – travelling incognito as "General Collingwood" – visited the Canadians near Raviscanina in the Volturno valley.

John Keefer Mahony was born at New Westminster, British Columbia, on June 30, 1911, and educated at the Duke of Connaught High School. He was a natural athlete and excelled at swimming and lacrosse. On graduation he became the local reporter for the *Vancouver Daily Province* and joined the Westminster Regiment of the militia. He was commissioned in 1938 and, on mobilization the next year, was the battalion intelligence officer. In November 1941 he sailed for England, where the Westminsters became the motor battalion of the 5th Canadian Armoured Division. He was a major and a company commander when they moved to Italy in November 1943.

After the war Mahony was promoted lieutenant-colonel and remained in the army. His appointments included director of public relations in Ottawa and Canadian army liaison officer in Washington. In retirement he was the director of the London junior achievement programme, which trained young people for careers in business and commerce. He married and had two daughters.

MAJOR-GENERAL JOHN
ROCKINGHAM

MAJOR-GENERAL JOHN ROCKINGHAM (who died on July 7, 1987, aged 75) won a legendary reputation for bravery and skilful leadership in the 1944 invasion of Normandy. Later, in Korea, his 25th Canadian Infantry Brigade was known to his comrades in the 1st Commonwealth Division as "Rocky's Army," an affectionate reference to his rugged appearance and character as well as to his name.

Rockingham's quality as a soldier first stood out at the Battle of Verrières, which, after Dieppe, was the Canadian Army's costliest day of operations in the Second World War. His battalion, the Royal Hamilton Light Infantry, was the only unit in the 2nd Corps to seize and hold its objectives that day, in large part due to his confident and aggressive leadership. At one stage in the fighting Rockingham's tactical headquarters was practically wiped out, his driver and his signaller beside him were killed and his nose was clipped by a sniper's bullet; but he had seen the smoke from the rifle shot. Grabbing a sten gun he stalked and shot the sniper, then resumed control of his battalion.

Ten days later, he was promoted to command 9th Canadian Infantry Brigade during the Battle of the Falaise Gap and the subsequent breakout. He personally led his brigade's patrols into the main square of Rouen, where he exchanged shots from his armoured car with the retreating Germans. Charged with taking the immensely strong defences of Mont Lambert, crossing the River Liane and clearing the southern half of Boulogne, Rockingham's audacious tactics threw the enemy off balance, which in the six days of fighting they never regained. The German commander surrendered to Rockingham, who soon earned the gratitude of the people of Dover by capturing the huge coastal guns at Cap Gris Nez, which had plagued their lives since 1940.

A month of bitter struggle to open the approaches to Antwerp followed. In a move which attained complete surprise, Rockingham's brigade landed in amphibious Buffaloes at the rear of the enemy division holding the south bank of the Scheldt. In conditions of appalling misery they then fought their way westward through the flooded polder country, capturing the key port of Breskens and finally reaching the sea at Knokke where, nearby, they captured the German commander.

In the Rhineland, Rockingham led his brigade in a series of successes, first through the floods between Cleve and the Rhine, then in capturing the southern spur of the Hochwald. By this time his brigade had two unofficial titles – "the Water Rats," which they shared with the remainder of the 3rd Division, and "the Highland Brigade," which led to their selection to cross the Rhine with the British 51st Highland Division. In the lottery of war, Rockingham, on the left, drew the area of the British front where resistance was fiercest. After two days of hard fighting he broke through and began 3rd Division's advance down the river's left bank. Turning away from it at Emmerich, Rockingham drove his brigade hard as they fought their way through Holland to the North Sea. By the end of April they had moved into Germany and crossed the River Ems to capture the port of Leer. On May 4, when operations ended, Rockingham was within a few miles of the Emden naval base.

Almost immediately Rockingham returned to Canada to take command of a brigade being readied to attack Japan, but with the early end of the Pacific war, he returned to civilian life in Victoria, British Columbia.

A staunch Canadian, John Meredith Rockingham was proud to have been born in Sydney, New South Wales, on August 24, 1911. He was educated at Melbourne Grammar School before moving with his father, who worked for the British company Cable & Wireless, to Halifax, Nova Scotia, Barbados and Victoria, B.C. For five years after he came out of the army he worked for the Vancouver transport authority, then, on the outbreak of the Korean War, happily accepted command of the brigade group which Canada offered to the United

Nations. That dispiriting conflict presented few challenges to his tactical ability, but the high morale which his troops maintained was a direct result of his confident leadership, to say nothing of his sense of humour. One example was an ice hockey match between Australian and New Zealand regiments on the frozen Imjin, which resulted from spurious challenges that he passed to their respective commanding officers.

With peace again, Rockingham attended the Imperial Defence College, then successively commanded the Canadian Army's 1st Division and its Quebec and western commands. On retirement in 1966, he joined a construction company.

Rockingham, who married Mary Carlyle Hammond in 1936, was awarded the DSO and Bar, the Belgian Order of Leopold and the Croix de Guerre with palms for his part in the European campaign and the American Legion of Merit for Korea. He was appointed CBE in 1945 and CB in 1952.

MAJOR-GENERAL DES SMITH

MAJOR-GENERAL DES SMITH (who died on October 11, 1991, aged 80) was the youngest brigadier in charge of an armoured brigade in Italy and the Netherlands during the Second World War, and later enjoyed a successful business career in England.

Smith first saw action in the Liri valley in May 1944, when, at 32, he was commanding the Canadian 5th Army Brigade as the Eighth Army opened its drive to outflank Rome. His leadership and coolness under fire in the fight for the Melfa River crossing were readily distinguished. When the battle for Rome ended, Lieutenant-General Sir Oliver Leese, Bt, commander of the Eighth Army, expressed his dissatisfaction with the performance of the Canadians' inexperienced 1st Corps Headquarters. Three brigadiers were replaced, but Leese grudgingly accepted that Lieutenant-General "Tommy" Burns, the corps commander, should be given a further chance. Smith became Burns's chief of staff.

During the next four months the corps drove up the east coast of Italy, broke through the Gothic Line, took Rimini and advanced into the Lombard Plain. They achieved all their objectives, moved faster and farther than any other corps in Italy and inflicted heavy losses on the enemy. The headquarters was seen to be operating smoothly and efficiently under Smith's energetic guidance, but relations between Leese and Burns became strained to breaking point. Worse, Leese's lack of confidence in his corps commander after the fighting in the Liri valley was common knowledge among subordinate Canadian commanders. By the end of October 1944, the situation had become so untenable that Burns relinquished his command. In the minds of some Canadians, Smith played Brutus to Burns's Caesar. Smith was replaced as chief of staff and sent as stop-gap commander to the 1st Infantry Division, pending the arrival of its new general. Under Smith's command, the division advanced into the Lombard Plain towards a succession of resolutely defended positions.

At Lamone, an attack by his 1st Brigade met with disaster. Smith had no opportunity to recoup the situation before his temporary command ended. However, the new commander did not last long and Smith took his place. In the bitter fighting of the Battle of the Rivers he was both aggressive and successful. In northwest Europe, during the final stages of the war, his brigade assaulted westward across the Ijssel River, captured Apeldoorn and advanced towards the great cities of Holland.

James Desmond Blaise Smith was born in Ottawa on October 2, 1911, and educated at St Patrick's School and the University of Ottawa before entering the Royal Military College, Kingston, where he was a cadet company commander, played rugby for the college and was runner-up in its heavy-weight boxing championship. In 1933 he was commissioned into the Royal Canadian Dragoons. At the outbreak of the Second World War, Smith was staff captain of the 1st Canadian Division, with which he sailed to Britain. He attended a staff course at Camberley before returning to the division as its GSO 2. He was then appointed brigade major of the newly raised 2nd Canadian Armoured Brigade. In 1942 Smith was promoted to command his regiment, then equipped with armoured cars. Four months later, he became GSO 1 of Canada's 5th Armoured Division – although for a while he commanded the 4th Armoured Brigade, stationed in Sussex.

After the end of the war in Europe Smith returned to Canada, where VJ Day found him training a brigade for the assault on Japan. His first peacetime task was to reorganize the Royal Military College. In 1947 he left to attend a course at the Imperial Defence College in London, and on its completion became military secretary of the Cabinet Defence Committee in Ottawa, before being promoted quartermaster-general. In 1951 Smith again came to London, as chairman of the Canadian Joint Staff, the work of which greatly increased under his direction. After three years he returned to Canada to become commandant of the National Defence College, and in 1958 he was appointed adjutant-general of the Canadian Army.

Four years later Smith's resignation was forced by the prime minister, John Diefenbaker, because he was having an affair publicly, and he moved to Britain. Determined to obtain firsthand knowledge of British industrial relations, he found himself a job on the shop floor of an engineering firm. After six months he joined the Thomson Organisation and became a member of the team that launched the *Sunday Times*'s innovative colour section. In 1964 Smith switched to Pillar Holdings and two years later formed Pillar's highly successful engineering subsidiary. He retired from active business in 1986 and became the first Canadian member of the Commonwealth War Graves Commission. Later he helped to organize the Canada Memorial in London's Green Park.

Smith was appointed CBE and DSO in 1944 and was twice mentioned in dispatches. He was also decorated by France, Greece, Italy and the United States, and in 1948 was awarded the Canadian Forces Decoration. Smith was twice married: first, in 1937, to Miriam Blackburn, who died in 1969; and secondly, in 1979, to Mrs Belle Shenkman. He had two sons by his first marriage.

GEORGE WOODCOCK

GEORGE WOODCOCK (who died in Vancouver on January 28, 1995, aged 82) was a journeyman author in the tradition of Daniel Defoe and William Cobbett. He wrote more than 100 books of poetry, polemic, history, biography and criticism which were deeply imbued with a deep-seated belief in anarchism. This took the form of a graduated dislike for all forms of government and, in the eyes of his English friends, a risible decision to move to Canada in middle age.

Woodcock at first had to spread manure for $75 cents an hour. But he built up a second career in the dominion, churning out several volumes a year and becoming a father figure for the growing "Can-Lit" industry. At the same time, he maintained a foot in the British literary scene, most notably with *The Crystal Spirit* (1957), which was considered the best commentary on his friend George Orwell before publishers decided to ignore Orwell's wish that there be no biography.

George Woodcock was born in Winnipeg on May 8, 1912, the son of unsuccessful emigrants who returned to Shropshire when he was a few months old. Young George went to Sir William Borlase's School, Marlow, Buckinghamshire, and, too poor to take up a half-fees scholarship to Oxford, became a clerk with the Great Western Railway. Woodcock started to write poetry strongly influenced first by Ernest Dowson and then W.H. Auden, and produced several novels which he subsequently destroyed as he drifted into the London literary world of Herbert Read, Dylan Thomas, Roy Campbell and Julian Symons.

During the Second World War he was a conscientious objector who was employed as a farm worker, but found time to edit the literary magazine *NOW* and the anarchist paper *War Commentary*, which continues as *Freedom*. Afterwards he published a pioneering biography of the 17th-century female playwright Aphra Behn, a ponderous study of Oscar Wilde and a much-praised biography of the pre-Marxian socialist William Godwin. Harold Nicolson singled out the latter's balanced tone and sympathetic treatment in *The Daily Telegraph* but concluded it was still a whitewash of an unworthy character.

In 1949 Woodcock announced that he was going to Canada with his wife Ingeborg to escape the claustrophobia of postwar Britain and fulfil his father's disappointed dream. One of the few to give the project qualified approval was Orwell, who said it would be all right for a time if he was keen on fishing. Woodcock built a wooden house and grew vegetables at Sooke on Vancouver Island, then moved to Vancouver, which he described as "a literary desert." But he kept his name before the British public with biographies of the anarchists Pierre-Joseph Proudhon and Prince Kropotkin. A young man threw his pamphlet "What Is Anarchism?" into the chamber of the House of Commons; the jazz singer George Melly found himself facing a court martial for possessing it on a warship.

To make ends meet, Woodcock lectured for a time at Washington University and the University of British Columbia. But it was as founding editor of the quarterly *Canadian Literature* that he played a commanding part in nurturing the developing awareness of Canadian literary and cultural identity. By the mid-1960s he abandoned academic life to concentrate on his writing, which had the advantage of being not only naturally stylish but needing little revision.

Woodcock's first travel book, *Ravens and Prophets* (1951), about the British Columbia interior, was followed by others on South America, India, the South Seas and the Far East, which rarely failed to show that colonialism meant big government writ large at the individual's expense. Although he never modified his English accent, Woodcock became increasingly Canadian in his outlook, placing strong emphasis on the importance of regional literature. He produced highly influential studies of the novelists Hugh MacLennan and Mordecai Richler, made documentaries for the CBC and wrote biographies of the eccentric British Columbia premier Amor de Cosmos and the Métis leader Gabriel Dumont. In his later years, he returned to poetry, employing a freer, more personal form favoured by Margaret Atwood, and produced works on Aldous Huxley, Herbert

Read and the Trappist Thomas Merton, which showed his preference for social rather than close textual criticism.

Despite trumpeting his dislike of politics in *Anarchism* (1962) and *The Rejection of Politics* (1972), Woodcock continually worked for small deserving causes, such as water pumps for Indian villages and helping young struggling writers. True to his principles, he refused the Order of Canada, but he accepted a Governor General's Award for his Orwell book and, on his 82nd birthday, the freedom of Vancouver. He was delighted at the thought that the party held in his honour enabled him to witness his wake while still alive.

NORTHROP FRYE

NORTHROP FRYE (who died on January 23, 1991, aged 78) bore considerable responsibility for the rampant proliferation of academic literary criticism.

It is hard to overstate his influence on university English departments around the world. "In some ways," one of his colleagues wrote, "he was more like the founder of a religion, a Swedenborg or a Marx, than a literary critic." Frye achieved this influence – the effects of which he viewed with not altogether unmitigated joy – in two ways. First, the consistently exceptional standard of his work helped to establish literary academia's sense of itself as a profession. Second, Frye provided a cogent explanation of why literary criticism was a distinct, intellectually respectable discipline. He made the business seem a necessary adjunct to the existence of literature itself.

Frye's first book, *Fearful Symmetry* (1947), was a study of the poetry of William Blake. Blake had hitherto been regarded as a marginal figure in English literature, an idiot savant, a lyric poet of genius but the author, too, of incomprehensible "prophetic books," illustrated with rebarbative engravings of his own manufacture. Frye's book combined a comprehensive knowledge of Blake's work with the fruit of broad reading in the period, and showed that behind the apparent chaos of the poetry was a sane philosophical system. The book relocated Blake at the centre of English Romanticism and made Frye an academic star. It struck Harold Bloom – who was to inherit Frye's mantle as the most influential critic in North America – as "the best book I'd ever read about anything."

Frye's next book, *The Anatomy of Criticism* (1957), was an even bigger success. In it he set out to provide nothing less than an account of the mythical, formal, generic and symbolic basis of all literature – an astonishingly ambitious project, undertaken in a deceptively straightforward manner. The book argues for the autonomous, ahistorical independence of literature. Frye saw all the literatures of the world as a coherent system of myth and imagery – a system which he explicated, not in terms of what books might mean, but in terms of the relationship between the books themselves.

Much of *The Anatomy* is preposterous, and much of it brilliant. Even opponents of its overall argument accept that it contains a dazzlingly large number of unexpected insights into specific works, and Frye's theory of "modes," which explains the difference between such genres as epic and romance, remains a powerful critical idea. Frye sometimes used to claim, not altogether convincingly, that the elaborate apparatus of *The Anatomy* existed solely for the specific insights it provided. But even if one does not accept that characteristically humble self-assessment, it remains his masterpiece, and almost everything else he wrote can be said to be a series of explications and extrapolations of its broad-brushed conjectures.

The son of a hardware salesman, Herman Northrop Frye was born on July 14, 1912, at Sherbrooke, Quebec, and educated at high schools in Moncton, New Brunswick. He then took a course in business studies, which involved a visit to Toronto to take part in a typing contest. Frye came second and liked the city so much that he decided to read English and philosophy at Victoria College, where he wrote a gossip column for the literary magazine. His next move was to be ordained a minister of the United Church, but after a brief period preaching on the Prairies he decided on an academic vocation.

He read English at Merton College, Oxford, before returning to teach at Victoria College, where he remained for the rest of his career. The college has strong links with Methodism, and Frye said that his time there was in a way a fulfilment of his ministry. His religious belief manifested itself in the implicit moral and ethical stance of all his work and also in the streak of prophetic, visionary imagery which sometimes surfaced in his writing: he once likened commuters driving home at the evening rush-hour to "ants in the body of a dying dragon." He became full professor in 1948, was principal from 1959 to 1967 and chancellor from 1978.

Frye's other important publications include *A Natural Perspective* (1965), which remains the best book ever written about Shakespearean comedy; *The Secular Scripture* (1976), a study of the structure of romance; *The Great Code* (1982), which looked at the Bible in terms of literary morphology and archetype; and *The Myth of Deliverance* (1983), about Shakespeare's "problem plays." He was also a keen promoter of his countrymen's work, both as literary editor of *Canadian Forum* and in his essays about Canadian culture, collected in *The Burning Bush* (1971). He was delighted to see Canadian literature emerge from its status as a fortnight's reading at the end of a course on American literature.

A short, stocky man, with rimless spectacles, grey hair and massive forehead, Frye had the appearance of an elder statesman. Exceedingly reticent personally, he once said that he arranged his private life so that nothing would happen, in order to foil biographers. Married to Helen Kemp in 1937, Frye claimed to be "a bit short on hobbies" but is believed to have enjoyed playing the piano and reading science fiction. He was appointed CC in 1972.

SHAUN HERRON

SHAUN HERRON (who died at Port Hope, Ontario, on April 16, 1989, aged 76) was a hell-raising journalist whose novel *The Whore Mother* (1973) was one of the most bitter to come out of the Northern Ireland conflict.

The story of a young IRA member who tries to escape the terrorist life after meeting a middle-class American girl, it caused several critics on publication to remark that its remorseless spirit of violence must be exaggerated. But both the power of the writing and the history of the next 20 years ensured that it has since lost little of its impact. The book was companion volume to *Through the Dark and Hairy Wood* (1972), in which a kidnapped right-wing member of the Northern Ireland Parliament becomes the pawn in a duel between the IRA and the B-Special police. But although Ireland was the dominating theme of his life, Herron's best novel was based on his experience during the Spanish Civil War. *The Bird in Last Year's Nest* (1974) is the tale of a family caught up in Basque terrorism 30 years after the war's end, and contains a heady mixture of love and sentimental liberalism destroyed by the unstoppable spring of violence.

Shaun Herron was born at Carrickfergus, County Antrim, on September 12, 1912, and went to Belfast Academy and Queen's University, Belfast, which he left to join a Basque battalion that fought alongside the International Brigade in the Civil War. He was wounded in the left leg but remembered more vividly a quarrel in a café with Ernest Hemingway. On leaving Spain, Herron went to Edinburgh University, where he contracted a brief and unhappy marriage, then was ordained a Congregationalist minister in 1940. After being sent briefly to Greenock, he joined up to work in intelligence; he was wounded in the neck while with the Green Howards in France.

After the war, Herron studied at Princeton and became a padre with the Christian fellowship movement Toc H. He served at Keighley,

Yorkshire, and then Llandudno in North Wales, where he first attracted widespread attention by offering a Welsh national eisteddfod a £200 prize for a choral work solely in English; the gesture was rejected with some ill feeling. Herron's friendship with the poet Louis MacNeice got him some work as a scriptwriter with the BBC, and in 1953 he became editor of *British Weekly,* an important voice of the Nonconformist movement. Almost immediately, he plunged into controversy by attacking the home secretary, David Maxwell Fyfe, for refusing to commute the controversial death penalty on the murderer Derek Bentley.

"One thing can always be said for a Tory minister. He can be trusted to show a proper contempt for the conscience and conviction of the public," wrote Herron in an editorial, which prompted resignations from the paper's board. Herron eventually had to retract his remarks, but he continued to cause further upsets, as when he told a congregation that not many Christian ministers had sufficient experience of life to be able to preach God's word effectively.

On resigning after eight years, when *British Weekly* came under new ownership, Herron announced that he was going "precisely where I want to go: a small town parish." This turned out to be in Weyburn, Saskatchewan. He settled down with his second wife, Gina, who bore him two children, but it was not long before the parish work was failing to satisfy and he was writing a humorous column for the *Winnipeg Free Press.* His links with the paper continued when he moved, less happily, to Toronto and then Lowell, Massachusetts. In 1960 he became its Washington correspondent and, four years later, its chief leader-writer.

Under the paper's Gladstonian Liberal tradition he moved steadily rightwards, excoriating socialists more than Tories yet also raising the standard of literary criticism on the Prairies. Winnipeggers were surprised by his sharp criticism of Hemingway and assurances that the playwright Eugene O'Neill's work declined from the moment he was deprived of his witty brother's company. At the same time Herron demonstrated a reawakened awareness of Ireland in a light-hearted column about the religious divide, *Herron's Folk.* His views began to take on a dark tinge, however, with the onset of the Troubles and the murder his cousin, the Protestant leader Tommy Herron.

Although already nearing retirement age, he launched into fiction with two straight thrillers, *Miro* (1967) and *The Miro Papers* (1970), which had an American secret serviceman hero. These had handsome sales in the United States, an experience that encouraged his near contempt for the Canadian literary scene, which in turn paid him little attention. His later works included the long but less successful historical novel *The MacDonnell* (1978) and *The Prince Peacock and the Kingdom* (1988), about North American evangelical preachers. Herron's plotting could be clogged and his descriptions flat, but he had an undeniable gift for vivid dialogue, while his best work was powered by a fascinated revulsion for violence.

On retiring from the *Free Press* amid a considerable libel case stemming from one of his last articles, he divided his time for several years between Spain and the village of Schull, County Cork, where he kept two vicious wolfhounds. A neat, disciplined man with a sharp tongue despite a fundamental kindness, Herron was not without a measure of self-esteem. His *Who's Who* entry declared that he held several lectureships but found entries in reference books "too dreary to read."

'FLYING PHIL' GAGLARDI

"FLYING PHIL" GAGLARDI (who died on September 23, 1995, aged 82) was a British Columbia highways minister with a weakness for speeding on the roads he had built.

His career was dogged by fines, and he lost his licence on several occasions. This prompted a celebrated picture of him reading a bus timetable while holding an unattached steering wheel; it neglected to allude to the chauffeur-driven car and an aircraft at his official disposal.

Gaglardi's standard excuse on being stopped by a Mountie patrolman was that he was "testing the curves," and he was fond of asserting that his roads were so good that a limit of 50, then 60 and 65 mph was too slow. No friend to road safety campaigns, which he considered did more damage than good, Gaglardi disliked radar traps and believed that policemen should "come out from behind the bushes and use the highway like the rest of us: make men of them." But a constable only had to give the minister a ticket, he complained, to win promotion as sergeant.

"I talk fast, I work fast, I never slow down for anything," he would say. "But even though I'm supposed to be a madman on the highway I stay away from everyone. I gamble a bit, but I don't take unnecessary chances."

The son of southern Italian immigrants, Philip Arthur Gagliardi (later spelled Gaglardi) was born on January 13, 1913, at Silverdale in the British Columbia interior and went to school at Mission before working as a bulldozer driver. When his family converted to Pentecostalism, he gave up drinking, smoking and swearing to study for the ministry at Northwest Bible College. After honing his skills as a peripatetic preacher, he settled first in Langley, B.C. Next he moved to the Calvary Temple in Kamloops, where ran a daily radio show, *The Chapel in the Sky,* and bought 13 buses to bring children to Sunday school.

When British Columbia's Liberal-Conservative coalition administration collapsed in 1952, fear of a socialist government led to the formation of a new conservative party purporting to believe in the "funny money" doctrines of social credit. Gaglardi had shown no previous interest in politics, but he half-reluctantly allowed his name to be put forward at a local meeting and won the nomination. When the Social Credit party triumphed at the polls with the slogan "Social Credit: You Won't Regret It," he was given the aid of an assistant pastor in Kamloops and rewarded with the Ministry of Public Works by W.A.C. ("Wacky") Bennett.

Immediately Gaglardi launched a programme to build freeways to the United States and metal roads into the interior which was so massive that it quickened the pace of the entire provincial economy. Never a man for detail, especially if it involved the mundane practice of detailed accounting, Gaglardi would declare when harried in the legislature, "If I'm telling a lie, it's because I believe I'm telling the truth." As a dual minister of religion and government, he believed it his duty to put the highways "in such shape that motorists will avoid the language which would deny them access to the highway to heaven."

Gaglardi commissioned vast schemes, prodded the engineers who said they could not be achieved, and swooped down on every aspect of the work. On one occasion, he spotted two men loafing, ordered his plane to land and fired them – only to be greeted by incredulous laughter; they were local farmers mending a fence.

He won widespread esteem for his then novel policy of apologizing to motorists for any inconvenience, which led to his early nickname of "Sorry Phil," and was greeted around the world as "the greatest of the Roman road builders." But he could never extinguish rumours about his relations with contractors and the free lifts he offered in his planes.

Gaglardi was able to weather the widespread suspicion that he was an amiable crook because he evinced little personal interest in money. Trouble grew, however, when his sons Bill and Bob started out as developers of land close to their father's roads. Eventually he was caught out when he denied that his daughter had taken a trip to Dallas in a highways department Lear jet; Bennett discovered that the woman concerned was Gaglardi's daughter-in-law and fired him.

For over a year Gaglardi languished as minister without portfolio, then was given the Ministry of Welfare. He embarked with a characteristic promise to be the roughest, toughest welfare minister in history, earning an opposition claim later that his policy consisted of throwing rocks at beggars. Gaglardi set up an alliance of businessmen to help the jobless, which promised some success. He demonstrated a willingness to stretch the rules both to exclude "deadbeats" and to aid deserving cases by buying tools for a mechanic and paying part of an overweight bricklayer's wages until he slimmed sufficiently to work effectively again.

But Gaglardi's brief success in reducing the welfare rolls vanished with the hint of recession and the arrival of flower children more interested in making love, not war, than in finding jobs.

After 20 years of prosperity fostered by the small-government, free-enterprise ambience of Social Credit, the Bennett administration showed signs of its age and the electorate flirted boldly with the socialist New Democrats. The realization that the party was in serious trouble came in the middle of the 1972 election campaign when Gaglardi told a reporter that it was time for the ageing Bennett to make way for him. Of course, he immediately claimed to have been misquoted; but he lost his seat and the government crashed.

Gaglardi's speeches – delivered in the cadences of the pulpit with good-humoured references to himself as "the little fella" and employing such dramatic expressions as "Jumping Jehosphat" – continued to contain a mixture of outrageousness and common sense that won headlines in later life. He condemned abortion, lambasted the young for their lack of the work ethic and suggested the speed limit be raised to 110 mph.

But his only return to active politics came with his election as mayor of Kamloops in 1988, which led to an uneasy term for both elected and electors. Three years later, when the Social Credit party was clearly dying, he announced his candidature for the leadership but failed to file nomination papers on time.

MAJOR-GENERAL DAN SPRY

MAJOR-GENERAL DAN SPRY (who died on April 2, 1989, aged 76) was a battle-tried and successful divisional commander before he retired at the remarkably early age of 32 to win international respect as a world leader of the Boy Scout movement.

In July 1943, as a lieutenant-colonel, he accompanied General Andrew McNaughton on a visit to Canadian troops in Sicily. There the CO of the Royal Canadian Regiment was killed in action and Spry replaced him. For five months he led the battalion through the arduous fighting for the island and the subsequent advance through the mountains of Italy until, in December 1943, they reached the outskirts of Ortona. There, when its brigadier fell ill, he became the acting commander of the 1st Canadian Infantry Brigade. His first battle to clear the approaches to the town was described in the official history as setting "a standard of almost faultless co-operation between artillery, infantry and armour not previously obtained in the Italian campaign."

Both during the fighting for Ortona and the spring battles southwest of Cassino, Spry showed what a bold, skilful and inspiring leader he was. In the difficult struggle to break through the Hitler Line and capture Pontecorvo, he was constantly with the forward troops as he co-ordinated their advance. During the summer of 1944 he was ordered to form a new infantry brigade in Italy from units converted from other arms. He had barely begun its training when he was summoned to replace the wounded commander of the 3rd Canadian Infantry Division in Normandy. At 31, Spry became the youngest general in the Commonwealth forces in the 1939–45 war.

Taking command as the battle of the Falaise Pocket ended, he led his division across the Seine to capture the heavily defended ports of Boulogne and Calais which were vital to the Allies' advance. After much heavy fighting, he forced the enemy in the ports to surrender. Spry's next task was to clear the south bank of the Scheldt as part of the Canadian Army's campaign to open the sea approaches to Antwerp. There, in appalling weather conditions, his men confronted one of the best divisions in the German army, fully up to strength in men and equipment. His first attack across the Leopold Canal made slow progress but became the focus of the Germans' defence. Realizing this, Spry launched an amphibious assault in the enemy's rear. Then, attacking relentlessly, he drove them from the waterlogged polders.

After the victory on the Scheldt the 3rd Division moved to the Nijmegen salient. From here in February 1945 Spry launched yet another successful water-borne offensive, this time to clear the western flood plain of the Rhine towards Cleve. At the end of a message to his men telling them that they were now being called "the Water Rats," he added: "Keep splashing."

Within six weeks of the end of the war, he was appointed commander of the Canadian reinforcement base in England, which after VE Day was to become responsible for repatriation of the army to Canada. Spry managed it so well that in 1946 he was appointed vice-chief of General Staff in Ottawa. The prospect of long service in a tiny peacetime army now held little appeal for the youthful general. He gratefully accepted the challenging position of chief executive commissioner of the Boy Scouts Association of Canada. In 1953 he moved to Geneva as director of the Boy Scouts World Bureau.

A major-general's son, Daniel Charles Spry was born in Winnipeg on February 4, 1913, and educated in Calgary and Halifax and at Ashford School, England. He joined the Princess Louise Fusiliers of the militia while at Dalhousie University and in 1934 obtained a Permanent Force commission in the Royal Canadian Regiment. A natural athlete, he soon gained a reputation as a football and basketball coach as well as a keen competitive sailor. He was adjutant of the regiment when it sailed for England in December 1939. Early in 1942 he attended the Staff College at Camberley, following which he joined the planning staff for the invasion of Europe. Later that year he became the military assistant to the commander of the First Canadian Army and in that capacity was present during the landings in Sicily.

He was appointed CBE in 1945 and was awarded the DSO for his gallant leadership near Pontecorvo. In 1965 he returned from Switzerland to live in Ottawa and was for eight years a director of the Canadian International Development Agency. He was colonel of the Royal Canadian Regiment from 1965 to 1978. Spry married, in 1939, Elizabeth Forbes, and they had a son and a daughter.

ROBERTSON DAVIES

ROBERTSON DAVIES (who died on December 2, 1995, aged 82) was strangely neglected until two brilliant works of his late middle age firmly established his reputation as Canada's wittiest and most talented novelist.

The Rebel Angels (1981) is a high-spirited work combining gypsy lore with an exploration of the medieval origins of a university, while *What's Bred in the Bone* (1985) deals with the nature of originality in a story about faking Old Masters. They suffered at times from the heavy tread of an elephantine narrative style, yet with their unrivalled energy, erudition and breadth of subject matter demonstrated a sureness of touch, depth of perception and largeness of mind.

A frustrated playwright who turned only reluctantly to prose fiction, Davies drew on experience as a newspaper editor, man of letters and academic. One of his novels would typically stretch back to early in the century and evolve through comic passages worthy of P.G. Wodehouse, sensitive delineations of adolescent self-discovery amid scenes set in exclusive boardrooms or the purlieus of civilized society; it would discuss such recondite subjects as the history of freak shows, the theories of Carl Jung and the significance of newspaper obituaries before arriving at its destination. Not the least of his virtues was a rare ability to portray the moneyed establishment as it goes about its discreet and private business.

There were reviewers who groaned at the arrival of another Davies confection: it would be too long, too learned, too clever. Davies shared none of the North American fascination with the minutiae of political life. He was too outspoken about Canadian insecurities to be as loved as he was respected at home. In the United States, his lack of feminist concern made him less appreciated than his fellow finalist on the 1985 Booker Prize short list, Margaret Atwood. In Britain there was a steadily growing number of admirers, led by the novelist-critic Anthony Burgess. Yet some seemed to be offended by his fecundity and confusing symbolism, and bridled at his well-bred, high-table assurance.

It was in Scandinavia, where there is little fear of long works or meditative passages, that his works inspired wholehearted enthusiasm. He was considered for the Nobel Prize for Literature several times.

William Robertson Davies was the son of a Welsh immigrant who rose from printer's devil to newspaper proprietor before becoming a Liberal senator given to returning regularly to Wales in later life to serve as High Sheriff of Montgomeryshire. Born on August 28, 1913, young Rob was educated at Upper Canada College and Queen's University, Ontario, where he did not take a degree because he never achieved the mathematical pass to become a conventional student.

Davies arrived at Balliol College, Oxford, at the mature age of 22, affecting heavy tweeds, large hats and a pince nez, to earn the distinction of being profiled as an *Idol* in the undergraduate magazine *Isis*. The sight of his almost Chestertonian figure proceeding up the Broad, it declared, made Davies seem the last of the real undergraduate figures.

He indulged a deep love of music by joining a choral society run by the future British prime minister "Teddy" Heath, read papers on the Victorian theatre to uninterested societies but concentrated on the Oxford University Dramatic Society. He was both stage manager and director, and made his mark as an actor with two performances. His Dogberry in *Much Ado about Nothing* was said to be the finest undergraduate performance since Robert Speaight's Peer Gynt in the mid-1920s; his Malvolio in *Twelfth Night* was still recalled 50 years later for its brilliant mixture of absurdity and precision.

At the same time Davies demonstrated his scholarly credentials with a pioneering thesis which became his first book, *Shakespeare's Boy Actors* (1939).

After coming down from Oxford, he went on tour, then was invited to join the Old Vic by Tyrone Guthrie, who found him bit parts, asked him to lecture on history at the theatre school and handed him rewriting responsibilities.

When in 1940 Davies was rejected by the Armed Forces because of his poor eyesight, he returned to Canada with a bride, the Australian Brenda Matthews, an assistant theatre director whom he had met at the Old Vic and who was to bear him three daughters.

He first became literary editor of *Saturday Night,* then editor and co-proprietor of his father's paper, the Peterborough *Examiner.* The small Ontario industrial town, with its stolid conservatism, made a marked contrast to life in London or Oxford. But hiving off most of the responsibility for writing about politics to deputies, Davies concentrated on reviewing books and the theatre and writing a quirky column, which was published in book form as *The Diary* and *The Table Talk of Samuel Marchbanks.* Although the paper only had a small circulation, it became one of the most quoted in Canada.

Volumes of his selected literary criticism and theatrical reflections demonstrated a sureness of judgment in championing the educated reader that was to establish him as one of North America's most perceptive critics.

Davies gave most of his spare energies to the theatre. He helped to set up the Ontario Stratford Memorial Theatre with Guthrie, and produced and acted in local amateur theatrical productions. However, although he gradually built up some Canadian following as a play-wright, his efforts to establish himself internationally were doomed. Manuscripts sent to his old acquaintances Laurence Oliver and John Gielgud gathered dust. His *Love and Libel* folded after six performances on Broadway. A play written for Stratford about Casanova was shelved in favour of another by J.B. Priestley. "You must realize that no one, but no one, has any interest in Canada," a member of the H.M. Tennent theatrical agency in London assured him.

Nevertheless, what appeared to be unbearably heavy erudition in a script proved digestible in novel form. First came *Tempest-Tost* (1951), an elaborate comedy of manners set in an amateur theatrical group. Then followed *Leaven of Malice* (1954), about a malicious letter sent to a newspaper, and *A Mixture of Frailties* (1958), delineating a woman's escape from her mother to become a great singer. *The Salterton Trilogy,* as they were collectively known, was well received, though it was more than 30 years before he had the satisfaction of seeing it published in Britain.

Although more than ready for a change, he turned down Roy Thomson's offer of the editorship of the *Scotsman* in Edinburgh, and finally accepted an offer at the new postgraduate Massey College at the

University of Toronto well in time for the arrival of student dissent. There were also other problems. The project was not firmly funded, his appointment was regarded as an affront by the massing ranks of professional Can-Lit specialists, and he was dogged by the college's failure to cater for women graduates – a matter made worse in his enemies' eyes by his belief that the matter was of little importance. Eventually, however, this large figure, with a white beard and flowing locks suggestive of a Welsh wizard, conquered the doubters to be recognized as both a prestigious figurehead and an infectious lecturer on theatrical history.

His next novel was *Fifth Business* (1970), in which a schoolmaster holder of the Victoria Cross traced the course of his life from the throw of a snowball. It revealed Davies's growing interest in Jungian psychology but, most impressively, demonstrated his ability to impose a magic coherence on a combination of comedy, tragedy, realism, fantasy and philosophy. By the time two further novels in *The Deptford Trilogy* appeared, *The Manticore* (1972) and *The World of Wonders* (1975), he had clearly developed a distinctive voice.

International recognition finally arrived, but it did not turn his head. When the sequel to *The Rebel Angels, What's Bred in the Bone*, was nominated to the Booker short list, Davies was bemused to find his arrival greeted as a major event by the London press, remarking that it had happily ignored him for more than 50 years. To balance the hype, he wrote an article in *The Daily Telegraph* about Swedes who doggedly disputed Canada's claim to be the world's most boring country. The third volume in *The Cornish Trilogy, The Lyre of Orpheus* (1988), an efficient work concerning the staging of an opera, closed Davies's most creative period.

Murther and Walking Spirits (1990) best demonstrated his strengths and weaknesses by brilliantly opening with a murder, then sagging with a long historical passage based on Davies's own family history, before picking up again at the end. Despite flat sections of narrative it was sustained by an authorial voice that had wit, erudition and pyrotechnical skill which lost little for being sustained by some loopy speculations on the post-Christian spirit world. All was presented with an effusion of energy that made him seem in many ways a displaced Great Victorian – as much a part of British literature as Canadian.

ROSS MUNRO

ROSS MUNRO (who died on June 21, 1990, aged 76) was the leading Canadian war correspondent whose most harrowing experience was the 20 minutes in which he witnessed the Royal Regiment of Canada's bloody attempt to land at Dieppe on August 19, 1942.

The fact that Munro had earlier heard talk of the raid being "a piece of cake" only made it worse when the bodies started to pile up on the ramp of the Royals' landing craft. "There was a young lad crouching six feet away from me," Munro wrote. "He had made several vain attempts to rush the ramp to the beach but each time a hail of fire had driven him back. He had been wounded in the arm but was determined to try again. He lunged forward and a streak of red-white tracer slashed through his stomach. I'll never forget his anguished cry as he collapsed on the blood-soaked deck: 'Christ, we gotta beat them, we gotta beat them.'"

This account appeared in Munro's book *Gauntlet to Overlord* (1945), which won a Governor General's Award. But at the time, he returned to England to find himself prevented from telling the true story for the Canadian Press news agency. Several accounts written in advance – "Dieppe Victors Come Back Singing" – appeared in British papers. The American news agencies, reporting on their country's first intervention of the war, hailed it as a triumph of American arms.

Munro went straight to his Fleet Street office, where he dosed himself with Benzedrine and set to work for the next 12 hours. In his dispatch, which was held up by the censors so that it did not appear in *The Daily Telegraph* until August 21, Munro conveyed some of the blood and excitement, but only the last paragraph mentioned that he had been in a spot where landing had been "temporarily repulsed." As the full extent of the tragedy became clear from the length of the casualty lists published in Canada, the still battle-shocked Munro was sent home on a nationwide lecture tour. He was unable say that the operation was a disaster, and even found himself telling 3,000 Calgarians how their tank regiment "fought their way clean through Dieppe." Nevertheless, he found some satisfaction in acting as a personal contact between the troops and their families.

Later in the war Munro filed vivid dispatches about the assaults at Sicily and on the Italian mainland. When Mackenzie King, the prime minister, grumbled that Canada's war effort was not receiving its rightful share of recognition, *Newsweek* remarked that Munro came close to undermining the complaint single-handed. Munro was with the first wave of troops on D-Day, June 6, 1944. There were still problems with censorship, but after an appeal to General Harry Crerar, he got through a dispatch reporting that the Black Watch had been "wiped out" at Verrières – when more than 400 men failed to return from a sortie. While covering the Scheldt campaign, Munro was particularly aware of the advantages he enjoyed as a correspondent. During the drive from Antwerp he spent his days with the Regina Rifles, whose rations were indiscriminately lobbed to them like grenades so that some received little but marmalade. At night he took a streetcar back to the city's Century Hotel where he would file his copy and be served by waiters in white tie and tails.

A lanky, tousled figure forever smoking a pipe, Robert Ross Munro was the son of a parliamentary press gallery reporter and grandson of the founder of the *Port Elgin Times.* He was born in Ottawa on September 6, 1913, and joined Canadian Press after going to Humberside Collegiate and the University of Toronto. He had his first taste of battle when covering the Spitzbergen operation in 1941.

After the war Munro stayed on in Europe to report the Nuremberg trials, then returned to Ottawa to join Southam News Services. He later covered the Korean War, though by now his enthusiasm for war reporting was waning. Many correspondents had neither tin hats nor identity discs, he complained, and a lot of "warcos" were being killed. On his return to Canada, Munro went into management; he became publisher of the *Vancouver Daily Province,* the *Winnipeg Tribune* and the *Edmonton Journal* and was also responsible for launching the *Canadian Magazine* colour supplement.

When he married Helen Marie Stevens, a Canadian Army physiotherapist, in 1943, Munro tried to alert his boss in Toronto by inserting a piece of "cable-ese" in a routine report, which said "Mainaisling HMS Wednesday," but the censors cut it out in the belief that he was passing on classified information about one of His Majesty's ships. After her death, in 1982, he married Beth Helleur, the widow of a colleague. Munro was appointed OBE in 1946 and OC in 1975.

PROFESSOR HARRY FERNS

PROFESSOR HARRY FERNS (who died on February 19, 1992, aged 78) was an idiosyncratic intellectual whose most important staging post, in a journey from Marxism to the imperatives of the Institute of Economic Affairs in London, was his pioneering study of Argentina.

He was encouraged to embark on his researches by Lenin's remark about Anglo-Argentine relations providing a classic example of unofficial colonial exploitation. But by the time *Britain and Argentina in the Nineteenth Century* appeared in 1960, the Marxism had been purged. Writing with rare verve for an economic historian, Ferns showed that the Argentinians got much more out of their relationship with the British than theory postulated. He came not only to blame the socialist policies introduced by General Juan Peron for Argentina's precipitous postwar economic decline, but to detect related viruses in the British body politic.

Although he was not the first to warn about the dangers of state interference in Britain's higher education system, his experience at Birmingham University – where he was professor of social science from 1961 to 1981 – led him to produce an influential pamphlet, *Towards an Independent University* (1969). This pointed out the growing power of the University Grants Commission and suggested there would be little difficulty in setting up a private foundation for £5 million. Ferns was considered vulnerable because of his utilitarian views on tertiary education, but the idea bore fruit in Britain's first private university, Buckingham, which opened in 1967. Characteristically, he protested at its insistence on seeking a royal charter.

The son of a minor civil servant, Henry Stanley Ferns was born at Calgary on December 13, 1913, and brought up in Winnipeg's North End, a hotbed of socialist ideology. He went to St John's High School and the University of Manitoba. It was on his voyage to Cambridge, where he had a scholarship provided by the Imperial Order of the Daughters of the Empire, that he met a retired Indian Army major who introduced him to Marx's *Communist Manifesto*.

When Ferns arrived at Trinity College in 1938, the Soviet "moles" Anthony Blunt, Guy Burgess and Kim Philby had left, but there was still an active Marxist cell for which he recruited with a voluble enthusiasm that made him unsuitable for secret work. After the outbreak of war, Ferns was rejected by the army because of his deafness and set off for New York. He had a letter from the Communist leader Palme Dutt, but could not find the American to whom it was addressed. On moving north, he was disappointed that Tim Buck, the Canadian Communist leader, failed to introduce him to any intellectuals.

According to his own account, Ferns simply let his membership slide when he was offered a job in the prime minister's private office. For four uninspiring years, he helped to prepare Mackenzie King's parliamentary answers, in the course of which he fell foul of several key bureaucratic figures. He did not help his future by dining with the KGB head from the Soviet embassy and by becoming close friends with another Communist recruit at Trinity, Herbert Norman, who was to commit suicide while Canadian ambassador in Cairo. After a brief period in the Department of External Affairs, where he earned a black mark by advocating independence for the Indian Empire, Ferns became a temporary lecturer at the University of Manitoba's United College. When his name was revealed as having been mentioned in the Moscow messages of the defector Igor Gouzenko, he was busy drumming up support for his brainchild, the apolitical daily paper the *Winnipeg Citizen*. But as Cold War panic began to grip Canada, Ferns was forced to resign as president of the paper's board, even before it embarked on its sickly year of life. He then learned that his teaching contract would not be renewed.

Ferns used his sudden four months' leisure to go to Chicago to resume the Argentine studies he had begun at Cambridge. Then a lectureship at Royal Roads naval college in British Columbia was withdrawn at the last minute. Ferns's wife, Maureen, who was to bear him four children, persuaded him to return to Britain; they duly set off, pausing only in Ottawa to collect $2,000 compensation, and he eventually found a post at Birmingham.

Ferns had little reason to be grateful to the Canadian establishment, and he duly prepared an attack on the area where it would hurt most. In the years since Mackenzie King's death, while his Liberal party continued to guide the nation, the former prime minister was still regarded with awe. But *The Age of Mackenzie King* (1955), which Ferns wrote with Bernard Ostry, wittily exposed King's heavy reliance on spiritualism, with its examination of tea leaves and consultations with his dead mother. The book showed how the young King had ratted on his fellow leaders of a student strike at the University of Toronto in 1895 and warned that it was always necessary to distinguish between what King "persuaded himself he was doing; what he persuaded others he was doing; and what he actually did." The resulting storm that greeted the book was a warning of the Liberals' approaching electoral defeat, but it caused Ferns some personal embarrassment when it emerged that Ostry, who did the basic research in Canada, had unsuccessfully demanded first place on the title page. A sequel was abandoned.

In the early 1960s, Ferns declared that he enjoyed far more academic freedom in Britain than in Canada, where he could earn 30 per cent more money. Nevertheless, the failure of his *Argentina* (1969) and *The Argentine Republic, 1516–1971* (1973) to exercise much influence reflected the extent to which his anti-Marxism was out of step with fashionable opinion. He discovered the new flammability of political passions when he cancelled a speech at Birmingham University by Enoch Powell shortly after the right-wing Tory MP's celebrated speech warning that the growing number of immigrants could lead to "rivers of blood." Ferns rather fancifully claimed that he had made the decision in the light of the assassination of Senator Robert Kennedy, and was accused of being both untruthful and scandalous by Powell. When the Labour MP who was due to speak the following week threatened to withdraw, Ferns was forced to reissue the invitation, with result that Powell was met by abusive mob when he arrived to speak on foreign affairs but emerged unscathed.

By 1971 Ferns was sufficiently incensed by the political forces at large in the academic world that he publicly complained about the way left-wing dons tried to ensure that their like-minded friends were appointed to university faculties. In his later years, he produced several texts on the subject of freedom and wrote a sensitive autobiography, *From Left to Right* (1983), that was considerably thinner by the time the lawyers had finished vetting it.

Lord Harris of High Cross writes: Harry Ferns was not an easy person to get to know. At first meeting, an amiable teddy-bear of a man, peering back through thick glasses, pursing his lips and turning his best ear to catch your conversation, he seemed shy, serious, gentle, emollient. On longer acquaintance, he could become assertive, forceful, even passionate, which explained why his children, to whom he was plainly devoted, used to call him the "Old Exploder." I still recall the shy chuckle with which, over pre-lunch drinks at the Institute of Economic Affairs 20 years ago, he confided that he had graduated to what he called "the IEA camp" from the ranks of the Communist party.

By the 1970s there was no novelty in academic economists from the left becoming disillusioned with the Keynesian-collectivist consensus and writing radical tracts for the IEA. But here was a Canadian political scientist – later to describe himself as having been "a Marxist missionary among the natives in Cambridge" – who became the famed author of the most outrageously free-market proposal imaginable to most life-tenured academics, namely the establishment in Britain of a university wholly free from state funding or control. His first airing of this radical idea in the *Political Quarterly* aroused no interest until Arthur Seldon invited him to elaborate his thinking for an IEA occasional paper, *Towards an Independent University.* On the first page he explained his prime purpose as restoring "the moral and social energy of the people [which] is diminishing through undue and prolonged entanglement in the web of government."

His wide study of the English, French and American revolutions in various ways confirmed his verdict on the postwar decline of rich Argentina under Peronist politicization. He came to see unlimited government not as the solution to the world's problems, but as their cause. Hence another title in 1978: *The Disease of Government.* Like Adam Smith in the *Theory of Moral Sentiments,* this quietly Christian thinker saw human nature universally as having a divine spark, but also a devil's streak. He therefore followed Friedrich Hayek in favouring constitutional checks on the power of politicians, forever hiding behind the exaggerated prestige of "government," by "doing to Parliament what Parliament did to the Crown in the late 17th century." I doubt if he would have thought Mr John Major's Citizen's Charter an adequate intellectual or practical substitute.

GEORGE IGNATIEFF

GEORGE IGNATIEFF (who died on August 10, 1989, aged 75) rose to the top of the Foreign Service after arriving in Canada as part of an impoverished princely Russian family with a distinguished record in the Tsar's government.

As ambassador to NATO, the United Nations and the Geneva Disarmament Committee at various times, he raised his new country's esteem both by his diplomatic skills and a transparent concern for peace, which he expressed in an accent strongly redolent of Oxford and old St Petersburg. Ignatieff was always edgy in the company of Soviet diplomats, who would occasionally introduce themselves with the words "As the son of a peasant I salute you." When Ignatieff was part of an official delegation to Moscow in 1955, Nikita Khrushchev kept calling him "Count" as he plied him with so much vodka that he was sick. An official drew Ignatieff aside to invite him to come "home" to continue his family's tradition of public work, rather than serve a small satellite state of America. But his Russian was rusty, and a meeting with a cousin who had deserted the White Russian cause to become a lieutenant-general in the Red Army was not a success. The discovery that the house in which he had watched the first demonstrations of the 1917 revolution had become the Leningrad House of Marriage hardly reassured his deep Orthodox faith, which went with a strong affection for his adopted country.

Georgi Pavlovich Ignatieff was born in St Petersburg on December 16, 1913, the fifth son of Count Paul Ignatieff, a rising administrator who had large estates in the Ukraine and was to become Nicholas II's last education minister. Count Paul was imprisoned in 1918, but students who had benefited from his reforms secured his release, and helped by a redoubtable London nanny, he escaped with his family from Odessa aboard a British warship. On reaching England he bought a farm near Hastings and sent his younger sons to St Paul's

School in London, where young George was called "a bolshie" by his fellows and developed a lifelong aversion to public schools.

When the father went off to Paris to work with the Russian Red Cross, the elder brother Vladimir sold the farm and took the family to Canada. George spent a year at Lower Canada College in Montreal, then got his first job as an axeman cutting wood for railway sleepers in British Columbia. He went on to study at the University of Toronto and, with a slight bending of the rules, won a Rhodes scholarship to New College, Oxford. In the last months of peace he visited Bulgaria to research a thesis on his grandfather, who had liberated the country from the Turks, and returned to London via Nuremberg, Munich and Vienna.

Since the Canadian Army would not take him in London he joined the Royal Artillery and then switched to photo-intelligence before being offered a post in the Canadian Foreign Service. As third secretary at Canada House, Ignatieff acted as personal assistant to the high commissioner, Vincent Massey, who would hear nothing against Britain and her upper classes. He made an important friendship with the future prime minister, Lester Pearson, with whom he firewatched on the roof of Canada House in Trafalgar Square. Posted back to Ottawa in 1944 and married to Massey's niece Alison Grant (who bore him two sons), he steadily built his career, being attached to the United Nations and the Atomic Energy Commission. Ignatieff served as counsellor in Washington, deputy high commissioner in London, ambassador in Yugoslavia and assistant under-secretary in Ottawa before becoming closely involved in what he regarded as his major task of working for nuclear disarmament. Although he had long retired from the service, his last post was as ambassador for disarmament in John Turner's short-lived Liberal government in 1984.

Appointed CC in 1973, Ignatieff became vice-chancellor and then chancellor of the University of Toronto. A fluent if not always precise drafter of dispatches, he published a platitudinous auto-biography, *The Memoirs of a Peacemonger,* in 1985.

Ironically, the post for which he was pre-eminently suited, the Canadian governor-generalship, was snatched from him. In 1979 his wife had served as lady-in-waiting on two royal tours in what was regarded as preparation for the post when the prime minister, Pierre Trudeau, opted at the last moment for the former socialist premier of Manitoba, Edward Schreyer. Coming to vice-regal rank at the comparatively young age of 44, Schreyer was unable to disguise his boredom, and he left Canadians with the realization that Ignatieff was the best Governor General they never had.

MAX DUNBAR

MAX DUNBAR (who died on February 14, 1995, aged 80) was a distinguished marine biologist and oceanographer, and an early expert on the effects of climatic change.

On his first polar expedition, in the summer of 1935, Dunbar was the zoologist on a four-man Oxford University expedition to survey for a suitable airfield site in western Greenland. He and his fellow student Michael Atter were "lining" their canoe up the Safartok River when it struck a submerged rock and capsized. Atter was on the towing line, and after making fast he went to help Dunbar salvage the cargo, only to be swept away in the rapids. His colleagues searched for him in vain for two days.

The three remaining surveyors found the resolve to continue their work and eventually produced a one-mile-to-one-inch map of the area, covering some 300 square miles. With help from this map an important military airbase was established in Greenland during the Second World War. Afterwards it became a key link on the route of trans-polar commercial flights.

Maxwell John Dunbar was born in Edinburgh on September 19, 1914, and educated at Fettes College and Brasenose College, Oxford. A year after his first expedition he returned to western Greenland with C.H. (later Air Chief Marshal Sir Christopher) Hartley. The two made hydrographic and biological studies in the waters off the Christianshåb region, particularly in the "feeding zones" at glacier faces. After graduating in 1937, he spent a year on a research fellowship at Yale University before moving to McGill University, where he gained his PhD in 1941. He had spent the summers of 1939 and 1940 as a scientific observer in the Canadian government's Eastern Arctic patrol ship, which served as a relief for remote stations.

From 1941 to 1946 Dunbar served the Department of External Affairs as Canadian acting consul to Greenland at Godthåb and Nuuk, a post for which he was ideally suited: he was socially adept, spoke fluent Danish and knew the region well. In addition to his official duties, he continued his biological work in Godthåb Fjord. In 1946 Dunbar joined the McGill science faculty and 13 years later was appointed professor of oceanography.

Every summer between 1947 and 1958 he organized marine biological expeditions to Ungava Bay and Hudson Bay, and from 1948 was able to deploy his team in the *Calanus,* the first Canadian-built research ship specifically designed for operations in Arctic waters. Some of the results were brought together in his important monograph *Eastern Arctic Waters* (1951). Dunbar later expanded his studies to cover the waters of all the northern regions. He recognized three zones of water – Arctic, sub-Arctic and Boreal – determined respectively by the exclusive presence, admixture or total absence of water from the Arctic Ocean. He showed that climatic change can cause shifts in these boundaries, with profound effects on marine species. He argued that the remarkable abundance of Atlantic cod off western Greenland between 1920 and 1970 was a direct result of climatic warming in the present century. Dunbar also put forward the controversial hypothesis that in much warmer Tertiary times there was a general faunal dispersal from the Pacific to the Atlantic via the Arctic Ocean.

He believed that the deductive method in science should be given as wide scope as the classic inductive method. To back up his argument he cited Wegener's theory of continental drift, which was derived in part from general observations on the configuration of the continents. Initially Wegener's hypothesis found little support, but by the 1960s it had been fully accepted by plate tectonics theorists. Dunbar also argued strongly for the recognition of the ecosystem, as well as species, as a unit of evolution within Darwin's principle of natural selection. In his long career – he was still publishing seminal papers in the 1990s – he received many honours.

Dunbar, who was married twice, was an amusing and convivial companion. He knew how to relax and was always welcome at parties, where he would play guitar and sing traditional Scottish songs.

ARNOLD SMITH

ARNOLD SMITH (who died on February 7, 1994, aged 79) was the first Commonwealth secretary-general, charged with the task of creating an organization for that disparate group of countries which shared only a language and some very different experiences of British rule.

It was no easy task. Smith's fellow Canadians were enthusiastic, the Australians and New Zealanders suspicious. The Africans were busily shedding their newly acquired Westminster democracies and only too delighted to demonstrate their grown-up status by publicly slighting the Mother Country. That they did not choke the new body at birth was due in large measure to Smith, whose 10 years in the post began in 1965 just as the Rhodesian crisis was coming to a head. With his soothing negotiating skills, voluble good humour and high-minded talk of the Commonwealth's benefit to mankind, Smith prevented the rebel colony splitting its members irreparably. He fought many a "battle of the agenda" at prime ministers' conferences to check the hotheads demanding immediate military action. Yet while ensuring that the matter was left in Britain's hands, he insisted that the British remain committed to reaching a settlement based on black majority rule.

Smith began with the considerable disadvantage of having no clear power base. The Queen personally did much to increase his prestige. But there were objections to him being addressed as "Your Excellency" at first, and the Commonwealth Relations Office viewed the secretariat as a rival best kept small and obscure. Smith found his office removed from the comforts of Queen Mary's old bedroom to the kitchens at Marlborough House, and he suspected that his telephones were bugged. With a team of talented public servants drawn from throughout the Commonwealth, he succeeded in making the secretariat an efficient bureaucracy and the Commonwealth an international talking shop which at least compared favourably with the United Nations.

However, there were few headline-making successes. He was adept at persuading leaders who made threatening noises on television to behave sensibly behind closed doors, and stopped the Organization of African States cutting diplomatic links with Britain. But an attempt to mediate in the Nigerian civil war failed; India and Pakistan went to war; and then the Ugandan Idi Amin, who committed horrifying atrocities, expelled his country's Asians and demanded to be made head of the Commonwealth, thereby reducing the image of African civilization to one of black comedy. Smith's readiness with the optimistic interpretation of events might have been necessary, but his flights of high-level humbug went down badly with outside observers.

Arnold Cantwell Smith came from a United Empire Loyalist family which had left America for Grenada before settling in Canada. He was born in Toronto on January 15, 1915, and educated at Upper Canada College, the Lycée Champoleon in Grenoble and the University of Toronto before winning a Rhodes scholarship to Christ Church, Oxford. In 1939 Smith answered an advertisement in a London newspaper for an assistant editor of the *Baltic Times,* a bi-monthly started in Tallin, Estonia, by local businessmen who saw English as the best vehicle for urging Estonians, Latvians and Lithuanians to unite against coming aggression. He was made editor, became a lecturer at Tartu University and, following the outbreak of war, press attaché at the British legation. A month after the Russians invaded in 1940, Smith and his first wife, Eve, were allowed to take an eight-day train journey via Moscow to Odessa on the Black Sea. They were given plenty of food; his only regret was that while champagne was available at every station the caviar ran out on the last day. Smith came to rest amid the delights of Cairo, where he worked for the Middle East department of the Foreign Office, writing pamphlets urging occupied Mediterranean countries to rise against the Germans.

In 1943 he transferred to the Canadian Foreign Service, which dispatched him to Kuibyshev, Stalin's wartime seat of government. Subsequent postings in Brussels and Indo-China and with various UN bodies gave Smith such a reputation for reliability that his superiors forgave his habit of dictating 10-page dispatches with a minimum of punctuation. A posting as minister in London, when Canada was trying to repair the damage caused by its divergence from Britain in the Suez crisis, led to the delicate ambassadorship to Egypt. On disembarking his plane in Cairo he astonished the Egyptians by wearing hula-hoops, gifts for his three children, around his neck. For the next 18 months he played a key role in restoring relations between Egypt and Britain.

When Smith was sent on to Moscow, he built up his collection of abstract paintings and even ventured to tell Aleksey Kosygin that such discredited, pre-revolutionary works were superior to what was being produced in the West. The future leader replied that if foreigners bought all the Soviet Union's *abstractni,* it would be rid of an ideological problem and also able to cover the defence budget. In September 1962, when the British and American ambassadors were absent, Smith received a tip that Khruhschev planned a showdown with the West. His warning was treated with scepticism in London and Washington until the Cuban missile build-up was discovered a month later.

As Commonwealth secretary-general, Smith combined infinite patience with the knowledge of when to lose his temper. He showed no awareness of anyone's colour and delighted in guiding less sophisticated leaders through the mysteries of Western bureaucracies with their phalanxes of what he dubbed "abominable no men." It was his success in promoting economic, technical, medical and educational projects of a kind which rarely attracted headlines that both justified the Commonwealth and enabled it to withstand the anti-British posturings of his successor Sir "Sonny" Ramphal.

Smith paid a price for his relentless efforts, which involved travelling some 10,000 miles a month, when a heart attack ended his ambition to serve a third five-year term. On retiring, he first went to the 70-acre vineyard he had bought in France, then became Lester Pearson Professor of International Law at Carleton University, Ottawa. He married Frances MacFarland Lea after the death of his first wife in 1987, and spent his last years undertaking a host of good works connected with the Commonwealth and the Third World.

His greatest problem as secretary-general lay in the fact that his declared aim of changing the Commonwealth from an Anglo-centric organization into a truly international body could only be achieved by weakening its essential British cement and exasperating British leaders. Harold Wilson was driven to explode on one occasion that Britain was now being treated like "a bloody colony," while his Tory successor Edward Heath, who was exasperated to find himself forced by Smith to drop some arms sales to South Africa, made it clear that he much preferred the company in the Common Market.

But Smith, who was appointed CH in 1975 and OC in 1985, never wavered in his appreciation of Britain. He supported the British right to seek closer links with Europe. "The people of the little island of Britain," he roundly declared, "have probably accomplished more social and political advancement in the world than any other people."

'HANK' WARDLE

"HANK" WARDLE (who died on January 31, 1995, aged 79) made a remarkable escape from Colditz, the 16th-century castle in Saxony where the Germans imprisoned the most troublesome prisoner-of-war officers.

On April 29, 1940, Flying Officer Wardle took off in an obsolescent Fairey Battle light bomber from 218 Squadron's airfield at Auberive-sur-La-Marne in France. The single engine burst into flames, and Wardle came down in Germany, where he was captured near Crailsheim by a soldier on a bicycle. Ten days later he was incarcerated in Oflag IX A at Spangenberg, near Kassel. That August he escaped while on the way to the camp gymnasium, only to blunder into a German patrol at a railway crossing. The Germans kicked him and battered him with rifle butts, leaving him with impaired hearing and a limp.

Wardle arrived at Colditz in November 1940. In May of the next year he tried to escape through a tunnel leading from a canteen manhole cover. But the Germans clamped down after finding some French officers filing through the bars of a window, and as Wardle and 10 others broke ground they were confronted by the *Kommandant*. Wardle irritated them by laughing. Tall and laconic, Wardle lay low and bided his time. To while away the hours he played chess with Captain (later Major) Pat Reid, who was to write *The Colditz Story* (1953). Roll calls and searches ensured that their games of chess lasted for weeks. Another distraction was Reid's position as "escape officer." This entailed numerous organizational duties and restricted Reid's own opportunities to break out of Colditz.

Reid thought Wardle's imperturbable temperament would make him the perfect escape partner. After he had relinquished his position as escape officer, Reid urged his successor to promote Wardle up the escape roster. "I've got nothing to do until the end of the war,"

Wardle said when Reid sounded him out, "so it's all the same to me. There's no hope of success, but we've got to keep on trying." Reid planned to make the break with Wardle and two other officers, Major R.B. Littledale and Lieutenant-Colonel W.L. Stephens. Wardle and Reid were to pose as Flemish workmen, as a means of explaining their poor German and atrocious French.

On the night of October 14, 1942, Wardle and Reid cut through the bars of a kitchen window, climbed onto a flat roof, then jumped to the ground. Littledale and Stephens followed. To help the men to evade the sentries, it had been decided that an accordionist should signal a coded all-clear. But the signal never came, and Wardle and Reid hid in the shadows for two hours. In desperation, they waited until the sentry's back was turned, dodged the searchlights and made for a cellar, from which they proceeded along a narrow flue to the outer courtyard buildings. Their next obstacle was a series of three terraces, which they descended with the help of a sheet. In his escape report for MI9, Wardle noted: "The top terrace was within a few yards of sleeping Germans, and the bottom one some 10 yards from the dog kennels. Twice during a descent, an alsatian was roused, and barked furiously, but no action was taken."

Finally Wardle and his companions negotiated a road through the guards' married quarters and scaled a gate topped with barbed wire. Once they were outside the castle, the escapers split up, and Wardle and Reid made for Switzerland. When Reid tired, Wardle carried him. Though the men were questioned by the police, their Flemish cover and forged papers served them well. On October 18 they crossed into Switzerland and made themselves known to the police. Littledale and Stephens also reached Switzerland. Wardle completed his "home run" by travelling through Spain to Gibraltar disguised as a hairdresser called "Raoul." Back in England he was awarded the MC and promoted squadron leader. He resumed flying as a ferry pilot to the Middle and Far East and across the Atlantic.

Howard Douglas Wardle, always known as Hank, was born at Dauphin, Manitoba, on August 14, 1915, and educated in Ontario. After working as a bookkeeper, he sailed for Britain and in March 1939 was granted a short-service commission in the RAF. In early November 1939 he joined 98 Squadron, flying Fairey Battles, and on November 27 was posted to No. 218, a battle squadron in the Advanced Air Striking Force in France.

After the war Wardle planned to remain in the RAF. But he was injured in a mid-air collision and returned to Canada. He worked for Sperry Gyroscope, retiring in the 1970s. Wardle was married and divorced three times. He had two sons by his first marriage.

GENERAL FREDDIE SHARP

GENERAL FREDDIE SHARP (who died on June 10, 1992, aged 76) was a principal architect of the ill-fated amalgamation of Canada's navy, army and air force in the 1960s.

An RCAF officer from before the Second World War, Sharp was not alone in believing that worthwhile economies in defence expenditure could be achieved by unifying the support services of the navy, army and air forces. But he did not stop there: following the lead of Paul Hellyer, national defence minister, he became convinced that the forces themselves would be more efficient as a single organization.

Sharp had been an air vice-marshal for less than a year when this metamorphosis began: a large number of resignations and ejections meant that he moved rapidly from AOC Training Command to taking charge of the unification programme, with the rank of vice-chief of Defence Staff. When in 1968 he was translated to the rank of lieutenant-general, it marked the amalgamation of the forces. The next year Sharp was appointed deputy commander-in-chief of the North American Air Defence Command at Colorado Springs, and then returned to Ottawa as chief of Defence Staff, a post he held for three years.

Frederick Ralph Sharp was born at Moosomin, Saskatchewan, on December 8, 1915. After going to local schools, he attended the Royal Military College at Kingston, where his burly figure earned him the nickname "Porky." He was destined for the army but changed his mind and in 1938 joined the RCAF. As a newly qualified flying instructor, Sharp became involved in the Commonwealth Air Training Plan in Alberta. The training organization was notoriously loath to release its best officers, but after five years of continuous flying duties, four of them as an instructor, he was selected for the war staff course at Toronto. This enabled him to break free from service in Canada, and in March 1944 Sharp joined No. 408, an RCAF Halifax squadron in Yorkshire.

As part of No. 6 Group, Bomber Command, his squadron was heavily engaged in operations to prepare the way for the landings in Normandy. After D-Day, Sharp flew several missions in direct support of the army, ending with the bombing of the German defences of Le Havre, Boulogne and Calais. Later he was involved in attacks on the heavily defended industrial centres of Germany. Sharp was soon promoted to command his squadron, and proved a determined leader, reaching difficult targets and maintaining the efficiency of his crews. He was awarded the DFC.

In June 1945 he returned to Canada, where at Yarmouth, Nova Scotia, he joined "Tiger Force," then preparing for operations against Japan. Two years later, after a stint in command of the Central Flying School at Trenton, he was chosen for a course in business administration at the University of Western Ontario, from which, in 1950, he came to England to teach at the RAF Staff College. In 1953 Sharp returned to operational flying as commander of the air defence fighter base at North Bay, Ontario. After he had been in the position for only 18 months, his management qualifications, which were then rare in the services, began to influence his career. His next appointment was at AFHQ as director of management engineering. He attended the National Defence College at Kingston and was then appointed deputy commander of the 25th Norad Region at Tacoma, Washington, before being transferred to Maine, to command the Bangor Sector of the 26th Region.

Back in Ottawa, Sharp was director-general of management engineering and automation, a title appropriate to his approach to human organization, which relied heavily on business jargon. The process of unification of the forces had elicited a heavy cost in morale and resulted in disillusion for both officers and men. The promised savings were absorbed by cuts in the defence budget, and human factors proved more potent than management theory. Sharp lived long enough to see new and distinct Canadian navy, army and air forces emerge from the unwieldy monolith he had designed.

In retirement Sharp had a second career in management consultancy. He married, in 1940, Elizabeth Weaver; they had two sons and three daughters.

BERNARD BRADEN

BERNARD BRADEN (who died on February 2, 1993, aged 76) achieved celebrity in Britain in the 1960s when he commanded television audiences of more than 12 million as the medium's first consumer ombudsman.

In such programmes as *Braden Beat* and *Braden's Week* he presided in a breezy and mildly facetious transatlantic style over a mixture of consumer reports and cabaret; one novel feature was the appearance of its researchers on the screen. However, his informality did not always agree with the BBC's digestion, and one series ended after he refused to stop making advertisements for a can of soup on ITV. His argument that he was a freelance and therefore free to take any work that he wished was not acceptable to "Auntie," as the BBC was known then.

The son of a Nonconformist clergyman, Bernard Chastey Braden was born in Vancouver on May 16, 1916, and went to Magee High School before beginning his career as a radio engineer, announcer, singer and actor. He moved to Toronto in 1946, where he wrote and produced radio plays, and then came to Britain to make a series on postwar Britain for the CBC. Three years later he and his wife, the actress Barbara Kelly, who bore him a son and two daughters, moved to London. Within a year both had won big West End parts; he in *Streetcar Named Desire,* she in *Male Animal.* At the same time he broke into BBC Radio with *Breakfast with Braden* and *Bedtime with Braden,* which made him sufficiently well known to benefit from the advent of television. By the 1970s Braden's company, Adanac (Canada spelt backwards), which he had set up with his wife 20 years earlier as a vehicle for their earnings, enjoyed considerable success in the presentation of business conferences. In 1976 he reappeared on ITV as the quizmaster of *The Sweepstake Game,* a programme in which sporting personalities were asked such questions as "What is the sacred river of India?" It prompted a critic on *The Sunday Telegraph* to write of "poor Bernard Braden … looking like the *Queen Mary* washed up at Long Beach, California, in that he was built for better things." The programme was axed the next year, when he also starred in Toronto in *Side by Side by Sondheim.* In 1978 he returned to BBC Radio 2 with a Saturday show called *Off-beat with Braden* and eight years later came back to the stage as the American ambassador in George Bernard Shaw's political comedy *The Apple Cart* at the Theatre Royal, Haymarket. In 1987 he was given both his own Radio 4 series, *Braden Beside Himself* (which he described as "a gentle stroll through the world of transatlantic humour") and *All Our Yesterdays,* an equally nostalgic programme on ITV.

A genial and relaxed figure, Bernie Braden spent his leisure hours "playing snooker with taxi drivers and people in a club in Great Windmill Street." He was a quondam honorary chancellor of the London School of Economics.

GROUP CAPTAIN GEORGE GRANT

GROUP CAPTAIN GEORGE GRANT (who died in Vancouver on August 3, 1990, aged 74) undertook the hazardous exercise, early in the Second World War, of flying down enemy radio beams in order to trace their points of origin in France and Germany.

The knowledge so gained greatly helped the evolution of measures to confuse the German bombers, by bending the beams, and also proved invaluable in the development of Oboe, the RAF's system of radar beams, which radically improved the accuracy of Bomber Command. In April 1943 Grant joined Air Vice-Marshal Don Bennett's Pathfinder Force, which was responsible for marking out targets for the bombers. Notwithstanding his lanky, cadaverous appearance, he proved a natural leader and in May 1944 was given command of No. 109, a Mosquito squadron.

The appointment was appropriate, for Grant had been a founding member of this squadron, formed in December 1940 from the nucleus of the Blind Approach Training and Development Unit at Boscombe Down – the organization that had investigated the German beams. In December 1944 Bennett further promoted Grant, still only 28, to group captain in command of the Pathfinder base at Gravely, an outfit comprising one Mosquito and three Lancaster squadrons.

George Francis Grant was born in Ottawa on May 31, 1916, and educated at the Lisgar Collegiate Institute. He began work at the age of 16 as a timekeeper and four years later became a foreman. In the spring of 1939 he sailed from Montreal, determined to become a pilot in the RAF, and in the summer he duly received a short-service commission. Early the next year he was serving with No. 612, a Coastal Command squadron flying Ansons on North Sea patrols from Dyce in Scotland.

Grant proved as courageous with the Pathfinders as he had been when tracking the German beams. On one occasion in particular he was lucky to survive, when his aircraft was attacked as the crew were relaxing on their way back from a bombing raid in Italy. Suddenly Grant found himself dazzled by a searchlight and under fire from all sides. The smell of cordite was so strong that he imagined his own gunners were trying to extinguish the searchlight; in fact, the Lancaster was discovered on landing to be damaged beyond repair.

In the wake of actions like these, postwar staff appointments seemed small beer. Furthermore, Grant was understandably irked when officialdom decreed that at his age – 29 when the war ended – he could not remain a group captain but must content himself with the substantive rank of squadron leader. In consequence he retired early in 1948, being given the rank of group captain for that purpose.

Grant then went home to Canada, where he built a successful career in heavy construction and allied businesses. In 1974 he took up cattle farming and gravel supplying in the Fraser Valley.

Grant was awarded the DFC in 1942, the DSO in 1943 and Bar in 1945. He was survived by his wife, Peggy, whom he met when she was a WAAF at Boscombe Down, and by their six sons and two daughters.

MAJOR-GENERAL NORMAN WILSON-SMITH

MAJOR-GENERAL NORMAN WILSON-SMITH (who died on March 7, 1992, aged 75) was a notably effective infantry commander and staff officer with the Commonwealth Division in Korea.

In September 1950 Wilson-Smith was given command of the 1st Battalion of Princess Patricia's Canadian Light Infantry in Calgary with an operational role in the defence of the Arctic. He found this regular parachute unit with its nose out of joint: though probably the best trained battalion in the Canadian Army, it had not been chosen for Canada's contingent sent to the Korean War. It was a time of great expansion when the number of infantry battalions in the Canadian Army quadrupled within a year. The 1st Patricias were milked of experienced officers and NCOs for the new units.

During this difficult period Wilson-Smith's energy and enthusiasm did much to maintain the morale of his frustrated paratroopers. In August 1952 he received only a month's notice to reorganize his battalion as line infantry and proceed to Korea as part of the British Commonwealth Division. The day they boarded ship at Seattle, they lost their parachutists' "risk allowance," but Wilson-Smith and his men shrugged off all this as bureaucratic bungling and got on with the job. Within a month of leaving home, one of his companies carried out a highly successful raid deep into the Chinese lines against strong opposition.

The front had stabilized north of the Imjin River, and conditions soon resembled those of the First World War. During the six months that Wilson-Smith remained with the battalion, it patrolled and raided aggressively, beating off three virulent Chinese attacks. The artillery of the Commonwealth Division was outranged by the Chinese guns and could not reach some attractive targets behind the enemy lines. Recalling the effectiveness of German "88s," Wilson-Smith brought forward the battalion's six 17-pounder anti-tank guns with high-explosive ammunition and arranged for a crash course in indirect fire.

He then borrowed an Auster from the division's liaison flight, from which the support company commander, a qualified pilot, directed the fire of the "infantillery" onto such targets as presented themselves. For a few days the Chinese were treated to high-velocity shells but a dispute with the head of the "Gunners Union" (otherwise known as the Commander Royal Artillery) put paid to the experiment. Thereafter, it was noticeable that more long-range support was available from the Americans.

Norman George Wilson-Smith was born at St Catharines, Ontario, on October 4, 1916, and was attending the University of Manitoba in Winnipeg when war broke out in 1939. He was commissioned into the Royal Winnipeg Rifles with whom he came to England. After the campaign in Normandy, he was wounded while leading his company at the crossing of the Seine at Elbeuf in late August 1944. He returned from hospital to a staff appointment in the First Canadian Army. He was given a regular commission in 1946 and was on the staff of the adjutant-general immediately before his posting to the Patricias.

In 1952 Wilson-Smith left the Patricias to become senior operations officer of the Commonwealth Division. His ingenuity and diplomacy were brought into full play in reconciling the demands of the American Corps Headquarters, under whose command the division was operating, with the tactical doctrine of its British and Canadian brigades. On his return to Canada, he became director of infantry. After a year at NATO's Northern Army Group in Germany, he commanded the 3rd Canadian Infantry Brigade in New Brunswick; then, in 1965, he proceeded to Nicosia as commander of the United Nations force in Cyprus. His next post was as military attaché in Washington. During two years there, he trained as a pilot in light aircraft and helicopters, a qualification which fitted him well for his final position as deputy chief of staff, Force Development, in Ottawa.

Upon retiring from the army in 1969, he moved to England as managing director of the London office of General Dynamics and Canadair. After five years, he became interested in shipping and moved to New York, where he developed a highly successful career in the international marketing of coal. Wilson-Smith was awarded a DSO for gallantry in Korea and appointed MBE for his service in northwest Europe in 1945. He was survived by his second wife, the former Beatrice Claire Carmichael.

SVEVA CAETANI

SVEVA CAETANI (who died at Vernon, British Columbia, on April 27, 1994, aged 76) was a painter of brooding allegorical watercolours whose life story could have inspired a novel by Henry James.

A member of an aristocratic Roman family, she was brought to Canada, aged three, by her parents. There were occasional family trips to Europe. She was educated first by English governesses and then at Crofton House School, Vancouver. But on the death of her father, the Duke of Sermoneta, in 1935 – when Sveva was a strikingly beautiful 18-year-old – she was forced to become a recluse by her mother. The older woman had never adjusted to life in the New World and threatened to die if she were deserted. She even insisted that her daughter share her bedroom until Sveva rebelled by moving her bed onto a landing. Sveva was permitted to read widely, but discouraged from writing or painting. Letters from her school friends and relatives were intercepted. A fence was constructed round the garden, and visitors, apart from tradesmen, were turned away. For 16 years, Sveva could not step outside the home. When she was then allowed out to attend to family business, she had to be accompanied by her mother's elderly Danish companion, Miss Juul, and to phone her mother every half-hour.

Fifteen years after her mother's death in 1960, Sveva started to exorcise her experience through a series of 56 paintings loosely modelled on Dante's *Divine Comedy*. These ethereally powerful pictures reflect scenes from her family's life set amidst a mishmash of allegorical symbols drawn from many religions. They demonstrate not only a highly developed sense of design but a luminous quality which she claimed came from a dry-brush technique that had been favoured by the Indian Moghul painters. Neither the British Columbian nor the Canadian art establishments were unduly impressed with the work which, despite its origin, had clear affinities with the sophisticated horror-comic art of New York and Los Angeles. Eventually, however, the collection was accepted by a Mr Ng of the Alberta Art Foundation in Edmonton, who had the pictures framed for exhibition as one of the most unusual stories in the history of Canadian art.

Sveva Ursilia Giovanella Maria Caetani de Sermoneta was born in Rome on August 6, 1917, into a family whose position had been entrenched with the election of Cardinal Benedetto Caetani as Pope Boniface VIII in 1294. Sveva's father, the author of an influential 10-volume work on Islam and a deputy in the Italian parliament, had married in 1901 a member of the Colonna family, centuries-old enemies of the Caetani. But the match had not lasted. Twenty years later, he took Sveva and her mother with him to British Columbia, where he had hunted grizzlies as a young man and now wanted to become a fruit farmer. The duke returned to Italy several times but fell out with Mussolini, who deprived him of his Italian citizenship.

When her mother died, Sveva was left so little money that she began to teach at a local elementary school. She earned a teacher's certificate at the University of Victoria, where she was encouraged to paint again, then returned to Vernon and taught at Charles Bloom School at Lumby. Sveva named her paintings, some of which were eight feet tall, *Recapitulation*. They took 14 years to complete, by which time she was working from a wheelchair. Afterwards she wrote a verse and prose commentary in English, Italian and French.

The Caetani home in Vernon, a 110-year-old wooden frame house, has been turned into an arts centre. It makes a marked contrast to the Renaissance Cachigi Palace on the Tiber, which houses the Caetani Foundation for Islamic Studies, which her father founded as part of Academia de Lincei in 1924. But even Henry James might have agreed that it was a not unfitting monument to the last of the Caetani de Sermoneta.

'Wally' Floody

"Wally" Floody (who died on September 28, 1989, aged 71) was the architect of the celebrated "Great Escape" from Stalag Luft 3 at Sagan, Silesia, in 1944, and later gave technical advice on the much-televised film of that name.

Floody surveyed, designed and engineered the tunnel through which 76 RAF and other Allied prisoner-of-war officers made their escape. His role in the project was so highly valued that the camp's leaders forbade him to join an earlier escape attempt with a delousing party. "We need you for the tunnels," he was told. "God, I am sick of them," he complained. "I seem to spend my life down a stinking hole in the ground. I want a change."

A large man of six foot three, Floody was a ferocious digger in the sandy and treacherous soil and was twice almost killed underground. On the first occasion he was buried under nearly half a ton of sand. On the second he was crawling naked through a tunnel when a section of it collapsed on him; luckily his face was just over a trapdoor to a secret shaft, so he could breathe, and he was rescued after an hour's frantic digging. After putting so much effort into the design and digging of the camp's three tunnels – "Tom," "Dick" and "Harry" – Floody was disappointed not to take part in the Great Escape. Shortly before the breakout he was moved to a nearby camp at Beria and so avoided the fate of 50 of his fellow prisoners, who were recaptured and murdered on Hitler's orders.

Clarke Wallace Floody was born at Chatham, Ontario, on April 28, 1918, and educated at the Northern Vocational School. He then entered the mining industry at Kirkland Lake, Ontario, which gave him the expertise so valuable in the prison camp. Commissioned into the RCAF as a pilot officer in 1941, Floody joined No. 401 Squadron (formerly No. 1 Squadron RCAF). That October, a month after he joined the squadron, its Spitfire Vbs – together with two other squadrons of the Biggin Hill Spitfire wing – were bounced by enemy FW190 and Me109 fighters while on an offensive sweep over Nieuport and Gravelines in France. Floody baled out and was captured.

The tunnel scheme began while the Germans were preparing a new compound at the camp, and Floody was all for it from the start. Seven hundred prisoners moved in on April 1, 1943, and by April 11 sites for the traps of three major tunnels had been selected. In the event the escape took place on March 24, 1944, through "Harry." To keep the tunnel straight – it was 336 feet long and almost 30 feet beneath the surface – was a considerable engineering feat, for which Floody was chiefly responsible.

After the Second World War he gave evidence at the Nuremburg Trials before launching himself into a hectic entrepreneurial career in Canada. Floody built up and sold numerous small businesses and was chief executive of several trade associations, including those for florists and the bottlers of carbonated beverages. He also helped to found the Royal Canadian Air Force Prisoners of War Association and was indefatigable in his work for less fortunate members. He was married and had two sons.

CAPTAIN TOM PULLEN

CAPTAIN TOM PULLEN (who died on August 3, 1990, aged 72) became a passionately devoted authority on the Arctic after he took command of the Royal Canadian Navy icebreaker *Labrador* in 1956.

Fuelled by the example of his naval forbears – who searched for Sir John Franklin's Arctic expedition in the mid-19th century – he drove *Labrador* so hard during 211 days at sea that she sailed through 37,000 miles of largely uncharted Arctic waters without dropping anchor once. The voyages led to the preparation of vastly improved charts and sailing directions. At the same time, Pullen made the first east-west transit of Fury and Hecla Strait and the first circumnavigation of Somerset Island. He rescued from the pack ice in the Gulf of Boothia the United States Navy icebreaker *Edisto,* which had lost a propeller; conducted the first survey of winter ice conditions in the Gulf of St Lawrence; and made the first midwinter entry into the port of Quebec. Pullen's command of *Labrador* ended after a year when, to his exasperation, she was transferred to the Ministry of Transport as a result of service cuts that left the navy with no surface ships in the North.

But on retiring in 1965 he began a second career as an Arctic consultant, spending several months of most seasons as either adviser or icemaster on the shipping routes being used with increasing frequency by oil and tourist companies. In 1969 Pullen played a key role on the politically controversial voyage of the American icebreaking tanker *Manhattan* through the Northwest Passage from Halifax, Nova Scotia, to the Chukchi Sea. Five years later he served as ice adviser in the specially strengthened ship *Lindblad Explorer* on the first cruise for tourists in the Canadian Eastern Arctic. Subsequently he lectured on the same ship during the first tourist cruises through the Northwest Passage. While he displayed a broad knowledge of the Arctic and a genial personality, Pullen's role called for considerable tact, as he had to give captains the often unwelcome warning that they were pushing their luck in the pack ice. He was obliged, too, to take a strong line with stout American tourists who started behaving like children when they approached icebergs in small boats.

Thomas Charles Pullen was born at Oakville, Ontario, on May 27, 1918, into a proud nautical family. His great-great-grandfather, Nicholas Pullen, was press-ganged in 1780; 16 descendants became naval officers, including four flag officers, two captains and two commanders. Vice-Admiral W.S. Pullen commanded the depot ship *North Star* on the 1852–54 expedition to find Franklin; his younger brother, later Captain T.C. Pullen, was his second-in-command. When Tom Pullen sailed in the Arctic a century later, there were four Pullen place-names to remind him of his great-uncles.

Educated at Lakefield College School, he joined the RCN and was soon sent to the British training cruiser *Frobisher*. He went on to serve on the patrol off the Iberian peninsula during the Spanish Civil War. At the outbreak of the Second World War Pullen was qualifying as gunnery officer at Whale Island, Portsmouth. Although he was later to complain that he had spent far too much time on training duties because of the rapid expansion of the Royal Canadian Navy, he had his share of excitement in 1942 when he was first lieutenant on *Ottawa,* which had a horrendous voyage across the Atlantic; at one stage he had to serve as a doctor's assistant during an appendicitis operation because nobody else could remain on his feet. Then the ship was hit by two torpedoes and broken in two off the Newfoundland coast with the loss of 114 lives. Pullen was one of the last to leave – having tried his sailor's luck by wanting to leave after the captain – and was fortunate to spend only five hours on a raft before being rescued. However, he had strong reason to survive, as he was on his way home to marry Elizabeth Wheelwright, who was to bear him a son and a daughter.

Pullen also served in *Chaudière,* which was involved in a 30-hour battle to sink one German submarine off the Normandy coast and another, a couple of months later, off Beachy Head. At 26, he became one of the youngest destroyer captains on taking command of *Saskatchewan.*

In the inevitable contraction of the service after the war, Pullen was a senior officer on one ship, but when it went aground off the Nova Scotia coast, he found himself transferred to another, which was retrieved from dock to take over the patrol. His later commands included being the senior Canadian naval officer in Korea and director of naval gunnery in Ottawa. His career ended with the amalgamation of the Canadian Armed Forces in 1964. Like most naval officers he regarded it as totally misguided, and hardly relished the prospect of wearing a bottle-green uniform and being addressed as "Colonel." Although he never personally vented his feelings to the Liberal minister of national defence Paul Hellyer, his mother, who met the minister on an aircraft without realizing who he was, made her son's opinions extremely clear.

Pullen was appointed OC and given the Massey Gold Medal of the Royal Canadian Geographical Society in 1984. His elder brother, Rear-Admiral H.F. Pullen, died in 1983.

JEAN MARCHAND

JEAN MARCHAND (who died on August 28, 1988, aged 69) was the Quebec trade unionist whose recruitment by the federal Liberals led to his long-standing associate Pierre Trudeau becoming prime minister three years later.

A small peppery man with an unruly shock of hair and a dapper moustache, Marchand was a fiery orator and a relentless "gut fighter." He first met Trudeau in 1949 when he was leading the union side in the bitter Asbestos strike. Gérard Pelletier, a journalist covering the dispute, had brought along his intellectual friend Trudeau, who made a moving speech to the strikers' families, not about their legal rights, as he was asked, but about their human rights. "Miners are not schoolchildren, you know," cautioned Marchand.

Sixteen years later the trio was invited to stand as overtly federalist Liberal MPs in 1965 when the party leader Lester Pearson was clinging to power with a minority government amid a continuing series of scandals. The invitation had originally been extended only to Marchand, but he insisted on coming with his two friends, a decision greeted by elements both inside and outside the party as evidence of its flagrant infiltration by socialism and communism.

As Pearson's acknowledged French lieutenant, Marchand made himself felt by supporting the nationalistic policies of the former finance minister Walter Gordon and the proposals for introducing a national health service which had been part of the Liberal platform since 1919. Yet he was no more successful than others in avoiding the humiliations that were a way of life in Pearson's ramshackle administration. On one occasion he bluntly told Pearson: "I'm not going to be treated as a puppet. I'm no *roi nègre*. There are too many messenger boys from Quebec."

But Marchand could never have been entirely happy in the capital. He had no chance to become used to parliamentary life before

222

being appointed minister of citizenship and immigration, and was said to have remarked that the best thing about Ottawa was the road to Montreal. His English was only adequate, his health poor. Also, when he was tipped as the French Canadian to succeed Pearson, he had recently received some severe criticism on the floor of the House for persuading the government to amend the make-up of a labour relations board to suit some of his old colleagues.

He therefore pointed to the sophisticated Trudeau, who had known his way around the federal capital from his earlier employment in the Privy Council Office and was making a strong impact as justice minister. It was not easy to persuade Trudeau, of course, whom he had had to push to consider becoming an MP and who had resisted his pleas for three days before agreeing to become Pearson's parliamentary secretary; but Marchand eventually won his friend's agreement.

The youngest of six children in a poor family where the oldest brother was the breadwinner, Jean Marchand was born in Champlain, Quebec, on December 20, 1918, and worked his way through Laval University. He first came to prominence in 1942 as an organizer for the National Federation of Pulp and Paper Workers and from then on was a central figure in the Quebec labour movement. He became the federation's secretary the following year. By 1960 Marchand's fearless and autocratic drive had brought him to the top of the Confederation of National Trade Unions (formerly the Confederation of Catholic Workers), and he was chosen as a member of the Royal Commission on Bilingualism and Biculturalism.

Once Trudeau was in power, Marchand had access to him at 24 Sussex Drive as an old trusted associate, and they collaborated closely in the effort to make Canada an officially bilingual country while fighting off the separatist pressures. But after a while he felt resentful of the way he was being shuffled out of central decision-making in favour of younger and more technocratically minded Quebeckers. He seemed so out of his depth as minister of forestry and rural development and then as minister of regional economic expansion that political commentators started to dismiss him as "more of a mouth than an administrator."

In 1974, during his time as minister of transport, he candidly described the country's transportation policy as "a mess." Two years later he caused a sensation by resigning in disgust over the government's "sell-out" to English-speaking pilots after a strike grounded air traffic for nine days. The dispute, which was prompted by a plan to introduce French at Quebec's international airports, was ended by a government promise not introduce the language unless a three-member commission ruled unanimously that it was safe. This was acting in defiance of the government's promise to encourage equal use of French, fumed Marchand.

Trudeau stood by Marchand to the extent of appointing him a senator and, much against the wishes of other Liberals in the Upper House, its leader. Marchand married Georgette Guertin in 1946, and they had a daughter.

LUCIEN CARDIN

LUCIEN CARDIN (who died on June 13, 1988, aged 69) was the justice minister in Lester Pearson's crisis-ridden Liberal minority government whose revelations of the Munsinger "sex and spying" affair proved that Canada was quite capable of producing its own sleazy equivalent of Britain's Profumo scandal.

A small-town French Canadian lawyer, Cardin received the justice portfolio on the grounds that he would – as Pearson told colleagues – at least keep the government out of trouble. But soon after taking up the post in July 1965, Cardin made some damaging admissions on television about a postal clerk who had been dismissed for – but not charged with – spying for the Soviet Union. John Diefenbaker, the Opposition leader, seized on the human-rights aspect of the case in the Commons and harried Cardin, who shouted back with equal venom. He claimed that the previous Conservative administration's record had not been blameless, and then said the word "Munsinger."

Press gallery reporters thought he had said "Monsignor" and set off in search of a heroin-smuggling prelate. Cardin came close to resigning when Pearson reversed his stand and agreed to set up an inquiry to look into the dismissal of the postal clerk. But when he called a press conference to say that he was remaining in his post, Cardin gave some details about a Montreal prostitute called Gerda Munsinger who had once been suspected of spying in Germany and more recently had been patronized by two ministers in the previous Conservative government. Munsinger was thought to be dead, but the *Toronto Star* traced the glamorous blonde to a Munich bar, where she turned out to be alive, well and – for the sum of $5,000 – willing to share with a CBC correspondent her cherished and undimmed recollections.

Like the Macmillan government in the Profumo affair, the Pearson administration survived. Fresh crises developed, and although no security breach was discovered, Diefenbaker was eventually censured by an inquiry along the lines Cardin had suggested. But Cardin, who enjoyed poor health, was quietly dropped to make way for Pierre Trudeau. When Trudeau, as prime minister, called an election in 1968, Cardin refused to stand again.

Louis Joseph Lucien Cardin was born at Providence, Rhode Island, March 1, 1919, and educated at Loyola College and the University of Montreal before serving overseas with the Royal Canadian Navy during the Second World War. Setting up in practice at Sorel, Quebec, he entered the Commons in a 1952 by-election and made little impact on the back-benches – except for a surprisingly vicious attack on Diefenbaker when his government's French Canadian support was in sharp decline.

Cardin was appointed assistant minister of defence in 1963, in which capacity he attended Sir Winston Churchill's funeral, and then served as minister of public works before taking up the justice port-folio. After giving up politics, he became a member of the immigration appeal board, chairman of the tax review board and then a judge in the Canadian tax court. He was survived by his wife, Marcelle, and four children.

GENERAL JACQUES DEXTRAZE

GENERAL JACQUES DEXTRAZE (who died on May 9, 1993, aged 73) combined the flair and gallantry of the French Canadian soldier with an incisive intellect which brought him from the ranks to head his country's forces.

He enlisted as a private in the Fusiliers Mont-Royal (FMR) in 1940 and became a sergeant before entering the Officer Cadet Training Unit at Brockville, Ontario. On receiving his commission, he joined his regiment in England, where because of their heavy officer casualties at Dieppe, he was given responsibilities beyond those usual for a newly joined subaltern. By the time Dextraze landed in Normandy in July 1944, he was a company commander. His first experience of action came in a battalion attack south of Caen, followed by a four-day battle against German panzers and SS troops.

The FMR's casualties had been so large that when they were ordered to resume the advance to a stoutly defended farm, they could muster only enough riflemen for a single company, with Dextraze in command. Such was the force of his personality that he was able to lead them in a classic pincer attack supported by armour and artillery, which drove a stubborn enemy from the farm. Less then a week later Dextraze again distinguished himself in a brilliant pre-dawn assault on the church of St Martin de Fontenay, a key strong point and observation post of the 9th SS Panzer Division. When machine-gun fire prevented his supporting sappers from placing charges to breach the church walls, he led his men around the building, where – with guns blazing – they swarmed over the wall into the churchyard. An hour-long battle ensued during which he and his company fought with grenades and bayonets to capture the church. At its end, apart from six prisoners, its defenders lay dead. Dextraze was awarded a DSO.

Following the battles near Falaise and the advance to the Siebe, a few days after his 25th birthday Dextraze was promoted to command

Les Fusiliers Mont-Royal. During the siege of Dunkirk and the battles on the Scheldt and the Rhine, he led his battalion with great panache. Typically, when the 2nd Canadian Division were battling their way into Groningen in northern Holland, it was Dextraze who drove into its centre and forced the surrender of the German commander – an action which earned him a Bar to his DSO. At the end of the war in Europe he returned to Canada to command the Hastings and Prince Edward Regiment of the Canadian Pacific Force. When Japan surrendered he went back to civilian life.

Jacques Alfred Dextraze was born in Montreal on August 15, 1919, and educated at St Joseph de Berthier College and the MacDonald Business College – where he returned after the war to complete his studies. He had become manager of forest operations of the Singer Corporation when, in 1950, General Charles Foulkes invited him to raise and command a new 2nd Battalion of the Royal 22e Régiment (the "Vandoos") to form part of a Canadian brigade to be sent to Korea. He accepted with alacrity.

In November 1951 Dextraze was holding the southern flank of Hill 33 ("Little Gibraltar") when its American defenders were driven off by a Chinese mass attack. "They went through my lines so fast," Dextraze remarked, "their cigar ends looked like tracer bullets." The ensuing battle went on for four days, during which the Vandoos beat off repeated attacks by an enemy suspected of being drugged. Refusing to take cover from fire, the Chinese were often seen to advance through their own supporting barrages. As one officer present observed, Dextraze was "always two jumps ahead of the Chinese in his thinking." For his services in Korea, Dextraze was appointed OBE.

Back in Canada he served as chief of staff, Quebec Command, and commanded the School of Infantry at Camp Borden. In 1963 he was commanding Eastern Quebec Area when he was summoned to be chief of staff of the United Nations Force in the Congo, then in a state of near anarchy, with Europeans, in particular, in danger of their lives. Dextraze planned and – often at considerable personal risk – supervised their rescue. In recognition of his leadership he was appointed CBE.

On his return to Canada he commanded the 2nd Infantry Brigade at Petawawa for two years, then moved to Mobile Command where in 1967 he became its deputy commander. From there he was posted to National Defence HQ in Ottawa and within a year had become chief of personnel. From 1972 to 1977 he was chief of Defence Staff. On his retirement he became chairman of the Canadian National Railways.

A royalist and a Canadian patriot, Dextraze was noted for his somewhat caustic wit. When Brigadier Dollard Menard, who had commanded the FMR in the Dieppe Raid, declared his support for Quebec independence, Dextraze joked to a press conference: "Poor Dollard probably declared himself in that fashion because at 8 o'clock that morning, that was the thing to do." He added that the real heroes of Dieppe were "the ones that are buried there." Unfortunately, the press interpreted Dextraze's remarks as suggesting that Menard's five war wounds had affected his political judgment. The consequence was a suit for slander; the case received wide publicity. Eventually Dextraze apologized and the two men shook hands.

Dextraze's interest in the forces and ex-servicemen never flagged. He was colonel of the Royal 22e Régiment, a staunch supporter of the Infantry Association and the Royal Canadian Legion, and also president of the Canadian Amateur Boxing Association.

He married, in 1942, Frances Helena Paré; they had four sons, one of whom was killed serving with the U.S. Marines in Vietnam.

COLONEL 'BUCKO' WATSON

COLONEL "BUCKO" WATSON (who died on February 6, 1992, aged 72) won a reputation for aggressiveness and coolness under fire in the Italian campaign during the Second World War.

Watson's baptism of fire came in July 1943 when, as adjutant of Princess Patricia's Canadian Light Infantry, he landed in the assault on Sicily. Halfway through that campaign he was given command of A Company, which he led into Italy in September. For the first three months the company's advance was opposed by skilful enemy rearguards. A third of the country was in Allied hands before the Germans decided to stand and fight at the Moro River, determined to block the advance towards Ortona.

During the night of December 5 the Patricias were to attack across the Moro and seize the town of Villa Rogatti. Watson's task was to clear the northern half of the town and defend it against enemy counter-attack. The river crossing was under continuous fire – which retarded supporting arms and the replenishment of ammunition – but by first light Watson's company had fought their way through the town. On the outskirts, they came under heavy fire from German infantry. Aware that ammunition was woefully short, Watson warned his company to make every shot count, and for two hours he and his men held off the 200th Panzer Grenadier Regiment, which was closing in through the mist. Just as the Germans were about to charge, a troop of the 44th Royal Tank Regiment arrived: the stream of their machine-gun fire was music to the ears of the hard-pressed Patricias.

When the position was secure, Watson, who had been hit by a mortar splinter, went to have his wound dressed. Two days later he led his company in the capture of San Leonardo. While he was consulting with his commanding officer in the lee of a tank, a shell struck the vehicle and he was again wounded. He was out of action for two months.

On May 23, 1944, Watson and his company led the attack on the Hitler Line. This product of the Todt organization – pillboxes, tank turrets embedded in concrete, a welter of mines and barbed wire – blocked the Liri Valley and the road to Rome. The approach to the enemy lay through dense undergrowth and was overlooked from the enemy-held town of Aquino on the right. The Churchill tanks of the North Irish Horse were in support.

As A Company advanced behind a crushing artillery barrage, the enemy opened a devastating fire from concealed pillboxes and from Aquino on the flank. Every man in Watson's command group was hit; communications with battalion HQ failed; supporting tanks were nowhere in evidence; and his platoons disappeared. Hoping to find his men at the objective, Watson pressed on alone. There was no trace of them, but the enemy were present in strength. By that time Watson had been wounded twice. He managed to evade capture and finally settled in what he later described as a "large and quite comfortable shell hole."

Intense enemy fire prevented all attempts by battalion HQ to communicate by liaison officers and runners. In an attempt to help, the North Irish Horse were trapped by a combination of mines and concealed self-propelled guns. During the night Watson again went forward to the objective, hoping that it might now have been taken. The enemy were still there.

All next day he lay concealed, until an old friend, Colin McDougal, found him, and greeted him with "Hello, Bucko." "Oh, hello, Colin." Watson returned. That was their entire conversation. The regiment's war diary records: "Major Watson was located in a shell hole, near an 88 mm gun, suffering from a wound in one arm, a piece of his helmet and a Schmeisser bullet in his forehead, and a tremendous appetite."

This time Watson was evacuated to England. Some months later he returned to the Patricias in Italy and, in early 1945, accompanied them to Holland. There he was posted to the Lincoln and Welland Regiment as second-in-command and, after advancing through northern Germany, finished the war near Oldenburg. The next year he commanded the North Shore Regiment (New Brunswick) in the army of occupation. He was awarded the DSO for his gallantry at the Hitler Line and an MC for his leadership at the Moro River.

A colonel's son, William de Norban Watson was born at Edmonton, Alberta, in October 1919. After graduating from high school, he joined what was to be the last class at the Royal Military College, Kingston, before it closed for the Second World War. Watson was commissioned in the Patricias in June 1940, and in October was sent to England as a reinforcement officer. He joined the regiment at Godstone, Surrey, and a year later was promoted captain.

On his return to Canada at the end of the war, Watson was second-in-command of the Patricias in Calgary. After attending the Staff College at Kingston and an appointment in Ottawa, he was given command of the 2nd Battalion of the Black Watch (Royal Highland Regiment) of Canada. In 1960 he returned to England to teach at the Staff College at Camberley. He was later promoted director of infantry in Ottawa, where he helped defend the regimental system against threats posed by the unification of the Armed Forces. His final appointment, after attending the National Defence College, was as military adviser to the Canadian high commissioner in London.

Watson married, in 1947, Katherine ("KC") Carlisle; they had four children.

CHARLES LYNCH

CHARLES LYNCH (who died on July 21, 1994, aged 74) created a journalistic legend when he waded ashore on D-Day carrying a typewriter and a basket of carrier pigeons on his head.

As a recently hired Reuters correspondent, the tubby 24-year-old had no experience of action and little idea of where Normandy was. He was placed under the tutelage of the veteran CBC reporter Matthew Halton, who showed no interest in fruitlessly trying to keep up with the action. Mumbling that there was a time to live and a time not to work, Halton led Lynch to a farmhouse where they were plied with Calvados, shown the farmer's pictures of himself in the 1896 Madagascar campaign and offered two feather beds for the night.

Next day they found the Canadian press camp, where they dispatched their reports attached to the pigeons' legs. Unfortunately, the birds flew inland. In desperation the last pair were launched from the beach. But after setting off in the right direction they veered round at the first breakers and headed off towards Berlin. "Traitors! Damned traitors!" shouted the exasperated Lynch.

It was a characteristic gesture. In the course of his long career covering Parliament Hill, Lynch was appreciated by readers as much for his ebullient personality as for his rare mixture of witty and perceptive writing, though his actions sometimes attracted not unjustified charges of buffoonery.

Charles Burchill Lynch was born at Cambridge, Massachusetts, on December 3, 1919, and brought up in Saint John, New Brunswick, where he went to the local high school. At 16 he joined the *St John Citizen* from which he graduated to the *Halifax Herald*. After a brief spell with the Canadian Press news agency in Halifax, he worked for British United Press in Vancouver and Toronto before being persuaded to join Reuters in London. Lynch's fast, fluid copy appeared regularly in *The Daily Telegraph* as he followed the front from Normandy to

Holland and finally to Hitler's bunker in Berlin. But there were incidents he did not report, his memoirs *You Can't Print That!* (1984) recalled, as when he encountered a queue of GIs outside a brothel. His French-speaking escort officer fell into conversation with Madam, who wanted a break from her duties. Let young Lynch take over while we adjourn for some tea, suggested the officer. Lynch found himself behind the till with instructions to allow them no more than two minutes and to double the prices every half-hour.

With peace, Lynch covered the Nuremberg war trials, a task that palled as the press warmed to Goering's laughter in the dock and cooled to the revengeful Russian judges. To keep their sanity Lynch and the American correspondent Walter Cronkite organized a nail-growing competition, which was won by the *Telegraph's* Ossia Goulding, who cheated by submitting part of a ping-pong ball. Lynch was next posted to Brazil, with the task of laying off the large staff hired on Foreign Office prompting to keep an eye on Axis agents. A trickier problem arose when Anthony Eden, on a private visit, suggested that the cheers he had received in the street should be reported. "This is news," said Britain's future prime minister, adding that he was on the board of a Reuters shareholder. London's advice was unambiguous: "No. Downhold harshly."

Lynch opened an office in Ottawa, became American editor in New York and covered the UN for the CBC before deciding to return to Canada. His daily syndicated column of shrewd observation and witty anecdote soon became one of the brighter features of the political scene. The logic might be dubious and the subject sometimes trivial, as when he devoted 600 words to pondering to whom Harold Wilson had asked him at a press conference to pass on best wishes. But he had a large and enthusiastic following among readers.

As a monarchy-loving supporter of the Anglo-Canadian connection, Lynch irritated the CBC while chairing an election-night programme by lighting up a cigar when it became clear that John Diefenbaker had driven the Liberals from power after 22 years. He also had an unusual scoop when Diefenbaker summoned him to confound rumours that he had injured himself in a fall. On entering the prime ministerial bedroom, Lynch watched Diefenbaker strip off his pyjamas to show there was not a mark on his body. "Now we'll have a chat and that will be off the record, " said Diefenbaker, going on to explain how he planned to call an election.

But Charlie Lynch's relations with those in official positions were rarely smooth for long. He alarmed diplomats in Kiev late one night by pulling out his beloved harmonica in a street and leading a crowd to the door of the Canadian legation, where a startled press officer dispensed Coca-Cola. While president of the Parliamentary Press Gallery he had the unique distinction of being expelled for reporting an announcement at a private party. When Pierre Trudeau tried to turn a meeting with provincial premiers into a private session, Lynch refused to move, pointing out that Trudeau had earlier admitted that he could live with an open session. "Yes, but I can't live with you, Charles," snapped Trudeau as he walked out.

Since Lynch incurred considerable opprobrium for questioning Trudeau about the break-up of his marriage a week before it was announced, many felt he only received just desserts when the press reported the collapse of his own marriage to Mary-Elizabeth Merkel, which had produced five children, and his subsequent remarriage to Claudy Mailly, a Quebec Tory MP.

Lynch was desperately ill and within weeks of his death when he returned to Normandy in June 1994, still slightly miffed that the film *The Longest Day* had assigned his legendary explosion to an effete Englishman. But he filed copy every day, ordered drinks with good-humoured sign language in cafés and enjoyed recounting one official cock-up: a commemorative stamp showed him interviewing a wounded soldier of the Royal Winnipeg Rifles in 1944. Lynch thus had the satisfaction of knowing that through an administrative oversight he was one of the few people in the Commonwealth, apart from members of the Royal Family, to appear on a stamp during his own lifetime.

LIEUTENANT-GENERAL STAN WATERS

LIEUTENANT-GENERAL STAN WATERS (who died on September 25, 1991, aged 71) played an idiosyncratic part in the search for a new Canadian constitution when he won the first election for a Senate seat in 1989.

Although he had no previous political experience and demonstrated all the political amateur's outspokenness – which in his younger days had gone with a notorious temper – Waters's exasperation with the Tory government in Ottawa lost little power for coming from a distinguished Second World War soldier and successful businessman.

As a recruit to the western-based Reform party, Waters entered politics, he was widely quoted as saying, because he was "damned mad at the tyranny of the minorities" that led to grants for black lesbians and groups working on banana horticulture. With his military bearing, ruddy complexion and no-nonsense haircut, Waters was a compelling figure on political platforms, appealing unashamedly to the party's "redneck" element. He had once been bilingual, he said, but had no intention of relearning French at his age. He was deeply opposed to large public debt. He strongly supported shareholders' rights and roundly declared that environmental dangers were exaggerated.

Waters's late chance of a political career came when the Alberta government grew tired of waiting for Brian Mulroney, the prime minister, to appoint a new senator and decided to call a vote to discover who Albertans would like to see chosen. A skilled and humorous speaker, given to lacing his speeches with quotations from Sir Winston Churchill, Waters found even his 69 years an advantage when offering himself as a Reform candidate. This meant he could only serve six years before compulsory retirement at 75 – a period which exactly matched the fixed period canvassed by his party for

Senate terms. In the face of derision and contrary to many expectations, Waters romped home with 265,000 votes – more than twice that of his nearest rival.

Stanley Charles Waters was born in Winnipeg on June 14, 1920, and educated at Strathcona High School and the University of Alberta before joining the 14th Army Tank Battalion (Calgary Regiment) as a private in 1940. After serving in England, he returned to Canada to be commissioned. He then volunteered for parachute training and was posted to the Canada-U.S. Special Service Force, a unique assault unit being formed in Montana.

Waters's first operational experience came in 1943 when the "Devil's Brigade," as it called itself, landed on the Aleutian island of Kiska, only to find that the Japanese had evacuated. The force next moved to Italy, where, as part of U.S. 2nd Corps, it attacked the German winter line. Using scaling ropes, Waters's company climbed the sheer cliffs of Monte la Difensa to help drive the 104th Panzer Grenadier Regiment from its heights. Several weeks of bitter fighting in the mountains opposite Monte Cassino followed until the enemy was cleared from the east bank of the Rapido River.

On February 1, 1944, Waters landed at Anzio, where the force held a section of the Mussolini canal against repeated German attacks. Casualties were so heavy that by the Allied breakout from the bridgehead four months later he was a major temporarily in command of a battalion. Waters's men were moving into position before an attack to cut the main coastal highway when they came under heavy machine-gun and artillery fire. Instinctively they took cover in a sunken road, but within minutes the leading tanks of their supporting armour appeared in the road. This was a dream target to the enemy, but in full view of the enemy Waters moved among his men, directing them to disperse and organizing the attack, which was duly launched on time. When the tanks' commander was killed, Waters walked under direct fire to co-ordinate the tanks with his infantry. The attack was successful, and Waters was awarded the United States Silver Star. The force's last operation before being disbanded was the invasion of southern France and the clearance of the coast from west of Cannes almost to the Italian border.

Waters and 100 of his men then joined the 1st Canadian Parachute Battalion, which as part of the 6th British Airborne Division had just reached Minden. Riding on the Churchill tanks of the 4th (Armoured) Battalion, Grenadier Guards, the Canadians met only sporadic opposition. Waters's last day of action came when the Canadian battalion joined the Royal Scots Greys in a dash to prevent the Russians sealing off the Danish border.

He returned to Canada and became chief instructor at the Joint Air Training Centre at Rivers, Manitoba, then held staff appointments in Ottawa. In 1953 he commanded the 2nd Battalion of Princess Patricia's Canadian Light Infantry in Germany and later returned to Canada to convert them to a parachute battalion. After a three-year liaison posting with the United States Marine Corps, Waters became an assistant chief military observer with the United Nations in Kashmir, then returned to National Defence HQ, Ottawa. He also served at SHAPE in Belgium before finally becoming commander, Mobile Command, at St Hubert, Quebec – in effect, the army's operational commander.

On retiring from the Armed Forces, he joined the Calgary-based Mannix group of construction companies, and six months later was made president of the Loram Group. When Waters was finally named to the Senate, eight months after his election victory, he continued to devote his energies to campaigning for his party, regarding the way he had arrived as more important than the job itself. He was criticized for having one of the lowest attendance records in the Upper House, but he played a vigorous part in resisting the controversial goods and services tax and claimed that he always took part in major votes. His point seemed to be confirmed the day before he died, when the Mulroney government unveiled for the first time official plans for an elected senate. The new debate over the constitution would ensure, Mulroney declared, that Waters's appointment was strictly "a one-shot deal."

BRIGADIER-GENERAL CAMPBELL MUSSELLS

BRIGADIER-GENERAL CAMPBELL MUSSELLS (who died on September 1, 1989, aged 69) played a key role in the Korean War airlift following a distinguished career as a bomber and Pathfinder pilot in the Second World War.

As a wing commander he was posted in 1949 from Air Force HQ to command No. 426 Transport Squadron whose Canadair North Star aircraft flew 600 Operation "Hawk" round trips, carrying 13,000 men and 7,000,000 pounds of freight and mail across the North Pacific between Vancouver and Tokyo without mishap.

Campbell Haliburton Mussells was born in Montreal on June 20, 1920, and educated at Westmount High School and McGill University. After training as a pilot, he joined No. 405, the RCAF's first bomber squadron formed overseas – known as the "Vancouvers" – and subsequently the only RCAF squadron to serve in the celebrated Pathfinder group.

Already awarded the DFC, Mussells received the DSO after an exceptional exploit in April 1945, less than a month before the end of the war. He had just completed his first run over the Englesdorf marshalling yard at Leipzig when his Lancaster was attacked by a Me163, an experimental rocket-propelled fighter. In one burst the Luftwaffe pilot killed the rear gunner, shot away the Lancaster's starboard rudder, smashed the port rudder and badly damaged both elevators. Its trimming controls useless, the bomber dived, as Mussells struggled desperately to level out. To keep the nose up he lashed the control column back and, escorted by Mustangs, flew the crippled bomber home. After crossing the coast Mussells ordered his surviving crew to bail out. Four did so, but the mid-upper gunner was too badly wounded to follow them. Mussells remained with him and managed to land, although his flaps were useless and the control column was still lashed back.

In 1952 Mussells was appointed OBE in recognition of his part in organizing the Korean airlift. His subsequent commands and appointments included a spell on the Canadian Joint Staff in London in the 1960s and director general of personnel services of the Canadian Forces Abroad and then the Royal Military College, Kingston. He retired in 1974, having been promoted brigadier-general in the controversial amalgamation of the Armed Forces. His marriage to Jean Molson ended in divorce. There were three children.

LIEUTENANT-COLONEL RAYMOND LABROSSE

LIEUTENANT-COLONEL RAYMOND LABROSSE (who died on December 6, 1988, aged 68) helped to spirit more than 130 Allied airmen and intelligence agents out of occupied France by his cool undercover work during the Second World War.

Yet Labrosse survived a series of mishaps and adventures before his operation there was successful. Recruited by MI9 – the intelligence arm responsible for organizing escape lines – from Canadian Military HQ in London, Signalman Labrosse was dropped by parachute near Rambouillet, 15 miles from Paris, on the night of February 28, 1943. His safe descent was a godsend, as it followed one abortive landing by a Lysander aircraft and eight unsuccessful attempts by Halifax pilots to find the dropping zone. Shortly afterwards Val Williams (the Anglicized name of the White Russian British agent for whom Labrosse was to be radio operator) was captured.

So Labrosse made his way to Spain and returned to London only to be told he was to be sent back to France as radio operator to another agent. The man who told him was Airey Neave, himself a celebrated escaper from the enemy's "escape-proof" fastness of Colditz – who had taken charge of Room 900, MI9's headquarters. Labrosse returned in October 1943 as No. 2 of the Shelburne escape line, which he helped set up to ferry escapers by sea from Brittany to Cornwall. Operating from Paris, he installed his radio in the dining room of the stationmaster of the Gare La Chapelle where he was assisted by his host's daughter Ginette – whom he was to marry after the war.

Joseph Raymond Marcel Labrosse was born in Ottawa on November 8, 1920, and joined the Royal Canadian Corps of Signals in 1939. His biggest coup during the war was his part in the rescue on March 24, 1944, of 30 airmen, 18 of whom were United States Eighth

Air Force Flying Fortress crews who had been softening up Germany and France for the coming invasion. The Shelburne Line managed to get some back to England within a few days of their baling out.

Labrosse was commissioned and awarded the MC in 1944, later receiving the Croix de Guerre and Legion d'Honneur. After June 1944, as Allied invasion forces pushed eastwards, the Shelburne Line folded and Labrosse and his team joined forces with *maquis* Resistance fighters. On coming out of the army in 1945, Labrosse went to France for a time, then returned home to join the Royal 22e Régiment, with whom he went to Korea. On retiring again in 1971, he worked for the solicitor-general of Canada. He had two daughters.

STEVE ROMAN

STEVE ROMAN (who died on March 23, 1988, aged 66) landed in Canada a poor Slovak immigrant and ended up as one of the country's most successful mining entrepreneurs.

Ruling his businesses with an iron hand, he remained firmly rooted in both his rural origins and strong religious conviction. He attended the Vatican Council as Canada's only lay observer and financed a large cathedral which serves as the Slovakian Byzantine rite uniate church.

Stephen Boreslav Roman was born at Kelky Rusov, Slovakia, on April 17, 1921, and went to Canada at 16. He worked on a farm and then in a factory before joining the Canadian Army during the Second World War.

After starting to play penny mining stocks, he built up a $10,000 nest egg which was invested in Alberta, where oil was found. Selling out for $2 million, he invested at 8.5 cents a share in what became Consolidated Denison Mines, which steadily rocketed upward after it opened the world's biggest uranium mine at Elliot Lake, Ontario. From then on, Roman steadily turned Denison into an operating company and then a global operation with a huge coal mine in British Columbia, uranium properties in Ontario and Australia, and oil interests in Greece, Spain and Italy.

Living on a 1,200-acre estate outside Toronto, in a 17-room mock Tudor mansion which still managed to retain a distinct Eastern European atmosphere, he was an enthusiastic breeder of Holstein cattle. As an unabashed defender of capitalism he twice ran for Parliament as a Conservative. But he had little sympathy for politicians after the prime minister, Pierre Trudeau, prevented a reverse takeover of Continental Oil by Denison Mines, with a threat to pass retroactive legislation in the House of Commons.

One exception was Richard Nixon, to whose 1968 presidential

campaign he contributed. But when Nixon telephoned him after the row with Trudeau to say that two U.S. consulate officials had been delegated to help him move to the United States, Roman replied: "No, I want to stay in Canada."

Although Roman believed that the Church should pay more attention to discipline and should remember that change could be seen as a sign of weakness, he dedicated much of his energy in later years to building the Cathedral of the Transfiguration, with a 20-storey central tower, which was blessed by Pope John-Paul II during his 1984 Canadian tour.

A stocky, round-faced man who had a tendency in conversation to drop the indefinite article from his conversation, Roman unabashedly maintained that there was a strong link between his religion and his business philosophy, saying he would be accountable for what he had done and what he had not done. He left a widow and seven children.

ESMOND BUTLER

ESMOND BUTLER (who died on December 18, 1989, aged 67) was a courtier on both sides of the Atlantic whose appointment as assistant press secretary at Buckingham Palace marked a significant phase in the Royal Family's adaptation to the modern world.

Until the late 1950s the Queen's press secretary, Commander Colville, had aimed solely to keep the Royal Family out of the news on the assumption that any journalist who did more than copy out the Court Circular should be languishing in the Tower. But after what was regarded as a sensational attack on the monarchy in a magazine article by Lord Altrincham, in 1958 Butler became the first Empire representative at the Palace.

On his arrival at Heathrow, the tall, handsome, pipe-smoking bachelor struck a new note by giving an impromptu press conference. "I hope to meet you all and be of as much help as I can," he told surprised reporters. "I am willing to learn – I think I can help." During his 16 months at the Palace, Butler showed occasional naivety, but he also demonstrated an unprecedented accessibility, even agreeing to accompany a reporter on a day out to Stratford. He brought over a Canadian Wren to help him in his office, and was to be found off-duty in parties accompanying Princess Margaret. It was while he was at the Palace that he met the flatmate of a Royal Household colleague, Georgiana North, the red-headed niece of the Earl of Guilford, and they married in 1960. They had a son and a daughter.

A clergyman's son, Esmond Unwin Butler was born at Wawanesa, Manitoba, on July 13, 1922, and educated at Weston Collegiate, Ontario, and the universities of Toronto and Geneva. During the 1939–45 war he saw service at D-Day and on the Murmansk run while serving with the Royal Canadian Navy in the destroyer *Algonquin* and the frigate *Stormont* (later Aristotle Onassis's yacht *Christina*). Afterwards he worked as a journalist with the British

United news agency in Geneva, then joined the Canadian government as an information officer, attracting Prince Philip's attention when the Queen opened the St Lawrence Seaway in 1957.

On returning to Canada from the Palace, Butler became private secretary to a series of Canadian-born Governors General, ranging from the proconsular Vincent Massey to the young ex–Prairie premier Edward Schreyer. The unstuffy Butler was ideally suited to help the office adapt to the more democratic style that Canadians expected from their fellow countrymen. At the same time he was careful to maintain essential dignities, particularly at investitures of the Order of Canada of which he was secretary-general. He was appointed CVO in 1972 and OC in 1986.

During his 26 years at Rideau Hall, Butler's vast knowledge, long memory and smooth administrative skills made him seem an essential part of the office, and it was not unknown for him to be mistaken for its viceregal tenant. Considerable surprise was felt, therefore, when he resigned after differences with Madame Jeanne Sauvé, the first woman Governor General, within two years of retirement; he was given the consolation of the ambassadorship to Mexico. The severing of many more royal links and the air of confusion that followed demonstrated all too clearly the valuable role that Butler played at Rideau Hall.

DON JAMIESON

DON JAMIESON (who died on November 19, 1986, aged 65) was the first Newfoundlander to succeed in Canadian politics after the island joined Confederation in 1949.

He served in Pierre Trudeau's cabinets during the late 1960s and throughout the 1970s, then was rewarded with the post of high commissioner in London, where his homespun humour made him sought after as a speaker. His fund of political anecdotes and Newfoundland stories made him a firm favourite with the Queen, who could often be seen summoning him to her side at receptions during his two years in the job.

Donald Campbell Jamieson was born in St John's on April 30, 1921. He left Prince of Wales College at 14 after his father died, leaving a widow with six children, and became a broadcaster while serving with the Royal Naval Reserve during the Second World War. Afterwards he operated a radio network on which he proved so fluent that he could recount the news without a script. At the same time, he had his first taste of politics when he fiercely supported an economic union between Newfoundland and the United States rather than confederation with Canada, which the island had first spurned more than 70 years earlier. When the majority vote in favour of confederation was announced, Jamieson became a close associate of Joey Smallwood, the new province's premier. Smallwood enabled him to set up a broadcasting company and helped him to become an MP in 1965, just in time to succeed to Newfoundland's necessary seat in the federal cabinet.

Jamieson headed four ministries – Supply, Transport, Regional Expansion and Industry – before being appointed external affairs minister in 1976. He took firm action in expelling 13 Soviet diplomats for spying, and was a severe critic of the United Nations, which he once described as a forum for "empty debates, futile resolutions and professional cynicism." On retiring from Ottawa in 1979, he took on the leadership of the ousted provincial Liberal party but resigned after 18 months.

Jamieson was one of that rare breed in any Parliament, a minister who did not fear to speak without notes. On a platform he delighted in wisecracks and would pause midway through an anecdote to light a cigar with all the polished timing of a professional entertainer.

RENÉ LÉVESQUE

RENÉ LÉVESQUE (who died on November 1, 1987, aged 65) was the romantic broadcaster whose dream of an independent Quebec, safeguarding French culture in the sea of English-speaking North America, has intermittently dominated the politics of Canada since the late 1960s.

During his premiership of the province from 1976 to 1985, he fought a battle of epic proportions against his fellow Quebecker, the prime minister Pierre Trudeau. But the effects of too much hope and passion, recession and the flight of English Canadian wealth to safer Toronto ensured that when, in 1980, he granted Quebec its long-promised chance to "rendezvous with destiny," the referendum met with a firm rebuttal.

A lawyer's son, René Lévesque was born in Campbellton, New Brunswick, on August 24, 1922, and brought up in the predominantly English-speaking town of New Carlisle, Quebec. A voracious reader, he took up broadcasting as a teenager and dropped out of Laval University's law school. Not wishing "to be ordered in English to peel potatoes in the name of His Majesty," he went to Europe as a liaison officer and broadcaster with the American troops. He covered the liberation of the Dachau concentration camp and was present when the two French leaders Daladier and Reynaud were released from their castle prison, where he had found them eating in different corners of a large room, refusing to speak to each other. Returning home, Lévesque joined the CBC's French network, Radio-Canada, for which he became a star reporter in Korea; later he covered the Coronation as a key member of an influential television current affairs programme, *Point de Mire*. With a reputation for honesty, based largely on emotional intensity, he took an important part in a French network strike from which English-speaking broadcasters stayed aloof.

In 1960 he joined the Quebec Liberal party just in time to become a key figure in the overtly nationalistic "Quiet Revolution" government of Jean Lesage. As minister of natural resources, he made an indelible mark by nationalizing the province's power companies, although significantly one of his strongest critics in private was Trudeau, who saw the whole business as an irrelevant and expensive waste of money. When the party was defeated after six years, Lévesque left to promote the idea of a sovereignty-association between Quebec and an acquiescent Canada similar to Benelux. The policy was outlined in *An Option for Quebec* (1968), a bestseller throughout Canada which soon found itself vying with Trudeau's stodgier yet out-and-out pan-Canadian *Federalism and the French Canadians.*

With his harsh voice, short wiry frame and long face that rarely seemed to be free of a dangling cigarette, Lévesque – for all the threat he represented to Canada – appeared the only person capable of standing up to the arrogant, if brilliant, Trudeau. Trudeau's invocation of the War Measures Act during the kidnapping of the British trade commissioner James Cross and the Quebec minister Pierre Laporte, together with corruption allegations against the provincial Liberal government over Montreal's Olympic Stadium, eventually helped to sweep Lévesque's Parti Québécois, with its promise of a referendum on Quebec's future, into power in 1976.

For almost the whole of his premiership, Lévesque seemed to be duelling with Trudeau; they sniped at each other in their parliaments, on television and from public platforms, arguing about statistics, philosophy, even over the relative degree of attention each received in Paris. More damaging for Lévesque, however, was a worsening economy exacerbated by a Quebec Act which made French the language of business and caused a business exodus. In the end Lévesque could delay no longer, and in 1980 he ordered the long-promised referendum on whether to hold talks on sovereignty-association – which was rejected by almost 60 per cent.

With his new, second wife, Corinne, standing beside him in tears, Lévesque accepted the inevitable. Yet he managed to win an election soon after and found himself battling with Trudeau again over patriation of the British North America Act from Westminster. Lévesque joined most of the other premiers in defending the status of the Queen (whom he was always careful not to insult publicly) and duly appealed to her and Margaret Thatcher while lobbying far more effectively in London than any other leader. In the end, the premiers' front collapsed, and he saw Trudeau's dangerously open constitutional proposals introduced. After the Conservatives won 58 Quebec seats in the 1984 federal election, Lévesque recognized that both country and province wished to be free of bitterness and decided to drop separatism from his party's aims, saying it should be kept only as an insurance policy. Party members ratified the decision by 2 to 1, but the change cost Lévesque the resignation of seven cabinet ministers, and afterwards he had noticeably aged.

In 1985 Lévesque resigned as premier and leader, six months before the Parti Québécois was defeated at the polls, and returned to broadcasting as well as writing a volume of memoirs. His last public appearance was at the launch of a book by his old opponent Trudeau. He had looked at the volume but would not read it, he said.

JACK PIERCE

JACK PIERCE (who died on June 8, 1991, aged 67) was the tough-talking Canadian oilman whose early hunch about the North Sea paid off in 1974 with the discovery of the 1.2 billion barrel Ninian field.

Pierce had opened an office in London during the late 1950s after buying a Royal Navy hydrographic map at Greenwich for five shillings. He tried to negotiate a concession for the whole North Sea and found his small company, Ranger Oil, treated coldly by the British giants that were also bidding for the first development blocks. One even accused him of stealing its survey results. But Pierce's professionalism never failed to impress officials at the Department of Energy. It was his willingness to gamble in the inexact science of seismic studies that led him to ignore his own geologists' advice and go ahead with an exploration programme with BP in the Ninian field off Shetland.

A wiry, weatherbeaten man with an egocentricity that bemused British oilmen, Pierce was a not atypical figure on the Calgary "Oil Patch." He owned a large ranch, loved fast planes and had a low opinion of all politicians except Margaret Thatcher. The Canadian government was conducted by ministers with "zero industry experience," he once declared, while the Alberta government operated at the IQ level of taxi-drivers – though this might be insulting to cabbies, he added. When a Jewish executive was blackballed by the Calgary Ranchmen's Club, Pierce, who was a member and himself of Jewish origin, said it had less to do with racial prejudice than with the fact that the fellow worked for a *government* oil company." Pierce had strong views on governments' foolishness in giving technological knowledge and capital to underdeveloped countries in Asia which were now competing with the West. Yet when he was accused of not doing enough for Canada, since two-thirds of his activities were overseas, he riposted that the North Sea's potential was so great that he would be negligent towards his shareholders if he stayed at home for patriotic reasons.

John Michael Pierce was born in Montreal on February 24, 1924, and educated at Westmount High School. He learned to fly at 15, after earning the money for lessons by selling stove lighters from door to door, and served with RAF Transport Command at the end of the Second World War. After studying geology at McGill University, he worked first for Sun Oil at Beaumont, Texas, and then for a small independent company at Tulsa, Oklahoma. He began a consulting business in the early 1950s before setting up Ranger in Wyoming. He also went on the board of a Canadian company, West Maygill, which subsequently took over Ranger and adopted its name.

Pierce took an early interest in Arctic exploration but was disillusioned by Conservative ministers who made a series of threatening statements about royalties in the House of Commons. "They were getting greedy," he later recalled. "I said, 'We gotta get outa here.'" Pierce had some big failures in Mexico and China. He almost lost his company after nine promising wells at Wyoming proved dry. But he retained iron control over the company – the stock of which ranged variously from $3 to $57.50. After correctly forecasting that the boom of the 1970s would not last, he guarded himself against takeover by retaining a large cash balance.

Pierce, who was married with five children, liked to fly his own plane on the 40-mile journey from his ranch to work in Calgary. He was a pioneer importer of the hardy French Salers cattle into Canada, but although he died of a heart attack while rounding cattle for branding, he had no doubts about his first love: "There is nothing more exciting than finding an oil well."

MARGARET LAURENCE

MARGARET LAURENCE (who died at Lakefield, Ontario, on January 5, 1987, aged 60) was the author of the *Manawaka* quartet of novels. Closely based on Neepawa, Manitoba, where she grew up during the Depression, they are set against an unrelenting landscape in conflict with a harsh spirit of Scots Presbyterianism.

Although the bulk of her best work was written while she lived in Britain in the 1960s, she never achieved the reputation she deserved there. But at the time of her death, Laurence's work was coming out in paperback – a recognition of the importance that her powerful female portraits played in the growing boom in feminist fiction.

In *The Stone Angel* she portrayed a 90-year-old woman, clinging wilfully to her clear memories and possession of her decaying body in the face of her family's determination to send her to an old people's home. *A Jest of God* (titled *Now I Lay Me Down* in Britain) was turned into the successful film *Rachel, Rachel* with Joanne Woodward. It was followed by *The Fire-Dwellers,* an occasion for some vivid satire on the application of American sales techniques in Canada.

The fourth in the series, *The Diviners,* was her last novel. Its banning from school libraries in Canada because of explicit sexual scenes, which even some critics thought unnecessary, deeply hurt her. For two years she tried to hit back at her traducers with another novel, but finally abandoned the attempt. "I realized you don't write fiction to get back at somebody. It was a lousy idea," she later admitted.

Jean Margaret Weyms was born on July 18, 1926, and brought up by an aunt after her parents died. She decided to become a writer as a girl, and first used the name Manawaka in a short story written for a competition in the *Winnipeg Free Press.* After graduating from United College, young Margaret worked as a reporter for the *Winnipeg Citizen,* a trade union-backed newspaper which had a brief flicker of life just after the Second World War. In 1947 she married Jack

Laurence, an engineer, with whom she moved first to England and then Somalia and Ghana.

Her African experiences led to several studies of African writing as well as to her first novel, *This Side of Jordan,* and *The Tomorrow Tamer,* a series of stories which showed the sufferings of both blacks and whites in the political sea change before the granting of independence.

After her second stay in England, she returned to Canada where her marriage, which produced two children, ended in divorce, but she found her reputation sharply rising. Laurence also published several children's books and had just completed the third draft of a volume of memoirs when she died. Her death came only days before the house in Neepawa where she had lived as a girl was to be opened to the public.

Although Margaret Laurence could seem formidable with her heavy features and black glasses, she had a friendly, hospitable personality and constantly worked to help younger, less well-known writers. Together with Margaret Atwood, Alice Munro and Robertson Davies, she did much in recent years to demonstrate that Canadian novelists were more deserving of critical appreciation than more famous authors to be found south of their country's border.

PROFESSOR GEORGE STORY

PROFESSOR GEORGE STORY (who died on May 9, 1994, aged 66) spent 25 years compiling the *Dictionary of Newfoundland English*.

For many Canadians the idea of a scholarly work devoted to the vocabulary employed by the 600,000 inhabitants of Canada's poorest province was just an example of that quirky genre "the Newfie joke." But Story brought an undeniable breadth of knowledge and power of definition to the words and expressions handed down, evolved and created by the islanders whose ancestors had emigrated from Southern Ireland and the English West Country. For three hours a day in their room at Memorial University, Story and his co-editors – the American-born linguist William Kirwin and the English dialectologist John Widdowson – drafted, revised and checked such definitions as *livyer* (inhabitant), *boniff* (piglet) and *chopping the beam* (expressing surprise).

The work, based on an exhaustive trawl of 17th-century books, 18th-century manuscripts, 19th-century ballads and 20th-century tape-recordings, ran to 700 pages when its first edition appeared in 1982. It entered Canadian non-fiction best-selling lists and was hailed internationally as a lexicographical triumph. More important, it became a cultural beacon which assured the people of England's first colony that they could never be subsumed into any amorphous Canadian identity.

George Morley Story was born in St John's on October 13, 1927, the son of an accountant and the grandson of a Methodist missionary and a sealing captain. He went to the local Bishop Feild College, where he failed his grade 11 exam, Memorial University College and McGill University before working briefly for the St John's *Evening Telegram*. In 1951 he won a Rhodes scholarship to Oriel College, Oxford. From then on, while retaining his lilting St John's accent, Story took on the tweedy, pipe-smoking persona of a compleat Oxford man, who would occasionally appear in downtown St John's wearing a deerstalker and knee-breeches. On his return home, he kept up his links with Oxford to produce with Dame Helen Gardner an edition of the minor Elizabethan poet William Alabaster in 1959, and seven years later there was a collection of sermons by the Jacobean divine Lancelot Andrewes.

Story joined Memorial, to rise steadily in its English department and to play a role in the university's expansion. His wit and erudition found their best public outlook, however, when he was appointed the university's first public orator in 1960.

Story's elegant addresses welcomed Eleanor Roosevelt, Malcolm Muggeridge, Field Marshal Montgomery, Lord Thomson of Fleet and the great constitutional scholar Eugene Forsey to honorary degrees. But he was also called upon to eulogize others, at the behest of the all-powerful premier Joey Smallwood, whose suitability was questionable. The dubious businessman John C. Doyle showed no sign of recognizing that Mercury, with whom he was compared, was the god of thieves as well as traders, but a hint that the banker William Mulholland's association with the Institute of the Future might be opening a modern Pandora's Box lost the university a $500,000 donation.

Story eventually gave up this outlet for his irony after penning a privately circulated paean to one Dame Belka, whom he described as having been attracted at a young age to Theology: Queen of the Sciences. Her career progressed from the Boston Theological Seminary to Berlin, Magdeburg and Basle before climaxing in an inaugural lecture "Is There a Synoptic Problem?" which immediately rendered her chair at Oxford obsolete. Dame Belka was the Story family's English setter.

In addition to the dictionary, Story wrote about Newfoundland's proverbs and tradition of Christmas mumming, the local balladeer Johnny Burke and the Atlantic Charter meeting of Churchill and Roosevelt in Placentia Bay in 1943. He chaired a provincial fisheries inquiry, was a member of the Canada Council and a valued consultant to the *Oxford English Dictionary*. He served on the international editorial board supervising publication of Erasmus's works. But Story made no great claims for himself. "Every writer has his particular metier," he would say. "Mine is the 10-word definition."

RICHARD HATFIELD

RICHARD HATFIELD (who died on April 25, 1991, aged 60) earned the nickname "Disco Dick" during an unprecedented 17 years as premier of New Brunswick.

A convivial, doll-collecting, jet-setting bachelor with a strong devotion to the monarchy, he was a regular patron of night spots in Montreal, New York and London, as well as some less salubrious German and Moroccan establishments. As a populist leader with a reputation for personal generosity, Hatfield enjoyed such standing at home that when a newspaper revealed he had spent 163 days of 1979 abroad, a friend dismissed any criticism by saying: "Just because Richard wants to be premier of New Brunswick doesn't mean that he wants to live there." In 1983 Hatfield the royalist astonished even the Prince of Wales when he rose at the end of a dinner in Saint John to declare: "Let the flame burn to warm hope, to cancel cynicism and despair, to heat the soul that remains and remembers. Yes, let the flame burn ... for the flame is *love*." After the Prince had hesitantly responded to this unusual toast by saying that he had no idea the premier was a poet, Hatfield accidentally knocked him into a steel door as they left the dining-room, and then called the Prince and Princess back to be blessed by the local bishop. Next day Hatfield explained that he had not had too much to drink, but rather that he had been up since 5 a.m. and could not remember how much alcohol he had taken – "I don't measure that perfectly."

The following year Hatfield found himself in far more serious trouble when Mounties found marijuana in his bag while searching the royal plane during a tour by the Queen. He was charged with possession, although the case was dismissed by a judge who suggested that the drug might have been planted by a television reporter looking for "the juiciest story ever to crack the media." In the interim a supporter of Hatfield's Tory government questioned the expenditure of

$123,000 on the premier's defence, since the fine would only have been around $50 if he had been found guilty. And his standing was further damaged when two young men recalled how he had produced marijuana at a party some years earlier.

Richard Bennett Hatfield was born at Woodstock, New Brunswick, into a Nonconformist family of United Empire Loyalist stock on April 9, 1931. He imbibed an early love of politics from his Tory MP father and studied law at Dalhousie University before being called to the Nova Scotia Bar. He served a brief term as assistant to the federal trade minister Gordon Churchill in Ottawa, and on his return became sales manager of the family potato crisp company. He entered the New Brunswick legislature in 1961.

Eight years later he became leader of the Opposition Tory party and won his first general election in 1970. Hatfield showed himself an efficient premier in his early years, during which he modernized social services and captured the support of the Acadian French-speaking minority in the province by championing the official use of French at the provincial level. Despite gallant efforts, however, he never managed to speak more than what was described as "polyester French." At the national level he first achieved prominence during a televised meeting of first ministers when he told the prime minister, Pierre Trudeau: "Come on, Pierre, you don't ask for credit, you just take it." When Trudeau began his ill-conceived move to reform the constitution, Hatfield was a key supporter as one of only two premiers in favour – although he insisted that the position of the Queen be made unassailable.

Hatfield also began cleansing the New Brunswick administration of the custom of kickbacks on government contracts, but he was dogged by a succession of scandals. A company which produced a gull-winged car, in which he campaigned, collapsed after receiving $23 million of government money; one of his ministers had to leave the country; and, finally, an attempt was made to stop an investigation into a Tory fund-raising scheme.

Hatfield enjoyed such an easy dominance over the Opposition, whom he liked to dismiss as "dissidents," that he was able to brush off his mistakes until the clucking began in earnest after the marijuana incident. Despite the urgings of colleagues, he nonchalantly went for a fifth successive election victory in 1987, saying he had called it after consulting numerologists and astrologists and checking his bio-rhythms. The result was a disaster: the Tories lost every seat, leaving their leader to bear his defeat with dignity, as he had long vowed to do.

Hatfield claimed that he had never taken a wife because he was married to politics, so it was only appropriate that in his last year he was appointed a member of the Senate, where he might have brought some badly needed energy and comic relief.

NICHOLAS PENNELL

NICHOLAS PENNELL (who died on February 22, 1995, aged 55) made a name for himself in the roles of handsome weaklings, vulnerable suitors, doubters and poor but honourable husbands on the London stage – then established himself as a stalwart of the Stratford Theatre in Ontario.

He was best known in England for his portrayal of the gentle and earnest Michael Mont in the 1960s television series of Galsworthy's *The Forsyte Saga;* elderly female viewers wrote to him expressing fear that Fleur (played by Susan Hampshire) was going to hurt him. But after moving in 1972 to Stratford, which offered him work almost every year and plenty of chance to play classical roles, he established a reputation as one of North America's leading exponents of the classics. His fine voice and handsome presence served Stratford for 23 seasons in which he took some 77 roles in Shakespeare, Molière, Sheridan and Wilde. Among his more memorable roles were the ineffectual Gaev in *The Cherry Orchard,* the wily Ulysses in *Troilus and Cressida* and the small but significant part of Quaker Smooth in *Wild Oats.*

Nicholas Pennell was born at Brixham, Devon, on November 19, 1939, and educated at All Hallows School. His mother encouraged his dreams of becoming an actor but insisted he should also learn shorthand and typing. He attended the Royal Academy of Dramatic Art and had stints in the typing pool of a Manchester paper manufacturer. Pennell did the rounds of provincial repertory and made his first appearance in London's West End playing a police guard at the Royalty Theatre in 1961. Later that year, he played Horne in Harold Pinter's *A Night Out.* His other stage credits included a season at the Oxford Playhouse as Dapper in Johnson's *The Alchemist;* the youthful suitor to Judi Dench's "shameless wanton" in Anouilh's *Roméo and Jeanette;* Nicky Lancaster in Coward's *The Vortex* (Yvonne Arnaud,

Guildford, 1965); and Tusenbach in Chekhov's *Three Sisters;* and Orlando in *As You Like It* (Bristol Old Vic, 1970).

In the 1960s and 1970s he appeared on television in *Maigret, The Brothers Karamazov,* Anouilh's *Poor Bitos, A Tale of Two Cities, David Copperfield, The Woman in White,* Tom Stoppard's *Neutral Ground, Only When I Larf* and Fay Weldon's *Poor Mother.* In Karel Reisz's film *Isadora* (1968) Pennell played a discourteous young man who found the heroine boring. and he was a young pilot in Guy Hamilton's *The Battle of Britain* (1969). In 1977 he toured the United States in two of his own productions, *Rogues and Vagabonds* and *This Fair Child of Mine.* His last West End appearance was with Maggie Smith in Edna O'Brien's *Virginia* (Haymarket 1981), which had been produced at the Canadian Stratford the previous season. Pennell played Leonard Woolf, the self-effacing husband who tremulously returns from the dead.

On the first day of rehearsals for the forthcoming Stratford season, Pennell sent a letter to the company saying that, to his regret, he would have to drop out. Two days later he died from cancer.

ROGER MARSHALL

ROGER MARSHALL (who was killed near the summit of Mount Everest on May 21, 1987, aged 45) enjoyed a reputation as "the bad boy of Canadian climbing."

One of the most forceful members of a group of British climbers which settled in the Columbia Valley in the 1960s, Roger Marshall was born in Kendal, Westmorland, on August 17, 1941, the son of a county librarian. He was introduced to the hills early after showing an enthusiasm for climbing railway bridges.

On leaving school he started work as a journalist in Preston, Lancashire, then moved to the *Hull Daily Mail*. At the same time he graduated as a climber in the hard school of Langdale's Wall End Barn, where fighting, drinking and crashing fast motor bicycles were as much part of the curriculum as activity on the cliffs. Mostly in partnership with Mick Burke (who died in an attempt on Everest in 1975) Marshall was in the vanguard of alpinists at a crucial phase of their influence on the sport.

But "Swinging Sixties" Britain, with its residue of class consciousness, was little to Marshall's taste. He left his job as a journalist with the *Daily Mirror* in Manchester and took his wife and two sons to British Columbia, where he was a journalist on the Vancouver *Province*, worked as a scaffolder, taxi driver, property speculator, textile manufacturer and built his own log house.

He was proud to have found a new way up Mount McKinley. In 1981 he made a winter ascent of Annapurna Four but earned considerable unpopularity by returning with T-shirts proclaiming "Moderation is for Woofters."

The following year he was sent home from Nepal for disciplinary reasons by the over-lavish Canadian Everest expedition. In 1983 he attempted Lhotse Shar with two companions on a lightweight expedition, and the following year reached the summit of Kang Chen

Junga, the world's third-highest mountain, alone and without oxygen. This was his major achievement and one of the ascents which characterized the new ethos of Himalayan mountaineering.

From then on, Marshall's actions were those of a man driven by compulsion and beyond reason. A winter attempt on Cho Oyu in 1985 ended with him being brought down by his companions from 24,000 feet suffering from the mountaineer's deadly ailment, cerebral oedema. He recovered sufficiently to attempt the North Face of Everest by the Northern Couloir in 1986 but was forced to retreat at 21,000 feet. Finally, he went back to Everest, where he died, alone and without oxygen – a fate that was predictable, if not inevitable.

Marshall had an erratic, not wholly pacific temperament which did not always endear him to other mountaineers. But he was thoroughly reliable and competent on a mountain and proved a driving force in any team. He spent his last years in Colorado.

ABBREVIATIONS FOR AWARDS AND ORDERS

CB	Companion of the Order of the Bath
CBE	Commander of the British Empire
CC	Companion of the Order of Canada
CH	Companion of Honour
CMG	Companion of the Order of St Michael and St George
CVO	Commander of the Royal Victorian Order
DFC	Distinguished Flying Cross
DSO	Distinguished Service Order
KBE	Knight Commander of the Order of the British Empire
MBE	Member of the Order of the British Empire
MC	Military Cross
OBE	Officer of the Order of the British Empire
OC	Officer of the Order of Canada
VC	Victoria Cross

INDEX

BY NAME

BY PROVINCE OR CITY